WHEN THE GODS CHANGED

PETER C. NEWMAN

WHEN THE GODS CHANGED

THE DEATH OF LIBERAL CANADA

RANDOM HOUSE CANADA

PUBLISHED BY RANDOM HOUSE CANADA

www.randomhouse.ca

Random House Canada and colophon are registered trademarks.

LIBRARY AND ARCHIVES CANADA CATALOGUING IN PUBLICATION

Newman, Peter C., 1929–
    When the gods changed : the death of Liberal Canada / Peter C. Newman.

Also issued in electronic format.

ISBN 978-0-307-35826-4

    1. Liberal Party of Canada—History. 2. Canada—Politics and government—2006. I. Title.

JL197.L5N49 2011   324.27106   C2011-906026-4

Text and design by CS Richardson

Printed and bound in the United States of America

10 9 8 7 6 5 4 3 2 1

This book is for DOUGLAS BEARDSLEY.
Best friend.
Enlightening Holocaust poet.
Fellow jazz drummer and Mulligan groupie.
Equatorial explorer.
Keeper of my conscience.

"We tell ourselves stories in order to live . . ."

"I am a child of the century,
a child of disbelief and doubt,
and will remain so until the grave.
How much terrible torture this thirst
for faith has cost me,
which is all the stronger in my soul,
the more arguments I can find against it."

FYODOR DOSTOYEVSKY

CONTENTS

PART FOUR BE CAREFUL WHAT YOU WISH FOR

IT WAS AN APPARENTLY INNOCENT MOMENT, but it revealed more about Michael Ignatieff's fate than his million (or so it seemed) personal appearances over the half decade since he'd first shown up on Canada's political radar. He had landed like a brick thrown through a stained glass window, abruptly assuming the mantles of Laurier, Mackenzie King, St. Laurent, Pearson and Trudeau as leader of the Liberal (read "Government") party. But instead of inheriting their thrones, he turned out to be an enemy of promise—the crown prince who was never to inherit the kingdom.

Fortunately, there was an Ottawa-based *New York Times* correspondent on the spot to record the chilly occasion of that chilly late winter afternoon in 2011 when this harsh verdict was confirmed. "Michael Ignatieff may have written 17 books, gained some fame on British television as a serious thinker and led a human rights center at Harvard—but all that appeared to count for little when he laced up his skates and headed out on the

19th-century canal this city uses as a giant ice rink," reported Ian Austen in the newspaper's March 11 edition. "As he skated through a bitter wind with ten children and a gaggle of adults for a photo opportunity, no one approached him or even waved. In a random sampling, few of the skaters that day even knew his name."

This incidence of non-recognition did not happen in Red Deer, Alberta, or in Amherst, Nova Scotia, but in the nation's capital, within sight and sound of the Parliament buildings. And this did not happen on some insignificant, lazy Wednesday afternoon. It happened on a hectic Sunday during the run-up to the general election of 2011, which turned Canadian politics upside down and inside out.

Ottawa is a company town.

Liberals invented the franchise.

It just expired.

Introduction: **The Enemy of Promises**

Despite Michael Ignatieff's best efforts—and at times he was unexpectedly impressive—when the 2011 election was called, the Grits were already dying.

THIS BOOK HAS TWO PURPOSES. The first is to reconstruct the Liberal party's Ferris-wheel experience under the stewardship of Michael Ignatieff, who was on watch for the brief revival of its hopes and its stunning crash to earth. His reign was compelling in its Wagnerian symmetry. His genuine dedication to the party's rebirth was offset by its state of disrepair, and the self-satisfied hibernation of its previous leaders. His failure was more a symptom of their careless stewardship than his doing—but try as he might, he could not halt the party's disintegration.

My second purpose is to reconstruct the nation-building significance of the Grits in Canadian history, starting with their founding saint, Sir Wilfrid Laurier. He picked up the torch originally lit by reformers such as the shy and introspective Toronto lawyer Robert Baldwin, who sat in the Assembly of Upper Canada for only one year but became an ardent crusader for responsible government. Baldwin influenced the visiting Lord Durham, eventually became co-premier of the newly united province of

Canada (today's Ontario and Quebec), founded the University of Toronto and reformed the judiciary. The alliance he established with Canada East's liberal reformer Louis-Hippolyte LaFontaine made them, in effect if not in name, the country's first prime ministers. As well as popularizing the notion of responsible government, LaFontaine and Baldwin were the founding proponents of a bicultural nation. Today, few remember their names or mark their achievements.

The demise of the Liberals, if it comes, will be nothing to celebrate. We have a polarized, two-party system to the south, an example to be avoided by anyone in search of relatively civil and efficient governance. Much will be lost if this ship goes down. But the unsteady hands at the helm have been those of the Grits themselves. This mélange of tragedy and inevitability reflects the current of events—the party's shining legends and hard truths on the one hand, and its most recent leader's descent into hell on the other. The two strands cannot be separated, even by those who wish to evade responsibility for the party's electoral collapse by doing the easiest thing: blaming Ignatieff. In the pages that follow, readers will taste the raw facts.

Ignatieff holds the narrative arc in place, but the book is less about him than about the looming disappearance of the Liberal party. Here was a man who had publicly blessed the worst of George W. Bush's extra-territorialism, yet was also endowed with passionate love for his home country—as he frequently demonstrated on his 2010 bus tour and his 2011 election town-hall rallies. Every evening, right to the bitter end of the campaign, he displayed aspects of the humanitarianism and intellectualism for its own sake that we had so (rightly) admired in Trudeau. Ignatieff was an evocative writer, a trafficker in ideas; his intimate personal experience with Iraq's gassing of the Kurds neatly paralleled Trudeau's adventures during Quebec's asbestos strike and his cohabiting with Central Asia tribesmen.

Why Ignatieff didn't catch on is not hard to guess. Most voters learned the details of Ignatieff's life and times through Harper's attack ads, which portrayed him as a cynical visitor who had come home only to further his career. The besieged professor only truly understood how to connect with a crowd at the very end of his time in Ottawa, and could never undo the impression that he was an academic trout out of water, unsuited to wooing the general public.* He took every attack personally—as he did everything that happened to him, including forecasts of foul weather when he wanted to throw a picnic. Although the Tories were successful in portraying his lengthy absences as disqualifying him for high office, viewing the dysfunctional status of Canadian politics, it was doubtful whether being here would have been an advantage.

It's a bit of a stretch to place Michael Ignatieff as a direct heir to that long line of distinguished men and women who were instrumental in most of the events and decisions that made Canada great. But whatever his faults, he was a patriot and optimist about the country's future, perhaps partly because he rediscovered Canada so late in life. Nothing stirs the blood more than "the return of the native." He realized first hand that the immature land mass he had left behind as a junior assistant professor at the University of British Columbia had become a far greater country than logic would suggest possible.

---

* *The former United States Democratic presidential candidate, Adlai Stevenson, a bona fide public intellectual himself, was advised to disguise his intellect, and so he took care to have himself photographed with his feet up on his desk to show the hole in the sole of his right shoe. In the same spirit, a photo of Obama in an identical pose circulated on the web during his first campaign, with a hole in his shoe in exactly the same spot.*

THE IGNATIEFF INCUMBENCY, of course, turned out to be less a game changer than a history-maker—well, *unmaker* really. The 2011 election campaign humiliated the Grits and allowed Master Harper, the triple-brick radical Tory, to attain a parliamentary majority—a personal achievement that he preferred to having been born a Beatle.

Harper's victory meant that the country will never be the same— might even have to change its name since it will no longer be recognizable. Maybe we'll end up living on the equivalent of George Orwell's *Animal Farm*, obedient beasties to Harper's command. The plain fact is that for at least four years Stephen Harper can do anything that strikes his fancy: his post-election moves to cut the funding for political parties—his own having an established financing system—and his appointment of Tory senators who were rejected when they ran for office speak to power wielded without regard to the consequences to the democratic fabric.

At the same time, its fourth defeat in a row (and I'm counting Paul Martin's short-lived minority government as one of those losses) changed the Liberal party from being an essential engine of social reform and economic progress to a swamped raft loaded with a newly endangered political species. Liberals made the country what it is—and understandably considered themselves to be its natural rulers. But their operational code belonged to another time and place—certainly not to the Canada of the second decade of the twenty-first century. Despite Michael Ignatieff's best efforts— and at times he was unexpectedly impressive—when the 2011 election was called, the Grits were already dying.

MICHAEL IGNATIEFF SHOWED UP in Belleville, the perky yet historic settlement on eastern Ontario's Bay of Quinte where I now live, toward the end of what would turn out to be his last campaign. He came to preside at a Liberal rally in the Greek Orthodox hall, which was jammed by local Grits ecstatically welcoming their standard bearer.

He was accompanied by four flacks tucked into white shirts, who looked as out of place as altar boys in a mosque. Around here, most locals reserve white shirts for funerals—usually their own. I slipped into the hall's back office where the Ignatieff entourage was preparing the leader for his gig. At that point he was still optimistic enough to believe he could salvage a sprinkle of grace from a hopeless dilemma, though I was pretty certain he was like the drowning man about to descend for the third time. It was my self-imposed mission to shock the candidate into some retroactive appreciation of reality. In grave tones I informed Ignatieff and his wife, Zsuzsanna Zsohar (rarely out of his earshot), that I needed to share some uncomfortable truths with them. Ignatieff appeared startled (his eyebrows shot into the stratosphere).

"I know your secret," I revealed. "In a past life, you were a torturer for the Spanish Inquisition." Though his expression didn't change, I could feel him thinking, "Who is this guy and has he finally flipped his lid?"

Once launched, I had no choice but to carry on. "Now you're paying for what you did in another life. That's why you get so little respect in the media, that's why you're so low in the polls. That's why your destiny is to be the last leader of Canada's once luminous Liberal party."

He stood his ground, even showed me his perfect teeth, but he started looking around for someone to gently lead me away. He was saved the trouble, though, because it was time for him to be rushed into the hall. And I was stuck with yet another incomplete verbal transaction with Ignatieff—an all-too-common occurrence between us since I'd started closely following him in 2006, when he first ran for leadership of the Liberals. Back then, I'd been certain that history and his own unusual qualities had combined to make Ignatieff the answer to the Grits' problems, and that he was destined to be our next prime minister. We had never met, but I had read a number of his books and had been impressed by both style and content. It was also blindingly clear that the party was lost in the woods, fractured by a decade or more of infighting, and bereft of new ideas.

Instead of a stump speech, that night in Belleville he gave the crowd a Dr. Phil-style psychology session on how the country might be improved and how the Liberal party could become relevant again. His prescription was so vague that I can't remember the details, but I shared the secret agenda of others in that hall: When will he tell us why he supported George Bush's invasion of Iraq? What had he been thinking? But that wasn't on his list of topics to be addressed—these reincarnated Spanish inquisitors are reluctant to speak to truth.

As I watched him perform, I realized that he had come a long way: the audience wasn't trading high-fives but they were attentive in a deferential sort of way. Justifiably known for the quality of his mind, he did have a few other moving parts: shoulders that swung from port to starboard and back again, and those semaphore eyebrows that signalled his mood changes. Despite my many solo interviews with him, on which this book is partly based, we did not connect easily. If I had to sum him up, even now, all I can say is that he is a swell bunch of guys who have never met. He seemed to operate on so many wavelengths that even when we were alone together, though he was always perfectly pleasant, I felt as if I was only receiving a tiny fraction of his attention—the part reserved for itinerant journalists with potentially toxic tape recorders— while his heart, soul and brain were otherwise engaged. His only brother, Andrew, says, "I will not go on record saying that Michael has multiple personalities. But his life is a particularly elaborate stage set, with sliding screens to protect the inner core of who he is, which is a rather quiet, deeply intellectual, thinking person of great affection." Not anyone's idea of a natural-born politician.

In the two previous elections, come hell or tar-sands-tailings high water, Canadian voters would not grant Master Harper a majority. Yet, by 2011, when faced with Ignatieff as the logical alternative, they not only blessed the Tory leader with a generous majority, but also gave Jack Layton the hope that he really might be Canada's next prime minister. The NDP leader's secret weapon was his smile, which could light up a room or a stadium; it was a horrible accident of fate that just as Layton reached a historic milestone of 103 seats for his party, he had to take a leave to concentrate on a round of treatment for a reoccurrence of cancer, and died on August 22, 2011, before he could truly take on the role of leader of the official opposition.

Still, even the Ottawa press corps had been surprised by how well Ignatieff campaigned. What we journalists didn't know—more importantly, what Ignatieff himself didn't realize—was that most of his attentive audiences were certified Liberal members who would most likely have voted for him if he'd turned out to be a yellow dog in disguise. That was why his final score—just thirty-four seats—was well below that of Stéphane Dion, whose almost comically disastrous campaign in 2008 had netted the Grits seventy-seven MPs.

With Ignatieff, some essential element was missing. No matter how hard and how well he campaigned (though he never was disciplined enough to stick to the script and as a consequence looked unfocussed compared to Stephen Harper, who was unrelenting in his hammering of the Conservative message), he could not dig his way out of also-ran territory. The voters sensed that he wasn't one of them—call it the Tim Horton syndrome. He clearly belonged not in the doughnut shop, chowing down with the rest of us, but in his own cloister.

I HAVE SPENT MOST OF THE PAST two years attempting to fill in the many blanks in the story line of this book: the narrative arc of Michael Ignatieff's rise and fall—and, more significantly, the not unconnected death spiral of Canada's Liberal party. Like it or not, the Liberals have long been our political gods, turning this awkwardly giant land mass into a field of realizable dreams. But the gods have changed. No smaller concept can encompass what happened to Canada in the spring of 2011—when for the very first time voters handed a clear majority to a government run by a politician whose ideals and goals seemed antithetical to the country I thought I knew.

The Grits were originally dubbed the "Natural Government Party" by Jack Pickersgill not because they were constantly in power, but because under Laurier, Mackenzie King, St. Laurent, Pearson and Trudeau—who between them ruled the country for sixty-six years—they created modern Canada. Yet after the shellacking of May 2, they were in danger of emulating the Progressive Conservative party in 1993. In one election, Brian Mulroney's once invincible political machine plummeted from double majority status to two lonely members, the tragic residue of the political movement that had founded the country and now could not mobilize enough hands for a rubber of bridge.

Having gone a couple of decades without renewing their mandate in any meaningful way—even with three majority governments under Jean Chrétien—the Grits paid a similar if not quite as drastic a price. But to place the burden of the blame on Michael Ignatieff is neither fair nor accurate. He was there, acting as the catalyst on the road to ruin.* But the catastrophe in party fortunes was less his doing than his inheritance

WHEN IGNATIEFF ARRIVED BACK in Canada in 2005, he was severely handicapped by not knowing the lay of the political land or any of its players. The adult Ignatieff had lived away from the country of his birth for twenty-seven years. But he'd also spent much of his childhood in foreign parts, as his father, the gifted diplomat George Ignatieff, moved up the ladder of postings. If you added in his boyhood, he'd been away from Canada for roughly four decades—more than half his life.

Before he returned to seek political office, he had devoted much of his time and energy to documenting the various atrocities of warlords on three continents (some cynics contended that this was a perfect apprenticeship for Canadian politics). But Ignatieff was tragically out of his element in the day-to-day rough and tumble of politics, even in the give and take of his own caucus. About the only way he could have won an election was if Canadian voters had discovered that Master Harper's frequent tactical bloopers coincided with the phases of the full moon.

It wasn't so much that Ignatieff was out of step with current political realities—he could analyze with the best of them—but that all too often he acted as if he took his inspiration from Talleyrand sitting in his Paris apartment, hearing the revolutionary crowd roar in the streets. He excitedly exclaimed to his adjutant, "Listen, our side is winning!" This confused the man, who demanded, "But Sir, which is our side?"

* *A catalyst is a useful substance that enters a chemical mixture, radically converts its character and accelerates its rate of change, but is itself not altered in the process. Just like Ignatieff.*

"Hush," Talleyrand replied. "Tomorrow I will tell you."

Ignatieff contradicted his own opinions often enough that when I opened one of our exchanges by quoting Talleyrand, he got the point.

Yet a little more than three years after he returned home, Ignatieff became the Liberal party's *de facto* leader in an immaculate conception (or bloodless coup) that made Canadian political history. His takeover of the Liberal party involved no public debates and no campaigning. He simply waltzed in, declared that the world existed to be put in order, and that he was the man to do it. The themes that had animated his life had been the struggle for democracy and human rights, and those of us who had studied his career believed that his coronation actually breached his usual regard for the proper order of things. But he accepted the tainted crown, and became interim leader after Dion's electoral loss in 2008. There was eventually the formality of a convention, held in Vancouver five months later, but by then there was only one candidate.

SINCE WE BOTH WERE BOTH FREELANCE WRITERS who sold our life stories to the highest bidders over and over again, I had felt instant empathy for Ignatieff. We were entrepreneurs, literary acrobats operating without safety nets. Every three or four years we emerged from our comfy hermitages clutching the rumpled pages of a manuscript that was turned into a book that nobody needed. Would someone actually buy it and read it? That was dangerously unpredictable, amounting to sorcery. I accepted his credo that he was a self-made man—even if he ended up worshipping his creator. (Nearly all of his prose, books, speeches and essays, included generous use of the first person singular.) During his political odyssey, when his detractors made fun of his aristocratic lineage—he was the grandson of a Russian count—I tried to comfort him, pointing out that this was strictly from envy, which is what makes Canada run. As a classic introvert—or as I preferred to think of him, a closet extrovert—Ignatieff must have been well aware that a sense of security comes from within. Still he laid himself open for voters to judge when he must have known their loyalties are as variable as the hues in a pigeon's neck feathers.

Late one evening, I sat in my study contemplating my latest subject's literary outpourings: four bulging file drawers' worth of clippings along with his seventeen books. Then, like the parting of the Red Sea in a costume drama, it came to me: the solution to the ongoing puzzle of Ignatieff, the mysterious stranger from everywhere. While he has in his time pontificated about everybody from Madonna to Mother Theresa, he was really in search of a hero. He had spent his exemplary career achieving more than most of us even dream of, but he was primarily in search of himself—and perhaps on a parallel quest, in search of home. I figured the hero in such a drama had to be *him*.

His return to Canada was like a grant of political asylum. His was a fierce, burning need to control his destiny and he saw his political incarnation as a way of setting new boundaries, then living by them. Deciding to come back home and enter public life also set his personal story alight, as it could have been and should have been, ruled by enlightenment instead of entitlement. Had he won the election, it would have been the perfect scenario. But democracy (and his too frequent public eruptions as the professor instead of the contender) got in the way.

ON ELECTION NIGHT, the emperor turned out to have no clothes—well, no empire. He lost both his own seat and the standing of his party. Ignatieff thought he had earned the admiration of a grateful nation by sacrificing his dignity to flip burgers at every pit stop in the vast Dominion, from sea to sea to sea. (Or to lead a conga line live on Toronto's CITY-TV.) What did he get for his troubles? The voters discarded him like a Zellers sweater they hadn't even bothered to try on.

Just as this isn't the future Ignatieff wanted, this isn't the book I was supposed to be writing. It was supposed to be *The Making of a Prime Minister*, its title a homage to Theodore White's 1961 classic on the presidential election of John F. Kennedy. It was meant to be the inside story of Ignatieff's coronation, which had seemed inevitable when I started my reporting. The election results unraveled my narrative arc and turned it into skywriting, scattered by the breeze.

Long before he lost the election, Ignatieff had lost the direction of his own caucus by achieving the impossible: the Harvard import made his hapless predecessor look good. But Ignatieff managed to drive the final nail into his political coffin all on his own, during a late election interview with the CBC's Peter Mansbridge. In the early days of the campaign, Harper had scored many points with voters by insisting that they had to give him a majority to foil an insidious plot by all the opposition parties to foist a coalition government on the nation. Ignatieff had actually managed to disarm that attack by issuing a powerfully worded disavowal of any such scheme. Now, on national TV, with only eleven days to go in the election, Ignatieff deliberately revived the coalition issue, not by saying that once again he had changed his mind and he was going to enter into one, but simply by discussing the possibility in minute detail. Like a gift-wrapped hand grenade, he gave his opponents the ammunition to blow up his political dreams. "We may not like the way politics is played, but for better or for worse the man who wants to be the country's top politician should display some skill at it," wrote Kelly McParland in the *National Post* after the Mansbridge interview aired. "Or at least an ability to recognize a burning gas bag when it's laid on your doorstep. Mr. Ignatieff didn't."

Still, I would argue that Ignatieff's Canadian caper did him honour, at least for trying so hard and remaining civil under impossible circumstances. But one thing: he ought to have known that any normal sense of patriotism requires only that you love your country. *It does not mean that your country must love you back.*

There will be few hands extended to him now, except Zsuzsanna's. This book is my attempt to understand his odyssey and to try to explain how the Liberals turned from the walking wounded to the walking dead. The pages that follow trace the downward spiral of both Michael Ignatieff and the Liberal party, who jumped hand in hand over a cliff of worthy intentions.

PART ONE

STORMING BABYLON

1. The Messiah Who Was Handed a Crown of Thorns

From the moment Ignatieff appeared on the scene, he was anointed as the messiah who would revive the miracle of papal succession that befitted a state religion such as Canada's Liberal party.

THE HISTORIC RISE and cataclysmic pratfall of Canada's ruling political party was anything but an overnight phenomenon and neither was my relationship with the Ignatieffs. That dated back to 1952, several lifetimes ago when I was in my early twenties, a bewildered and certifiably insecure graduate student at the University of Toronto. I had been unsuccessfully trying to stay awake during my MBA classes and had finally decided to give up my ill-fated attempt to become an apprentice capitalist. Instead, I spent the rest of my university sojourn slumped in one of the red leather chairs at the Hart House Library, the student hangout where I hungrily morphed into a reading machine, absorbing nearly every non-fiction volume on its shelves.

I had another compelling reason for becoming a Hart House brat. There I came under the spell of Nicholas Ignatieff, the all but forgotten, charismatic warden of Hart House who was the first adult to tutor me in the occult world of politics—as it was and as it could be—a poisoned chalice or a healing art.

3

We were both European Slavs under siege in the WASP-dominated Toronto of that faraway time when multiculturalism was a choice between Patronizing English Exiles, Fisticuff Tavern Irish and Rock-Ribbed Scottish Money Pinchers (otherwise known as bankers). Nick Ignatieff took them all on and enjoyed the jousts. He was an overbearing Russian aristocrat with a hair-trigger temper relieved by a wondrous sense of the bizarre. Under his enlightened autocracy, the once-staid Hart House, where tea had been served on doilies and no one used adverbs after dark, became an evolutionary safe house. It was where students went to learn about the real world and how to survive in it. There were no courses or textbooks on that lost art. As a rootless Czechoslovak refugee destined in my mind to be ever the stranger, I was awed by my encounters with the redoubtable Ignatieff. He was hard-ass and real life; older than his eminent diplomat brother George, he was the toughest of his litter.

My family had escaped from the Nazis and found a haven in Canada; my brain reverberated with the four languages I had learned to speak, misplaced vowels, obscure consonants, rogue verbs and drifting diphthongs refusing to jell into recognizable vocal patterns, sensible thoughts or acceptable behaviour. Nick became my anchor. To a questing rabble of youthful Hart House reprobates like me, he provided shelter—not in any parental sense, but as a wise and welcome worldly presence in our lives when we needed one most.

He lectured widely, wrote regularly for *Saturday Night*, then the country's leading journal of opinion, and had served with the Russian section of British intelligence in London during the Second World War, where he was picked to personally brief the reigning British monarch on the conflict's progress. His nephew, Michael, described him as, "moody and difficult—hard to live with, hard to forget." Yet Nick was our role model. He taught us that our life forces need not be denied. (At that age, life force in its several manifestations was about all we had.)

A windy day in March of 1952 was the occasion for Nick's annual Hart House lecture. To the jammed Great Hall he recalled a shimmering sunny afternoon during the local wars that followed the Russian Revolution. He had watched from a hillside as the Red and White armies massacred one another in the battle over Kislovodsk, a southern spa town of little strategic value. "I remember thinking acutely for the first time what pitiful fools these grown men are to do this to each other—and on a day like this," he recalled, his voice bouncing off the Great Hall's rafters. "What blasphemy! When my father, all our friends and relations said that Communism could only be fought by force and that to hang a Communist was a service to society, I was disturbed and refused to accept the explanations of my elders. I was haunted by the spectacle of a young mother who happened to be an active party member, hanging for three days from a gibbet erected on a hill in the middle of town."

The lecture, given at a time when being anti-Communist was the white man's burden, made an indelible impression on me. Though his audience consisted mostly of student-acolytes, toilet-trained in deference to authority, raised on porridge and piety, Nick had the courage to speak out: raging against smugness in all its guises, condemning the bizarre cult of McCarthyism then sweeping the United States, attacking the insipid parochialism of a Toronto that still didn't allow tobogganing in High Park on Sundays, and defending lapsed students like me who had decided to follow their own muse.

My memory of Nick's courage and the way he inspired us is particularly poignant because on the afternoon following that

Hart House lecture, while changing a tire on his car, he had a massive heart attack and died instantly. He was only forty-eight.

I mourn his spirit to this day and can't help thinking about that other Ignatieff while writing about the hall of mirrors that is Michael—who also occupied his own vibrant intellectual universe with distinction, and lived to tell the tale.

AS AN ACADEMIC, Michael Ignatieff had made his mark at Harvard, Oxford and Cambridge, using his young adulthood, from age twenty-two to thirty-five, to establish his academic roots. Then, as a columnist for London's *Observer*, he belonged to a period when British journalism existed in a close relationship to literature; in my opinion, two of his three novels (*Scar Tissue* and *Charlie Johnson in the Flames*) as well as *The Russian Album*, his memoir of the prerevolutionary Russian history of his family, were masterpieces. During his time in London he won a respectful following but remained an outsider because he was, after all, a colonial. Unlike most expats, he had maintained his Canadian accent instead of slipping into the plummy tones of BBC regulars. Unlike most voluntary exiles, he never turned himself into one of those mid-Atlantic Canadians who belong to neither shore nor nationality. While he was never a man of the people, he could legitimately claim to be a man *for* the people, especially if they were being victimized by the horrors of ethnic cleansing, which turned so much of post-Tito Yugoslavia into a killing field.

Becoming a politician in a country where he had lost his points of reference after being in foreign parts for most of his life, he was forced to revise his academic view of the political process as the art of making the necessary possible. In Canada, successful politics required alchemy in order to turn the dross of circumstance into the glitter of golden opportunity. It was a tough gig. In a country that covers more than one fifteenth of the earth's land surface, diversity was a given and regional discontent a daily plague. While Stephen Harper, Ignatieff's nemesis, was dedicated to reducing the public sector, Ignatieff never questioned the political function or usefulness of federal government. He was shy of rigid creeds but he maintained that politics was not about the exercise of power, but about the *will* to power—the willingness to utilize the resources and opportunities of political power to subdue the obstacles that interfere with individual rights and collective liberties. Almost from the moment he appeared on the scene—despite what surviving Liberals are saying now—he was anointed as the messiah who would revive the miracle of papal succession that befitted a state religion such as Canada's Liberal party.

BACK IN 1990, WHEN IGNATIEFF was on his trajectory as a significant figure on London's A-list of public intellectuals, he was featured on the cover of British GQ, the men's magazine, dressed in a rust-pink silk double-breasted Nicole Farhi suit, with an impressive mop of dishevelled hair, worn in the new romantic style then in vogue. The cover line asked, "London's bionic liberal, is he for real?"

"The thing about that cover," noted the *Guardian* more recently, "is that you would not have to alter the magazine much to bring it up to date. Simply photo-shop the hair to make it short and greying, add a few worry lines to the face, and tweak the cover line to read: 'Canada's bionic Liberal, is he for real?'"

He was for real, in the sense that he knew exactly what he wanted every time he changed incarnations, which was roughly once every nine years, give or take a month or two. But unlike most talented *machers* he didn't merely switch jobs but acquired new personalities and new friends to suit each vocation: academic

7

professor to television host, to journalist/commentator, to novelist and author, to human rights advocate, to politician. Only in the most recent of his choices, attempting to breathe life into the once invincible Liberals, did he stumble.

If Ignatieff turned out to be the unwilling agent of the Liberals' demise, it was mainly because he went against a law of life that has seldom been broken: intellectuals seek truth while politicians seek power. Not only do these lines rarely intersect, their purposes are diametrically opposed. Ignatieff ultimately opted for power by allowing himself to be co-opted by the existing Liberal power structure. That was an untenable position from the start because it soon turned into a struggle between power and honour. Ignatieff had the misfortune of remaining a rational reformer and never becoming an ardent revolutionary like his Uncle Nick. Instead of issuing polemics and shaking up the ragtag remnants of a once glorious political movement, Ignatieff for a very long time remained the elegant incarnation of common room civility and self-deprecating humour. That served little purpose, since the hostile press took care of more deprecation than he deserved or could handle.

Ignatieff's initial forays into the political abattoir were chilling. Canadians blamed his inability to connect on the arrogance that he seemed to exude before anyone had been exposed to his ideas. He had been a winner for so much of his career that he had never learned to act or look like a loser—in other words, to admit that he was not superior to everyone else. During the early part of his transition, there were many gaps between what he said and what he thought, papered over by the inevitable corrections that followed most of his pronouncements. His worst gaffe was his pledge to renew the constitutional wars that had so drained the country's vitality during Brian Mulroney's attempts to rewrite history. That was when Ignatieff's lengthy absence from Canada created a stumbling block for his worthy intensions. Anyone who had lived through the Meech Lake and Charlottetown accords, tests of endurance and sanity, reacted with horror at the thought of reviving those masochistic exercises in constitutional masturbation.

Ignatieff was multitalented but he lacked the instinct for detecting onrushing danger. If you lack such an instinct in politics, you get pounded again and again. You pay in lost self-confidence—and eventually defeat.

He found himself facing in Stephen Harper an impressive opponent who was not so much a politician as an ideologue of cutting-edge cunning, capable of treating a routine statistical form as toxic to human consumption. The Harper regime's fuss over dumping Canada's expensive but useful long-gun registry reminded me of Robin Williams' line that if, under the U.S. constitution private citizens are permitted to bear arms, Americans ought also be allowed to arm bears.

There could be little doubt that a blood feud developed between the two men; they expected the worst of one another and were seldom disappointed.

BY ANY STANDARD the shift in Canadian society following the 2006 election that put Harper in office was without parallel. Once upon a time, one of the Liberal party's big thinkers was Tom Kent, the suave former journalist whose compassionate ideas forged modern liberalism in Canada; the Conservatives' stalking horse was often Ezra Levant, the neo-con who gave raucous voice to the reactionary new wave, vilifying human rights commissions and inventing the concept of ethical oil. From being a compassionate society of left-leaning progressives, Canada is becoming the preserve of Stephen Harper, who is out to transform the character of the country into the cowboy capitalism of downtown Calgary.

The Liberals ruled over a one-party state. Harper's government—despite the John Bairds, Jason Kenneys, Jim Flahertys and Peter Kents—is a one-man band.

The only joke I've heard repeated about Harper is this one. Harper decides to take his cabinet ministers to dinner at Ottawa's best restaurant. (Yes, I know this seems out of character right off the start.) They are all seated around one large round table when the waiter arrives to take their orders.

"What would you like, sir," he asks the prime minister.

"I'll have the steak."

"How would you like it cooked."

"Medium rare."

"And the vegetables?"

"Oh, they'll have the same."

OKAY, SO THERE WAS NO PUFF of white smoke when Stephen Harper toppled the Liberals in the election of January 23, 2006, to form his first minority and completed the rout on May 2, 2011. His victories—and they were well earned—established a new political dynasty and humbled an old one. If the earth didn't move, it sure as hell trembled.

Most of this happened in the context of the tainted ethical record of the Grits under the wobbly command of Jean Chrétien and Paul Martin, as exposed by the Quebec sponsorship scandal and the Liberals' clear loss of political mojo. Using the guise of federal funding to promote national unity, leading manipulators of the Montreal advertising community had pocketed illegal millions and thumbed their noses at Ottawa's naiveté. Though neither Chrétien nor Martin was directly implicated, the scandal reached into the PMO. And the monkey business took place on their watch. The Liberals had ruled for all but one of the previous four decades. Now the jig was up and the disgrace of a few had finally caught up with the smugness of the many.

Although Martin had dislodged the Chrétien gang, voters ultimately rejected his lame brand of sweaty Liberalism because they sensed that he had lost touch with his better self and his behaviour seemed more desperate than deserving. He acted as though he was destined to govern but he never seemed certain of what he wanted to do. He claimed several dozen policy options as his highest priority items, which meant that he didn't have any. None of his good intentions went unpunished. After all, he had been preparing for this position all of his life—his bedtime stories must have been the collected speeches of his father Paul "Oompah" Martin, Sr., whose career followed a similar avalanche into irrelevance. Both men—to their peril—treated the Tories, in Liberal bigwig Pickersgill's immortal phrase, "like a case of mumps, an unwelcome disease that you put up with once, then forget about, and never want to experience again." The Liberal disease was a lot worse than mumps; as guardians of the public purse, the party's movers had abandoned their mandates and eventually their integrity.

THE PORTRAIT OF CANADA as painted by the voters on that seminal 2006 election night when Paul Martin took the fall for the scandals, was that of a nation digging for its soul and finding no reassuring panaceas. Canadians appear to be political eunuchs, not giving much of a damn about what goes on in Ottawa, and yet collectively the voters almost always do the right thing. Certainly they were right to send the Liberals packing, just as they were correct to award Harper minority mandates until his superior organizational skills and iron determination overwhelmed the hapless Grits.

The 2006 campaign, which revealed the Liberals' steep descent, was characterized by the usual sandstorms of half-truths that added up to more noise than substance. Paul Martin went into arm-waving hysterics that Harper aptly described as "his windmill thing." Hardly a belief system worth voting for. The Conservative leader kept his cool and that was recommendation enough. By describing his policies in numbing detail, including a $1-billion plan to combat the mountain pine beetle plague in B.C. forests, Harper raised the status of his party above that of the Liberals. Try as they might, the Grits couldn't break out of the public perception that they were a disorganized gang of desperadoes with an insatiable appetite for power. By that stage of the party's disintegration this was true, but it was equally the case that the Conservative and Liberal party platforms matched like they were competing in a synchronized swim contest. They were using almost the same strokes at variable speeds and in different packaging.

I distinctly recall that Harper, at the climax of his original run for office in 2004, chose to reassure the voters—many who were terrified of the possibility that he might win a majority—that they need not worry because a *Liberal* Senate, a *Liberal*-appointed judiciary and a *Liberal*-tinged public service would provide "the necessary checks and balances." That was a dumb proposition since these same *Liberal* institutions failed to prevent or clean up the Adscam scandal. But the fact that Harper felt compelled to issue such a pre-emptive reassurance signalled that he had learned a great deal about federal politics, and Canadians' overly hesitant attitude about being rushed into reform—or even change.

Be strong only in moderation, the historians had cautioned, because this is a country governable only by compromise. Harper initially heeded that advice, even if his adherence to moderation was tactical and fleeting. Despite his root convictions, which dwelled somewhere over the rainbow of reactionary despotism and extended back to his apprenticeships with both Ernest Manning's Social Credit dogma and his son Preston's Reform party benedictions, Harper pretended that being right or left wing in Canadian politics had come to mean as little as which hand one used for a tennis serve. But of course it means everything.

IF POLITICS IS A FEVER IN THE BLOOD, arrogance is the Liberals' genetic code. I witnessed this trait first-hand in the mid-1960s as an Ottawa columnist who happened to be within earshot of a brief exchange between Prime Minister Lester Pearson and Keith Davey, then executive director of the Liberal party. Pearson had marched his party backwards through four campaigns, never earning a majority mandate. Late in the evening, on election night in 1965, when it was clear this would be his final attempt, I overheard Davey apologizing to the PM for another Liberal minority.

"We let you down," Davey lamented.

"No, Keith," Pearson replied, sighing. "The country let us down."

Pearson was in effect complaining that the Liberals had tested the Canadian people and found them wanting, and this remained the predominant party outlook during Michael Ignatieff's leadership four decades later.

The 2006 election was fought at a time when Canadians sensed that history was accelerating. Their world was changing faster than their comprehension of it. They felt dispossessed, rootless and angry. The peaceable kingdom they inhabited might be filled with wonders, but it seemed to provide no sanctuary from violence, domestic or imported.

That tumultuous campaign, which so dramatically altered Liberal prospects, featured one great moment of truth. During the first television debate, a spunky lady from Lac-Simon, Quebec, called in to ask a simple question: would the participants be willing to swear on a Bible, or whatever was dearest to their hearts, that they would keep their promises? Instead of replying, the quartet of party leaders shot off in all directions: Stephen Harper said that he didn't understand the question; Paul Martin pointed out that he had balanced the budget; Jack Layton rhymed off his party's platform; Gilles Duceppe used the occasion to discuss the softwood lumber crisis.

The correct answer would have been "Yes."

By the end of 2006, with Paul Martin in the dumpster and the party winding up for a leadership conclave, thoughtful Liberals slowly, much too slowly, realized that their party would require not only inspired leadership but new gods, freshly minted mentors motivated by values as the source of their experience—instead of experience as the source of their values. In other words, people who tested their values against real-life needs and concerns as opposed to political marketability.

That was the reason some Liberals figured that Michael Ignatieff just might provide their ticket to ride.

2. Provence Interlude

"In Canada the silence among the great trees was
menacing—no light for miles. I had no quarrel with
the place. I just wanted to get out."
                            —MICHAEL IGNATIEFF

IT IS AFTER MIDNIGHT in August, 1984, at the Ignatieff family villa in Les Martins, a notch among the hilly indentations of Provence, the fabled playground of the privileged in Southeastern France, wedged between the Alps and the Riviera. A modest dwelling, it was only ten minutes from Gordes, where François Mitterrand, the president of France, kept a summer hideaway for his mistress.

"They are all in bed except me," Michael, the eldest son, wrote in the British magazine *Granta* at the time. He was thirty-seven, and visiting the family's summer place along with his wife Susan and his infant son.

I have been waiting for the rain to come. A shutter bangs against the kitchen wall and a rivulet of sand trickles from the adobe wall in the long room where I sit. The lamp above my head twirls in the draught. Through the poplars, the forks of light plunge into the flanks of the mountains and for an instant the ribbed gullies stand out like skeletons under a sheet. Upstairs I can hear my mother and father turn heavily in their sleep. Downstairs our baby calls out from the bottom of a dream. I smooth his blanket. His lips pucker, his eyes quiver beneath their lashes.

Susan is asleep next door, the little roof of a book perched on her chest. The light by the bed is still on. Her shoulders against the sheet are dark apricot. She does not stir as I pass. At the window, the air is charged and liquid. The giant poplars creak and moan in the darkness. It is the mid-August storm, the one which contains the first intimation of autumn, the one whose promise of deliverance from the heat is almost always withheld. The roof tiles are splashed for an instant, and there is a patter among the trumpet vines. I wait, but it passes. The storm disappears up the valley and the night sounds return—the cicadas, the owl in the poplars, the rustle of the mulberry leaves, the scrabble of mice in the eaves. I lean back against the wall. The old house holds the heat of the day in its stones like perfume in a discarded shawl. I have come here most summers since I was fifteen . . .

His memories stir sweet reminiscences about his boyhood ambition to be a musician and play slide guitar like Elmore James, to be muscular with fine bones and to be fearless, acting on impossible wishes. This is the only place on earth he can call home. While he was growing up, his father's diplomatic assignments changed the family's circumstances every two years. Michael went to Provence to renew his sense of belonging, to be surrounded by family and this fabulous landscape. His pilgrimages cured whatever homesickness he might have been feeling. London was his habitat; the literary world, his playground; Provence his field of dreaming.

The villa is a former wash house where villagers once scrubbed clothes on slanted stones when they weren't raising worms for the Lyons silk trade. In more modern times, it became a shepherd's shelter, housing a retarded son and his father who beat him until the boy, crazed by the assaults and by loneliness, smashed in his father's skull. After they took the boy away and buried his victim, the house fell into disuse.

In 1962, when they first came to look over the place one day after sundown, his father sent Michael up the back wall to check on the state of the roof tiles. "The grass and brambles were waist-high in the doorway," Michael wrote. "A tractor was rusting in the gallery and a dusty rabbit skin hung from a roof beam. One push, we thought, and the old adobe walls would collapse into dust. But the beam took my weight and there were only a few places where the moonlight was slicing through to the dirt floor below. The tiles were covered with lichen and I could feel their warmth through the soles of my feet." When he jumped down, Michael could see his parents had made up their mind to buy it.

Many years later, he noted: "This will always be my father's house. I cannot sell it any more than I can disavow the man I became within its walls, any more than I can break the silences at the heart of family life."

IT IS NEARLY DARK, that same summer of 1984, and the lights have been turned on across the valley. Alison, Michael's mother, twirls her wine glass between her fingers and says to no one in particular, "When I was seven, my father once asked the family, "Who remembers the opening of the *Aeneid*? Anyone?" This reminder of Virgil's epic poem about a Trojan warrior was Michael's cue. "They were all better scholars than me, but *I knew*," he recalled. "*Arma virumque cano . . .*" he repeated from memory.

Everyone cheered—Leo, the cook, his mother and her sister, even his father who was the lodestar of his journey through life, somewhat reluctantly offered approval instead of his usual cool regard. "My father slowly put down the knife and fork and just stared at me. I wasn't supposed to be the clever one. There is some hurt in this story, a boy's grief at never being taken seriously, never being listened to, which has lasted to this moment next to me in the darkness."

His parents had sent Michael away to Upper Canada College, the famed Canadian establishment finishing school, when he was eleven, and except for a month each summer at their Provence hideaway, they ceased living as a family.

He pretended to resent the exile but his notes for that period contradict any sense of grievance: "The truth is I loved going away from home, sitting alone in a Super Constellation shuddering and shaking high above Greenland on the way back to school, watching the polar flames from the engines against the empty cobalt sky. At the College, I won a first-team tie in football [soccer]. I listened to Foster Hewitt's play by play of *Hockey Night in Canada* on the radio under my mattress after lights out in the dorm."

It was at UCC that he first realized that his mere presence meant something—that other boys would gravitate to him as a natural leader, a role model—and he did nothing to discourage such celebrity, minor as it was. One of his ostentations at the time was to walk around the school with the latest copy of the *Economist* or *Paris Match* tucked under his arm. Out from under his father's stern eye, he blossomed, becoming a steward (one step up from a prefect), editor of the yearbook, captain of the college soccer team and debating society both. As a boarder—in residence all but three weekends of the school year—he was deeply imbued with the fundamental ethic of the place: the notion that duty and responsibility were man's highest calling; no master ever stressed the importance of spontaneity and joy.

I went to UCC for five years, in a much earlier era than Ignatieff's, but even then it seemed to me that the college prepared its graduates for a world that no longer existed — if it ever had. A surprising number of alumni believed their time there was the emotional high spot of their circumscribed lives, nostalgic for the days of black-gowned masters who kept canes in their desks, for the borders of rustling rhododendrons, for the smell of the common rooms' red leather chairs, the cold glass of morning milk that we all believed contained a dose of saltpetre to keep our raging hormones under control. I feel no nostalgia at all, but there was a positive side to all this, even for me. The school stretched us, pushing us to discover our potentials, showing us that the hardest limits to overcome are generally self-imposed.

Since the disruptions and priorities of his father's diplomatic postings left little opportunity for Michael to experience an authentic boyhood with his family, his time at UCC became one of the formative influences of his life. And yes, of course, the college inspired a sense of privilege and elitism that made it hard for him later to masquerade as any form of ordinary Joe a voter could connect with.

The harshest aspect of his seven years at UCC as far as Ignatieff was concerned may have been having his younger brother there at the same time. The story has it that when Andrew arrived, Michael told him, "If you see me you must turn the other way and not acknowledge my presence. You are not to recognize that I am your brother. You don't exist as far as I'm concerned."

That sounds harsh to adult ears, but Andrew forgave his brother long ago. "Look," he says, "Michael was a fifteen-year-old boy, and I was twelve. That comment didn't make him heartless, it made

him an adolescent." Still, the younger brother loathed his time at
UCC, partly because he loathed the fact that the other boys per-
sisted in calling him Iggy. "I hated it," he says. "So when [after
Michael got into politics] those good-intentioned young Liberals
put out a website describing Canada as the 'Iggynation,' I categori-
cally rejected the idea." He remembers the yearning he had to be
like the others, to speak the language of privilege. "That's how
I became an Anglican," he says. (His father had been raised in the
Russian Orthodox faith and his mother was a Presbyterian.) "The
school principal said, 'Peter's an Anglican, Mark's an Anglican—
where does that leave you? I wanted to assimilate, to be part of the
gang." After UCC, Andrew trained to be an archeologist and participated in several important digs in Peru, before moving on to rural
development work and a career in benevolent non-governmental
organizations. "Not wanting to overpsychologize," he declares,
"I was in a place where no one knew what an Ignatieff was."

After Michael graduated from UCC, he attended Trinity College
at the University of Toronto, where he had a similarly glowing
time. His most lasting impact may have been in his role as co-
organizer of the historic teach-ins held at Varsity Stadium, the
first of which—held in 1965 to protest the Vietnam War—he says
occupied his first three months as an undergrad. At later events,
his partners were his closest university pal, Bob Rae, and Jeffrey
Rose, a whip-smart scholar who described the extracurricular
brainteasers as "revolutionary experiments in group introspec-
tion." Eventually a fellow at the London School of Economics,
Rose became national president of the Canadian Union of Public
Employees (CUPE) and deputy minister of intergovernmental
affairs for the province of Ontario. The list of speakers that
Ignatieff et al. recruited included U Thant, Secretary-General of
the United Nations; Reverend Ralph Abernathy, successor to the

assassinated Martin Luther King Jr.; Krishna Menon, the foreign minister of Pakistan; Conor Cruise O'Brien, the essayist and Irish diplomat; and Garfield Todd, a missionary and former prime minister of Southern Rhodesia who had attempted to extend the national franchise to blacks.

In those same heady days of the sixties, Ignatieff became politically involved, campaigning for Mike Pearson's Grits in 1965 and for Pierre Trudeau three years later, as a delegate to the convention that chose Trudeau as leader. In the election that followed, Ignatieff was in charge of organizing the youth vote for Trudeau, was invited to ride on his campaign plane and was one of the few campaign functionaries invited to the new PM's victory celebration at Harrington Lake. Offered several sinecures in government, Ignatieff opted instead to take up a Harvard fellowship because, as he put it, "I didn't know a damn thing about anything."

He performed brilliantly at Harvard, but he was passed over for an assistant professorship for reasons that his friends attributed to reverse snobbery. Martin Peretz, the editor-in-chief of the *New Republic* who had taught at Harvard back then, editorialized that Ignatieff "has more than fulfilled the promise some of us saw in him when, years ago, we argued unsuccessfully that he be promoted to assistant professor. His key opponent remonstrated that, given his advantages as a scion of the aristocracy, and an especially handsome one too, his accomplishments were less than they appeared." Theda Skocpol was chosen over Ignatieff, and after a rather bumpy and contentious ride that saw her leave Harvard for a period of years, now holds a chair in government and sociology there.

Instead, Ignatieff accepted a two-year appointment to teach history at the University of British Columbia—then left it, and Canada, to take up a six-year teaching fellowship at Cambridge in the UK.

THAT EVENING IN PROVENCE in 1984, musing about his past for his *Granta* piece, his reveries shifted from love of his school days to chronicling love of another kind—his introduction to sex and romance. "I went to my first dances and breathed in that intoxicating scent of hairspray, sweat, powder and the gardenia of girls' corsages that promised lush revelations in the dark. I became an adult in a tiny tent on a camping ground north of Toronto. The gravel was excruciating on my knees and elbows. The girl was very determined. She guided my hands in the dark. Afterwards she slapped my face, like a caress. I did what I wanted. Because I was at school, I didn't have to bring her home; I could keep sex a secret— but I clung to the grievance of banishment." (A writer to the bone, he later published a slightly different version of this encounter.)

His first real love was Susan Barrowclough, a stunning young British film historian who was working for the British Film Institute and had trained under Federico Fellini in Rome. They had met at a street dance in London and within two weeks he had brought her to Provence where they pledged themselves to one another. His favourite photo of her was taken that week: she was on the terrace walking towards him, wearing a white dress and a red Cretan sash. "She is smiling, her gaze directly into mine, shy and fearless," he wrote. "It is the last photograph in which she is still a stranger, approaching but still out of reach, still on the other side of the divide, before we fell in love."

On the way down the hill from the village, through the vaulted tunnel of the plane trees, white and phosphorescent in the headlights, Susan sang Verdi to him. Flat as always—her head leaning back, her eyes gazing into the trees.

"I am *not* flat," she insisted, reading his thoughts. He laughed.

She ignored him and sang on in her husky voice. "*Libera me . . . de morte aeterna . . .*"

At the time of this visit to France, she had been Michael's wife for eight years. His brother's verdict: "She is an incredibly intelligent, very beautiful woman of great charm, with marvelous skills." Andrew also says, "Theirs was a complex, intensely emotional connection, but both were extremely competitive." Michael dedicated his first major book, *The Needs of Strangers*, to her: "To Susan who teaches me my needs." A slim volume that redefined the aid relationship between donors and recipients, it contains his first aphorism: "Being human is an accomplishment. It takes practice."

CARESSED BY the breezes that sing through these elegant hills, Michael remembered the boy who grew into a man. There had been happy times, such as the family (three generations gathered under one roof) singsongs in which they'd all belt out one of "Fats" Waller's crazy ditties:

> *There's no disputin'*
> *That's Rasputin--*
> *The high falutin' lovin' man . . .*

Here in Provence, he had been a student, then a professor, then a cosmopolitan man of letters, then a humanitarian witness and activist: the prodigal son who became not quite British, then almost a Yank. But most of all, he was an exile from Canada who identified with the exotic undercurrents of Serbian history and created a readership that valued his intellectual flights into unclaimed territory. "In Canada the silence among the great trees was menacing—no light for miles," Michael had written. "I had no quarrel with the place. I just wanted to get out."

THE MOST PERVASIVE INFLUENCE on Michael Ignatieff—his life pattern, the private wars that raged inside him, the public thoughts and writings that brought him fame, then notoriety, his ethics and his personal priorities—was his intense relationship with his father.

A difficult, highly talented, individualistic presence, George Ignatieff became one of Canada's defining postwar diplomats, having served in such high-profile positions as president of the United Nations Security Council when Canada sat as a member and as Canada's Chief Permanent Ambassador to NATO, as well as Ambassador for Disarmament back in Ottawa. He also very nearly became the nation's Governor General. Offered the position by Pierre Trudeau, he would have filled that role with distinction and grace—but it was not to be. Word got out before the official announcement, and Trudeau withdrew the appointment. He chose as Ignatieff's replacement Edward Schreyer, the dependably pedestrian former NDP Premier of Manitoba—as about as far a cry from the urbane George Ignatieff as one could get.

Within the family he was as much of a hero figure as any to be found in Latin or Greek mythology—all powerful, all wise, and distant beyond belief. Having lost their aristocratic legacy in the Russian Revolution, the clan (which was a more accurate description than "family") arrived in Canada in 1928 with limited funds and indifferent prospects. George, born in 1913, eventually became the patriarch, and ruled the roost with love and the strict manner of a Russian count still in charge of his, and the family's, destiny.

"Old age is not for cowards," the senior Ignatieff reminded his eldest son that summer in Provence. "He paced slowly at the other end of the long room, at the distance where truth is possible between us," Michael recalled. "We are drinking *tisane*, a nightly ritual usually passed in silence. There are thirty-four years between us: two wars and a revolution. There was also his success that made it difficult for us to understand each other."

As George grew older, he scoured the past looking for something to hold onto beyond the ravages of time. That quest increased the distance, if not the love between them. "I try to think about him historically, to find the son within the father, the boy within the man," Michael wrote. "His moods—the dark self-absorption—have always had the legitimacy of his dispossession. Exile is a set of emotional permissions we are all bound to respect."

That night at the cottage, his father broke the silence. "I don't expect to live long," he said.

"It's not up to you, is it?" the son rejoined, then wrote,

He stokes the prospect of his death like a fire in the grate. Ahead of me the prospect beckons and glows, sucking the oxygen from the room. He says he is not afraid of dying, and, in so far as I can, I believe him. But that is not the point. In his voice, there is a child's anger at not being understood, an old man's fear of being abandoned. He does not want a son's pity or his sorrow, yet his voice carries a plea for both. A silence falls between us. I hear myself saying that he is in good health, which is true and entirely beside the point. He says goodnight, stoops briefly as he passes through the archway, and disappears into his room.

The encounter sets off a nocturnal reverie in the son about the force of blood ties: "There is nothing more common, more natural than for fathers and sons to be strangers to each other," he writes. "It was only on those silent beach walks together, our voices lost in the surf, our footprints erased by the tide, our treasure accumulated mile by mile, that we found an attachment which we cannot untie."

When Michael Ignatieff exiled himself from Canada, he didn't realize that you are always exiled from, not to. That meant his new domiciles, however pleasant, inevitably left something to be desired. Instead of freeing him from extraneous concerns, becoming an expat felt peripheral and embargoed: he was out of reach—a gypsy in alien landscapes. When he settled down in Canada following his political gambit, Ignatieff was still running, but now he was running to, not from. He was running home.

Interview Excerpt: Ignatieff on his father

"My dad was physically big, powerful, tall, aristocratic, irascible, irritating, charming . . . an incredibly loveable, very affectionate man. I never once doubted his love for me. Everything I've ever done had that ground under my feet. People talk about me being privileged: that was the privilege. I've earned everything I have. But the privilege was having those parents . . .

There was a period in my twenties when I was having a very hard time at Harvard. I couldn't get my thesis done. I didn't know why I was doing it. People were out in the world, doing interesting things, and here I was, sitting in the library. I remember my father being very upset with me, very aggressive. *What are you doing? Just make up your mind.* I can remember it as a kind of primal moment when I thought I had to stand up for myself and for the path I was going on, which was the lonely path of academic scholarship. That was a tough period. There was frankly conflict. I felt he often dominated my mother, and was so needy, and so demanding of my mother that he just took all the oxygen out of the room for me and my brother. And that produced conflict. I remember an eight- to nine-month period in my twenties when I just didn't see him at all. But when I think about where my sense of Canada comes from it was from him and her. There's no question. I can't emphasize it enough, how much assurance they gave me. I'm a sentimental person, but I don't think I'm a fool about this. I felt absolute granite with their support which is unbelievable."

3. Recruiting the Action Intellectual

Ignatieff expressed enchantment at the
ease with which his nomination had come about.
"The team put itself together," he gushed. "One of
the wonderful things about this experience is that
I don't think I had to make a single call."

LURING MICHAEL IGNATIEFF to take on the leadership of the
Liberal party was a bit like nurturing a tulip, never sure whether
its fragile tip would be destroyed by a late frost or if it would survive
to full bloom. He was wooed and courted as no novice politician
in Canadian history.

It all began in the minds of a trio of Liberal lieutenants who
had participated in an unsuccessful and short-lived run by John
Manley for the party's leadership, a footnote to the footnote of
Paul Martin's belly flop as prime minister. Manley, who had been
Jean Chrétien's finance minister as well as the deputy prime minister, was one of those right-wing Liberals who should have been a
Tory but preferred being in power. Decent and intelligent, he had
never, as they say in the upper reaches of the Grit Establishment,
"blotted his copybook." In fact he was conscientious to the point
of being boring.

The initiating agent was Ian Davey, whose legendary father, Keith, was one of the founders of Canada's modern Liberal party. A bushy-tailed provocateur, Davey the younger became the champion not only of bringing in a new breed of leader but of creating a new kind of party. "Our aim," he told me at the time he was launching his daring plan, "is to change the political culture of how public policy is developed in this country. What's happened of late was that we didn't stand for anything except winning elections. Too many people in the Liberal party were basically in it to make a living, becoming lobbyists who peddled their influence. That was the culture that had to be changed."

To that point, Davey's idealism had seemed like a dead end because fundamental reforms of the party were considered by its influential decision-makers to be a greater threat to the existing power structure than anything Stephen Harper might dish out. Those partisans who blame the Conservative leader for the Liberal setbacks and defeats suffered from tunnel vision. If the Liberal party does vanish, it will have perished mainly from self-inflicted wounds. But Davey and his allies were able to seize the moment. The horror stories of Liberal fraud in the Quebec sponsorship scandal were making headlines daily, and it was alarmingly obvious that Paul Martin could only walk on water in swim trunks.

As chief agent of an intended revolutionary shift, Davey enlisted two co-conspirators—Dan Brock, a policy hawk who had spent a decade as a producer on Peter Gzowski's CBC morning radio programme, and Alfred Apps, a Bay Street lawyer who had been John Turner's chief Ontario organizer during his 1984 leadership campaign and was said to have become a Liberal backroom boy while still in swaddling clothes. He was known inside the party for lengthy and often astute strategy memos that nobody read, and for the fact that his breakfast menu was often betrayed by the evidence spotting his ties.

To this point, Davey had spent most of his time making prize-winning TV documentaries, such as *September 1972*, on the epic Canada-Russia hockey summit series. He'd helped with marketing campaigns for the Liberal party in the 1970s and 1980s, had been marginally involved with Dalton McGuinty when he was opposition leader at Ontario's Queen's Park, and he'd done the final edit on Chrétien's red book for the 1993 federal campaign. After Chrétien made it clear that he would relinquish his role and open the party up for a leadership contest in 2003, Manley had called Davey up and asked to see him at his Toronto office. As Davey remembers, "John comes in looking like an executive for Microsoft or something, with these big glasses, and he says 'I'm interested in running for leadership, and I'm told you can help me. What do you think?'"

"I think you're a Tory," Davey replied, and Manley started laughing. "In a funny way, we just hit it off because I don't think he had a lot of people shoot straight with him before," Davey says.

A little later, Manley convened a meeting of twenty-five advisers in Ottawa to discuss whether he really should take a run at it the leadership. "I got on a plane to Ottawa thinking it would be madness on his part, and I was planning to tell him so," Davey says. "Down the aisle comes Alf Apps, with his tie askew, breakfast on his shirt. You know Alfred—he's a mad professor." Apps was clutching a letter he'd prepared, headed "Ten reasons why John Manley shouldn't run for Leadership." So Apps and Davey at least were of like minds.

Davey picks up the story: "We sat in a large room with a bunch of senior Ottawa players, and when we went around the room, twenty-three of the twenty-five people present, said 'You've got to run for the leadership.' Until it was my turn. 'Lookit, John,' I told him. 'You can't win. I don't think you should run, but if you do, you've got to make Paul Martin lose. You may have a shot at that, but it's a small shot.' "

Manley decided to go for it, but three weeks later he called a meeting with Davey and Apps, confessing that though he was about to launch his bid, nothing was organized. He asked for their help. Davey pulled no punches. "If you're serious about winning, you've got to run hard after Martin, and here's how you do it," Davey remembers telling him. "Go after the money. He has raised $20 million for his leadership run. Who's given it to him and what do they want from him?" Davey told Manley he was worried about what was happening in the Liberal party, which had turned into a closed shop where money talked instead of the issues that mattered. "I'm prepared to help you, because I think that's wrong," Davey told Manley, "but you've got to understand the downside. If you fail you're done for." Within two weeks, the story about the level of Martin's funding was everywhere, as was the story that he was refusing to disclose the contributors. The Manley campaign was on the radar.

"I went into the Manley campaign," Davey said later, "because I was worried about what the Liberals had become. I grew up in a family that put their lives into this thing, and had done so with the belief that the party had to be constantly renewed with younger and better recruits. But it had become a family compact—actually two warring family compacts—and had slipped under the overwhelming influence of professional lobbyists. Manley was a good, decent, honourable guy, and quite a bright, able public servant." Manley stayed in the campaign, and Davey with him, until his money dried up, but it was Paul Martin, the head of one of those family compacts, who triumphed—for what that victory was worth, either to himself or to the country.

DAVEY HAD BIG SHOES to fill, but came by the desire to make a difference politically by birth. Though his father, Senator Keith Davey, had stepped down from the Senate in 1996, and was now suffering from Alzheimer's, there is no doubt that Ian in his way was about to try to enact a big-time solution to the Liberal party's problems, just like his father might have done. Except that he only had the memory of his father in action to call upon, as his father's memory no longer functioned.

If Canada's Natural Government Party in its heyday had a patron saint, it was Davey's dad, a former Toronto advertising genius who transformed the farm team into a smoothly professional operation. A big, hunched, handsome Eagle Scout, Keith Davey was the most widely liked and respected presence in Ottawa, where, as national campaign director of the Liberal party under three prime ministers—Pearson, Trudeau and Turner—Davey supplied the enthusiasm that kept the political machine alive.

Davey and his fellow Liberals regarded Ottawa as a company town—and they owned the company. They assumed that they alone knew what was good for Canadians, and that it was just plain dumb to vote for any other party, except as occasional comic relief. For Liberals, the political ideal was to do as little as possible, but as much as necessary. And for most of three decades, they followed Davey's sage advice, as expressed in his Ten Commandments of Canadian Liberalism, summed up in his memoir, *The Rainmaker*:

1. Revere the Leader.
2. Remember a leader is never cooked until people start to laugh at him.
3. Stay on the road to reform; keep left of centre.
4. Hang together.
5. Build a local poll organization worthy of the name.

6. Lead to your strength in campaigns; to your weakness in conventions.

7. Never negotiate through fear; never fear to negotiate.

8. Remember that in politics, perception is reality.

9. Recruit new, bright young people.

10. Avoid public humour, but laugh a lot in private.

Walter Gordon, then Mike Pearson's campaign manager, had hired Davey in 1961, following a groundbreaking Liberal policy conference in Kingston. Flowing out of that pivotal event, the volunteer wing of the party developed tactics and policies that were new to Canada, including a national pension plan, the implementation of Medicare and other schemes that were responsible for the Grits regaining power in 1963. Keith's job was to sell the new approach. The genius of Pearson was to reach out and recruit new talent to implement the innovative agenda, opening the party to fresh ideas and waves of outsiders.

Davey set about rebuilding the rusty Liberal machine, which would soon lose its third straight election to John Diefenbaker's Tories. Cog by cog, he rebuilt the apparatus, instilling it with his own enthusiasm and ideas cribbed from the New Frontier songbook of John F. Kennedy, the recently elected, charismatic American president.

I was an Ottawa columnist then, and at least once a month, Davey and I would lunch at the Granada Café, a cozy greasy spoon around the corner from the Liberal party's headquarters on Cooper Street, where he would give me a peek into Liberal affairs over hot hamburger sandwiches. Although he carried a button pinned inside his wallet that read, "stifle yourself," he seldom did. For example, he once gave me the heads up on his plan to modernize the party by importing President Kennedy's private pollster,

Lou Harris, to helped boost the Liberals in the 1962 campaign. Harris displaced existing do-it-yourself surveys with a professional approach, which had to be kept a deep dark secret because it was very American, and therefore highly suspect. He was registered at the Chateau Laurier hotel under a pseudonym.

I ABANDONED OTTAWA in 1969 to become editor-in-chief of the *Toronto Star*, but kept in close touch with Davey and his wonderful wife, Dorothy.

Most Ottawa Men of that era—and at the time they were nearly all men—pretended to have a devil-may-care approach to politics, treating it as a game, not as a religion. But once they had been excommunicated (i.e., their phones stopped ringing), they weren't so sure. There was an inner glow that illuminated the faces of political journalists, lobbyists and hangers-on when they were collecting useful and occasionally classified information. In those days, nearly every member of Ottawa's media elite was plugged into one brain, which told them what to think, write, broadcast— how to judge who was hot and who wasn't.

Political Ottawa was a place without weather. It had moods instead of climate, and the barometer was always falling. Allister Grossart, the Ottawa operative who had been the brains behind John Diefenbaker's bluster, once told me that "governing is a series of occasions." That was a valid observation but it was the Liberals who best exploited the occasions that presented themselves. And it was Keith Davey's particular genius they relied on.

During those first ten years of his Ottawa sojourn, influence became increasingly significant in Ottawa's decision-making mix. Power accrued to people according to their precise position within a formal hierarchy. Influence was a much more subtle phenomenon, since it manifested itself by the willingness of people to take seriously observers or players who lacked formal sanction. Imposing your agenda: that was the only power that counted. Davey mastered that art. Most Canadian universities still teach a subject they insist on calling political science. Its successful practitioners know that it might be an art or a game, but never a science—more a form of alchemy. And Keith Davey, during his years in Ottawa, was Canada's chief alchemist. His like will not come again, but his son Ian was willing to give imposing a new Liberal agenda a shot.

PAUL MARTIN WENT ON TO WIN the Liberal leadership and he promptly led the party into an election in which they squeaked out a minority mandate, hardly the crowning of the new Liberal messiah that his cadre of loyal supporters had predicted. After Martin's dismal showing at the polls, Ian Davey believed more strongly than ever that only an outsider with special talents could rescue the party from itself. So Davey, Brock and Apps assigned themselves the task of recruiting someone who could fit the bill.

Ignatieff's name was first mentioned to Davey by Rocco Rossi, then a popular power broker who became the party's national director and then ran for mayor of Toronto. (In the fall of 2011, still looking for an active role in politics, he ran in the Ontario provincial election as a Progressive Conservative.) Rossi said, "I only have one idea. It came from your dad, who was at a Victoria College lecture given by Michael Ignatieff. As I was leaving, your father walked up beside me and said, 'That guy should be prime minister.'"

That hadn't been just a lecture, but the second in a series financed by Davey's family as a living tribute to the man. It had been Keith himself who suggested that Ignatieff should follow Harvard's John Kenneth Galbraith, who had given the inaugural speech in 1996. Michael Levine, the ace entertainment lawyer, had gone to the lecture, too, and ended up sitting between Davey and John Ralston Saul.* During Ignatieff's talk, the senator kept leaning across Levine to murmur to Saul, "He'd make a great prime minister." Whereas according to Levine, Saul kept muttering things such as, "He's not that tall, he's not that handsome, he's not that smart."

After Rossi mentioned Ignatieff, Ian Davey tried his father's idea out on Apps. Apps liked the thought. "So what do we do?" Davey asked. "We'll call him," said Apps.

THEY DIDN'T HAVE A CONTACT number for their quarry but Davey was a client of Michael Levine's, and he knew Ignatieff was too. When Davey called his lawyer, Levine shot back, "You're nuts. Michael's at Harvard. He has the job of a lifetime. He's writing a book for me right now about his family and Canadian history. There's just no way. But I'll set it up for you."

Before Levine could work his magic, Apps got impatient and cold-called Ignatieff at the Carr Center for Human Rights Policy at Harvard, which Ignatieff headed (though his five-year term was about to expire). He arranged for them to meet in Boston on December 13, 2004, then sent Brock an e-mail: "Just spoke to the

---

* *Levine, who probably represented everyone in the hall except the ushers, remembers introducing his client and friend Michael Ignatieff to another couple he knew well, Charles and Andy Bronfman. Levine says, "On the way over to meet them, Michael was doing the Russian equivalent of oy veh, because he considered them to be the king and queen of Jews and his own great-grandfather had sponsored Russia's horrific pogroms of the Jews. So when we arrived, Ignatieff immediately launched into a convoluted defence of his ancestor. At which point, Andy, Charles's wife, turned to him and said, 'Michael, cut the shit. If my great grandfather had been minister of the interior in Russia in 1881, he would have thought the Jews were a big pain in the ass too.'"*

Russian. He has been waiting for our call all of his life." Then it turned out that Ignatieff had to come to Toronto sooner, so instead they met on a rainy Saturday afternoon in Apps's law office. As well as the original three, the meeting was attended by Lorna Marsden, an academic who had been a vice-president of the Liberal party (as well as president of York University) and Sachin Aggarwal, then gaining a reputation in Liberal ranks as a shrewd operative. A Toronto native, Aggarwal had graduated with a degree in biochemistry from McMaster, then went on to law school followed by an MBA from the University of Toronto. He cut his teeth as a corporate lawyer at the eminent Toronto-based firm Torys.

Ignatieff had come with Zsuzsanna, his second wife and his partner in all things. After the introductions, he leaned back and said, "Okay. This is your meeting, tell me a story." So they proceeded to go around the table, talking about themselves, their concerns for their country's future, their worries that their party seemed to be drifting out of contention for power. "Michael was very attentive to what we were saying," Brock recalls. "You could tell he was almost desperate to get this kind of first-hand insight into what was going on in Canada."

After three hours of these recitations, Ignatieff responded. He described his work at Harvard, how he loved his job, what he was working on, and what he was writing. Then he confessed that despite it all he longed to come back and be part of the Canadian experience again. "But what you have to understand about me," he concluded, pointing to Zsuzsanna, who had been quiet throughout, "is that nothing happens with me without her. So this decision is not my decision to make. It has to be *our* decision. And if that woman says she's not in, I'm not in. Full stop. We come as a pair. I'm going to take away all that you told me and think about it. Maybe in the New Year, we can talk again."

By the second week of January, none of them had heard anything more from him. Apps, getting antsy, phoned Ignatieff in Boston and invited himself and his two cronies to dinner on January 13, at the Charles Hotel on Harvard Square. There, in the Rialto dining room, which according to its proprietors offers "whimsical interpretations of regional Italian cuisine," they discussed their joint futures. Apps recalls, "It immediately became clear that for Ignatieff the issue was no longer 'if' but 'when'—and 'how.' The story he would tell about his return to Canada and his entry into public life was well rehearsed. He just didn't have a clue what the mechanics of that re-entry might be, and neither did we. So we ended up spending three hours of our dinner grilling him on his decision to support George W. Bush in the invasion of Iraq. There was a lot of 'How could you?' But the conversation always came back to him asking us, 'So how do I do this? What do you have to do? What's the life of a politician? What's the life of a politician's wife?'" They drank copious amounts of wine and, at the end of the evening, Apps remembers Ignatieff saying, "Listen, you told me a lot of very interesting things, but I'm not greenlighting anything yet. Go away and think about what the next steps might be, then give me a call."

"We went back to Canada and thought, well, at least he's interested," Brock recalls. "But we had no idea if we could actually do this, though we certainly talked a good game and convinced him that we knew what we were doing. Now we had to convince ourselves."

As far as Ignatieff was concerned, he told me later, "Davey, Apps and Brock appeared at the right place at the right moment. I was ready. I'd been away a long time, and was aware that no matter what I did, I would always be an expatriate in the United States. I had come to a fork in the road. I was pretty engaged. This was something I wanted to do. . . . It was about having been a spectator, and wanting to become an actor—wanting to take responsibility."

The example of his father was also a huge part of his decision to go for it. "I'd seen him represent the country, speak for Canada. His death and my mother's death so closely after in 1990–91 was the most difficult period of my life. Their voices were inside me saying, 'We did our bit, now it's time to do yours.' There's no question about it. The price of expatriation was going up and I was starting to ask myself, 'Where the hell do I belong?' And the answer was, I belong back in Canada. I remembered what happened to my dad, who signed up for the foreign service in 1940, worked for Mike Pearson and Vincent Massey in London, was abroad until the early 1970s, and then he came home too, which in many ways became the most creative period of his life. He was a homing pigeon. We were both homing pigeons."

AT THE TIME, the Liberal party was preparing for its policy convention in Ottawa in the spring of 2005. A good first step to bringing Ignatieff home, the trio thought, would be to wangle an invitation for him to give the keynote address in which he could say something substantive about his ideas of Liberalism and about Canadian politics, and thereby test the waters. With the blessing of Paul Martin, then leading a minority Liberal government, they approached Ignatieff and he agreed. "We thought we were off to the races," says Brock.

The core three-person Ignatieff recruitment team had expanded to include Aggarwal, Alexis Levine—Michael's son—Milton Chan, Mark Sakamoto and Leslie Church, a group of highly aware youthful Liberals with no place to hang their idealism, who coalesced around the idea of attracting someone with

Ignatieff's credentials into Canadian politics. At this point, it wasn't billed as a leadership gambit, or at least so everyone maintained.

The Ignatieff team had reviewed the speech before he gave it; he was speaking directly to fellow Liberals, and indirectly to Canadians, about the party's heritage and success, stressing its essential role in national unity, Canadian sovereignty and social justice—and also weaving in his own roots in the party, as a Trudeau delegate in the 1968 leadership convention, and then as the head of Trudeau's youth wing throughout the election that followed. The text had moved at least one team member to tears. Brock says, "It was a call to arms to remind Liberals who they were, where they came from, what ought to matter to them, why we were in government and what we should be trying to accomplish." (One of Ignatieff's most telling lines in hindsight was never reported: "Academics are supposed to be tremendously smart, but one of the things about academics is that they often comically and cruelly lack good political judgement.")

On the Saturday morning of that convention I published a column in the *National Post* that identified Ignatieff's appearance for what it really was: an attempt to move the Liberals into the twenty-first century by recruiting a highly touted outsider to take over the party's reins from a fumbling Martin.

"Oh my God, who's been talking to Peter C. Newman!" Brock remembers exclaiming. "We've been outed: the jig is up. My first thought was that this wouldn't be well received by Paul Martin and his people. They would see it as a power play designed to destabilize them. Now there was no more back-door entry. Either he came in through the front door with the blessing of the leader, or not at all."

Needless to say, that night as Ignatieff rose to speak the eyes on him were extremely beady. And the recruiting effort came close to self-destructing before it was even truly in motion. Ignatieff was about halfway through his speech, when he looked puzzled, and stopped. Then he said, "You are now looking at what a professor looks like when he is scared to death. It appears that I have misplaced some of my speech." He had left six pages of the podium copy in his hotel room and there was no teleprompter. From that point on, he spoke extemporaneously, reaching to gather the threads of the speech he had written. It was a public display of a man comfortable in his own skin but who still had a lot to learn, about politics, about the party, about the country and about how to draw in a crowd. It wasn't that Ignatieff's body language was inadequate, it's that there wasn't any. If he wanted to come back home in a political role, he needed to immerse himself in the cadence of Canada's life and times as if he was returning to his youth, a time of dreams and shadows that had suddenly taken on a startling new reality.

THEN CAME DINNER AT IL POSTO, the expensive pasta joint that was a popular Toronto Liberal establishment hangout. The host was David Smith, the Liberal senator from Yorkville, whose presence signalled that this dinner was really an audition.

Smith was the chief power broker of Grit-Heaven-on-the-Rideau, at the epicentre of that once-omnipotent party machine for as long as records have been kept. With a figure on the way to being chubby, and a smile you could auction at Sotheby's, Smith was still the reigning godfather. Until the senator agreed to dine with the candidate at the unofficial watering hole for testing potential potentates (Stéphane Dion had a bolognese with him there), Ignatieff's political birth was only a rumour.

Brock wrote in his diary entry about that night: "Ignatieff was intrigued, you could just tell by watching him. It was a testament to David being impressed that he quickly moved on to telling the visitor: 'If you're serious about doing this, this is what we'd need to do. I would call the Prime Minister, and tell Paul that you're thinking about doing this. And what did he think? Let him know. That's the way to do this—it's the appropriate thing to do.'" Smith was offering to act as the enabling ambassador for what was represented as the possible enlistment of an interesting new Liberal recruit. No one explicitly mentioned that there was a long game in play designed to replace Martin as party leader.

When they finished dinner, Smith spontaneously invited them back to his condo off Bay Street. It turned out to be a secular shrine to the Liberal party, the walls adorned with pictures of the party's saints—both the many who were canonized and the few who became cannon fodder. The unexpected invitation was a testament to how much Ignatieff had impressed Smith. But when Smith spoke to Paul Martin about the idea of Ignatieff running in the next election, the PM's reaction was decidedly tepid. He expressed technical concerns: "Where does he run? How do I find him a riding? Who do I ask to step aside? Do I have to guarantee a nomination somewhere?" But he did tell Smith, "You know, in principle, I'm supportive of this. If Ignatieff wants to run, can find himself a riding, build an organization, get himself elected, then as leader, I'm supportive."

The good news was that the PMO wasn't going to shut the recruiting process down; the bad news was that they weren't going to help much either. In fact, they weren't going to help at all. Brock soon received a call from Karl Littler, the PM's deputy chief of staff, which he recalls going like this: " 'So, Dan,' " he said, 'I understand that Michael Ignatieff wants to run. I have to be honest with you upfront, I'm not a big fan of the idea. You can tell me whatever you want about this—that it isn't about the leadership and all the rest of it—but I have to tell you, the notion of this guy coming from outside and having something handed to him on a silver platter just personally offends me. Meanwhile, you are free to do what you want. If there are ways in which the party could be helpful in terms of the setting of the timings of nomination meetings, we'd look at possibly accommodating that. That's as far as we might consider going. . . . I'm not having my people carry Mr. Ignatieff's water.' "

If Ignatieff was going to run, his recruiters needed to guarantee that he could get his feet wet in a riding he had a chance of winning. The best fit for a man of his background had to be a Toronto constituency, where at least he could say he'd gone to school and where his family did have some roots. So Smith had to find a winnable seat for his new protege when all the ridings in Fortress Toronto, as the Grits then liked to describe it, were occupied by Liberal members or confirmed claimants. The godfather was likely the only man who could find Ignatieff his toehold.

SMITH'S EMERGENCE AS OTTAWA'S dominant backroom influence was forged over two decades of faithful but not very spectacular service to the party. Born in Toronto, Smith enrolled in Carleton University in the early 1960s where instead of trying to become Big Man on Campus he devoted his spare time to going to the Hill to watch parliamentary debates. "I got to meet Mr. Pearson at 24 Sussex, and that was where I felt comfortable," he recalls. He became a Liberal first and a professional politician second. While studying for a law degree he met Keith Davey, who said, "Look, I know you're going to law school, but postpone it a year. I'll make you the national youth director, but you'll really be my right-hand guy." Smith took Davey's advice and spent the next twelve months meeting the party's insiders. His Rolodex still rules.

"Pearson was particularly kind to me," Smith recalls. "My father and grandfather, as well his father and grandfather, were Methodist ministers. Preacher's kids called themselves PKs. So Pearson would put his arm around me and say, 'We double PKs, we have to stick together. You know, there are quite a few PKs, but there aren't that many doubles.'" (When Smith told that story to Jean Chrétien before the 1993 election, the then Liberal leader replied, "I've been thinking a lot about it. The reason you were out there at Sussex Drive so much with Pearson wasn't because you were Keith's assistant, or the national president of the Young Liberals, it was because you're a double PK!")

Smith finished law school, articled, then joined the payroll of several ministers in succession, learning the ropes. At twenty-seven, he became one of the organizers of John Turner's unsuccessful 1968 leadership run. Smith then entered his schizophrenic phase, directing a rapidly expanding Toronto legal practice, while becoming the party's indispensable *über macher*. "Check it with David," became the signal that something important was afoot. He was Jack Pickersgill's political reincarnation: the old phrase had been "Check it with Jack," and had signaled similar clout. They ruled on matters that were important but not quite important enough to require the direct blessing of the leader.

With Chrétien, Smith came into his own, chairing each of his federal election campaigns. He acted as a kind of exofficio deputy leader, doubling as a translator of the Shawinigan politician's broken French and dysfunctional English, getting things done "the better the sooner," as his boss liked to say.

In the 1993 campaign in which Chrétien became prime minister, Smith's organizational skills led to the Liberals nabbing ninety-eight of Ontario's ninety-nine federal seats. U.S. President Bill Clinton came up from Washington the following year and when Chrétien told him the story, Clinton said, "Yeah, ninety-eight out of ninety-nine—I'd settle for that. Listen, David, I'd like you to come to the White House. I'm offering you a job. Can you report next Monday morning?" Clinton went on for several minutes longer, really getting into the gag. "But you know what?" Smith confided. "Chrétien never teased me again about winning only ninety-eight out of ninety-nine seats."

Smith ranked Ignatieff as the most intelligent among the Liberal leaders he's worked for—and the fastest study. "It's fair to say that his knowledge of politics has been from an academic perspective. Most people outside politics who've established good reputations for themselves just can't make the jump to give up the career they've got, and take the risk. But he did. To say bye-bye to Harvard—that was really something."

Smith was willing to back the dark horse because he knew the challenges his party was facing. The ground had been shifting for some time. "I don't want to put too much emphasis on religion, but you must understand this," he says. "Ever since the days of Laurier, if you were a French-Canadian, you were a Liberal. And if you were Catholic, you were a Liberal. And if you were an immigrant you were a Liberal, because you knew who made your entry happen. . . .

"Hardline Catholics are certainly a harder sell for us now." Combined with the rise of the Bloc in Quebec, the Liberals couldn't count on Quebec seats anymore. "Those shifts were the two big ones," Smith says. "The third is that a lot of young people have moved into the business world and they don't necessarily think, 'We've got to vote Liberal.' Some have gone right wing, I suppose. Those are all challenges. The sort of base that we inherited and kind of took for granted is not the same and probably will never be the same. Being French, being Catholic, and being the second and third generations of immigrants no longer guarantees votes for Liberals. Also, the Liberal party has never represented the far right or the far left. We've always had people on both sides of the spectrum. We're small 'l' social, progressive liberals and this is a liberal country. That's our heritage. That's our legacy. That's what we represent." All true, except for his use of the present tense.

SMITH AND THE IGNATIEFF TEAM soon fixed on the Toronto riding of Etobicoke-Lakeshore, which they thought was probably winnable if they could persuade the sitting Liberal member, Jean Augustine, to step down. Augustine was a popular MP who had been born in Grenada and had been an outstanding public school principal before she ran for public office. "At this point she had reached a certain age, and was ready to step aside, and I kind of helped make it happen," Smith admits.

When Apps and Smith approached her about her intentions, and confided that they were looking for a riding to launch Ignatieff, it turned out that Augustine had been thinking about not running again. In the previous year, her riding association had been taken over by a group of Ukrainian activists who had put her on notice that they didn't want her as the candidate anymore; the riding was home to one of the largest concentrations of Ukrainian-Canadians in the country and they wanted their day in the sun. She had fought such battles before and won but she wasn't relishing the idea of fighting them again. She met Ignatieff, and was impressed, and agreed to step aside. (She was encouraged in her decision by the fact that Senator Smith had already arranged a sinecure for her as Ontario's first Fairness Commissioner, working on behalf of foreign-trained professionals who immigrated to the province.)

On November 25, 2005, she informed the riding president, Ron Chyczij, and the rest of the executive of the Etobicoke-Lakeshore Liberal Association that she was resigning the seat she'd held since 1993. Anyone interested in contesting the nomination would have until 5 p.m. the following afternoon to file the required application along with thirty supporting signatures at Ontario Liberal headquarters in downtown Toronto. Chyczij and another potential candidate, Marc Shwec, brought their proper documentation to the Liberal office well before the deadline, and were shocked to find the doors locked. Though the aspiring candidates tried hand signals to attract the notice of staffers they could see inside, no one came over to unlock the door. Chyczij and Shwec finally slipped their papers under the door, and that was the last either saw of their perfectly legal applications.

(The only Liberal who behaved honourably in this debacle was the national director of the Liberal party at the time, Steven MacKinnon, who later told a CP reporter, "My understanding is that the nomination papers of the two Ukrainian-Canadian candidates were deposited at the office and that there's no dispute that they were there within the time frame prescribed.")

Meanwhile, over at the Valhalla Inn in Etobicoke (Valhalla, according to Norse mythology, being the hall in which the souls of heroes slain in battle are received by the gods), five hundred people had gathered for the nomination meeting, and they were definitely not there to welcome Michael Ignatieff.

I was there that night and I am still surprised no one was hurt. The problem was that the local activists had unearthed some pride-shattering quotes from his 1993 book, *Blood and Belonging*, and had been passing them around. For instance, Ignatieff had written, "I have reasons to take Ukraine seriously indeed. But, to be honest, I'm having trouble. Ukrainian independence conjures up images of peasant-embroidered shirts, the nasal whine of ethnic instruments, phony Cossacks in cloaks and boots." And: "My difficulty in taking Ukraine seriously goes deeper than just my cosmopolitan suspicion of nationalists everywhere. Somewhere inside I'm also what Ukrainians would call a great Russian and there is just a trace of old Russian disdain for these little Russians. . . . From my childhood, I remember expatriate Ukrainian nationalists demonstrating in the snow outside performances by the Bolshoi Ballet in Toronto, chanting, 'Free the captive nations!' In 1960, they seemed strange and pathetic, haranguing people who just wanted to see ballet and to hell with politics. They seemed fanatical, too, unreasonable. Hadn't they looked at the map? How did they think Ukraine could ever be free?" Since this was long before he'd ever thought of becoming a politician, it added credibility to the charge that he just might be plainly anti-Ukrainian.

After the Liberals' Ontario campaign co-chairs announced that only Ignatieff's name should be allowed to stand, and Ignatieff began to speak, riot police moved in. Fists were waved at him, and he was booed and continually interrupted. People yelled that Ignatieff should go home, which must have been confusing for him since he'd just committed to coming back to the country that was his home. Half the audience walked out, and after they were gone he was anointed the Liberal candidate by acclamation.

Ignatieff himself, the veteran observer of how the political world really works, ended this less than glorious episode with the most naive comment since Stockwell Day reminisced about the age of the dinosaurs. He expressed enchantment at the ease with which his nomination had come about. "The team put itself together," he gushed. "One of the wonderful things about this experience is that I don't think I had to make a single phone call." Who was this guy? How did he write all those pithy, trenchant books alive with authenticity?

When asked by the press to defend the nomination process, Ignatieff intoned, "I cannot speak to the process by which the party designated me as a candidate."

What was Senator David Smith's comment on how his man Ignatieff was launched into Canadian public life? "There was a little tension there, but it all worked out."

You've got to admire the sang-froid of a lifelong Grit who can define a fixed nominating procedure and a riotous nominating meeting that required a hefty police presence as "a little tension."

Interview Excerpt: Ignatieff on leaving teaching and going into politics

I felt kind of good about being a professor. I absolutely loved it. I felt confident in the arena. I would go into class and know exactly what I wanted to do, how to do it, how to get things out of students. I must have been nuts that I thought I could go into politics, because politics would be just like that. Politics is completely different. Words are weapons. The great thing about Socratic teaching, which is what I was doing, is not laying down the law but asking, "Why do you think that?" The musing, the thinking aloud thing was just so exciting to me. That had to stop, from one day to the next.

It takes a very long time to learn the discipline of getting up in the morning and saying to yourself, "What do I intend to say? What is the message? What issues should I take a position on? What issues should I stay away from?" I can't begin to tell you how difficult it was for me to learn. It's been very humbling. There have been moments when I've asked myself, "Why exactly did I think I would be good at this?" I really had to learn it from the bottom up in the full spotlight of public criticism. And so, there have been moments I haven't been terrific.

I don't think I've been arrogant realizing how much I had to learn. You can be a communicator all your life, as I've been, but working politics is a totally different art. In a classroom, what you say and what you mean can sometimes come a little bit apart. People give you the benefit of the doubt. In politics, the rules are literal. The words that come out of your mouth are words that matter, right? You have to respect that discipline. There are the rules, I play by the rules, and I accept the rules. If I don't learn them and don't follow them — my fault.

4. Just What the Party Needed

He was recruited as a Liberal foot soldier,
but it was an open secret that he had a field marshal's
baton tucked into his airport carry-on.

SANITY IS MADNESS put to good use. So Michael Ignatieff must
have thought as he arrived in Toronto on a mission from . . . well,
the Liberal press gang of three recruiters who had journeyed, if
not to a manger, at least to the Charles Hotel on Harvard Square.

At that point, Ignatieff had been in and out of university class-
rooms, as both student and professor for thirty-odd years, forging
an enviable reputation as a rare intellect and designated heavy
hitter in the field of journalism and letters. He was protected by
the prestige of the institutions where he lectured—Harvard,
Cambridge, Oxford and *École des Hautes Études*—and his only
constituents (other than his readers) were students who owed their
future careers to his indulgence. But now he was moving from
intellectual pin-up and raconteur to his latest manifestation as a
man of action. The idea was that his crusading spirit would find
release as he grasped the most daring of his many gambits: becoming a Canadian politician, then as dysfunctional an occupation as
any on this side of the law. Well, not exactly a politician, perhaps,

more a statesman—*le grand fromage*—even though there were few welcoming signals from anybody in the party, other than his original cadre. Nonetheless Ignatieff had been recruited as a Liberal foot soldier, so the official communiqués insisted, even though it was an open secret he had a field marshal's baton tucked into his airport carry-on.

Turning to politics drastically changed the pace and cadence of his life. Once he and his wife stepped off the flight from Boston he found himself immersed in an auto-flash-like sequence of events:

November 29, 2005: The Paul Martin government having been defeated, Martin, as his final act, calls a general election for January 23.

November 30: Michael and Zsuzsanna Ignatieff land in Toronto in the afternoon, later than intended because he had stayed to teach a final class to a group of Harvard students completing their semester. All along, he'd told his recruiters that he wasn't going to abandon his students before the end of term and that if they needed him sooner in Canada he'd either commute back and forth from Boston, or he wouldn't run at all. That evening he attends the raucous Etobicoke nomination meeting, which approved his controversial nomination.

ONCE HE WON the nomination, it became imperative to obtain his Canadian residence papers fast; he couldn't run for election with Harvard as his home address. His three musketeers found him a trim condo in the heart of Yorkville, on Scollard Street: problem solved.

At this point Paul Martin's Liberals were scoring in the mid-thirties in terms of popular support in the polls, so that a Liberal victory looked possible, even though a majority still had to be earned. If Ignatieff was uneasy about his own or the party's prospects, he didn't show it. The candidate didn't have his own wealth that he could plough into a campaign: he was living on what he could earn from his books and his academic appointments, and his divorce settlement with Susan had dug him a large financial hole. (Once when interviewing him I noticed that the lining of his jacket was tattered; the only extravagance in his Yorkville condo was books.) His run for office was funded by Davey (who contributed a $125,000 loan) and the riding association. "One of our early challenges," one of his mentors recalled, "was to get Michael to donate to his own campaign and to join the Laurier Club, as all candidates were asked to do that year." (The Laurier Club was a clever fundraising scheme: for $1,000 annual membership fee, you got invited to a series of Liberal VIP functions. Every MP was supposed to join. Nobody recalls whether Ignatieff actually did.)

The team also threw a couple of local fundraising events, as well as a larger one at the National Club on Bay Street. Former Ontario Liberal premier David Peterson introduced Ignatieff at that one, revealing one of his admonitions to the virgin politician, whose answer to even a simple greeting could be somewhat wooly. His unwillingness to deliver sound bites frustrated his camp early on, Peterson said. "I told him, I'm going to kick you in the nuts if you give a profound answer to 'How are you?' The answer is 'Fine.'" Ease of moving through a crowd was superhard for the candidate to learn; you could almost see him consulting an internal oracle on small talk (perhaps his wife) as he launched an awkward compliment on the shoes a woman was wearing, before gratefully elevating again into the world of issues and ideas.

His handlers described their approach to promoting their once and future candidate as a slow striptease—build the mystique and keep the media largely at bay. The prevailing thinking was that his win in the constituency would inevitably move Ignatieff into Martin's Cabinet. It took a Herculean effort to slim down media requests; to a large degree the coverage was already touting him as the next prime minister.

Sachin Aggarwal, a brainiac organizer with three degrees and an open, welcoming manner, ran the actual campaign while Davey and Apps more or less carried on with their lives. Then a couple of days before Christmas, Aggarwal called Davey to tell him, "We're in trouble." This was a shock. The recruiters had uprooted Ignatieff and now he was in danger of losing his seat. From that point on, says Davey, it was all hands on deck, though it had also become clear that the Liberals were going to lose nationally, so that there wouldn't be a Martin Cabinet for the newcomer to join.

"I went door to door so often, there were three people who told me 'If you promise not to come back, we'll vote for Michael Ignatieff,'" Davey says, insisting "I'm not joking!" Ignatieff's first political campaign was successful in part because Davey and Apps as well as Senator Smith heeded Aggarwal's call and had cajoled swarms of Liberals to canvas along with them; the other part was that the media coverage portrayed him as not "just a visitor" but as a visitor with touches of chutzpah. The Ukrainian vote stayed home but Ignatieff proved to be decent at engaging house-owning voters' attention and ballots. The result was that on January 23, 2006, Paul Martin and the Liberal party lost the national election but Michael Ignatieff won the riding of Etobicoke-Lakeshore.

And the next whirlwind was upon him.

- January 23, 2006: Stephen Harper gets his first minority mandate. Ignatieff wins his constituency, but instead of becoming a minister in a Liberal government, he is now a backbencher in a feckless opposition.

- February 6, 2006: Harper takes over the government; Ignatieff assumes his seat in the House of Commons.

- April 7, 2006: Ignatieff launches his bid for leadership of the Liberal Party—allowing a gap of only seventy-four days between being elected as a member of Parliament and deciding that he was fit, ready, willing and politically capable of governing the world's second-largest country by land mass—an empty land filled with wonders, but also a troubled nation state that required street smarts, exquisite care and constant tending.

WHEN MARTIN UNEXPECTEDLY resigned on election night, it changed everything. Instead of having the advantage of starting slowly and then accelerating as was deemed appropriate, the Ignatieff organizers found themselves having to mount a full-scale leadership campaign from a standing start. At first, there were few candidates from the caucus, so that the Ignatieff operatives quickly returned to their original strategy of portraying him as an outsider who could persuasively disown the party's recent past—specifically the Quebec sponsorship scandal, since he wasn't there when all that *merde* exploded. Even without a political apprenticeship, the Harvard import found himself ideally placed and for months his handlers felt the leadership was theirs to lose.

Ian Davey shakes his head when he thinks about it now, but also feels a certain pride at what they almost pulled off. "He'd just been elected, hadn't sat in the House yet and we're talking about him being prime minister . . . But my theory was that we were going to drive an agenda not on issues, we're going to drive an agenda on ideas. We're going to get people interested and excited within the Liberal party in a way they hadn't been in ages. So that's what we did. My theory was to keep driving an agenda, let everyone else play catch-up. Michael was confident without being cocky. He was composed without looking ahead into the spotlight. He was a lot of things but he wasn't a politician."

Ignatieff had no understanding of the party, its structure, mentality, and apparatus, but he was a quick study. Because of the link through his father, Davey was able to enlist such Liberal icons as Marc Lalonde, John Nichol, Jim Peterson, Pablo Rodriguez, Rodger Cuzner and Geoff Regan into the Ignatieff camp. He soon became the front-runner for two reasons: the vacuum of stellar candidates and because his handlers were careful to not overexpose him in order to maintain his mystique. That way people saw what they wanted to see . . . and didn't see what they didn't want to see.

Ignatieff supporters weren't necessarily Liberals; many were activists who wanted to be involved in something new and exciting. When the website went live, Davey says, "We got fifteen thousand to eighteen thousand people volunteering to be part of the Michael Ignatieff campaign. Most of them saying, 'I'm not interested in common politics, but this is a guy I'm interested in and I want to help.' So, organizationally, the campaign went all young and all new—not to say there weren't some who weren't either—but young and new was the focus."

They got so many people wanting to help, in fact, that their website briefly crashed. But it wasn't only the newbies driving things. Liberal godfather David Smith clearly also calculated that this candidate could win. Smith's support turned out to be both a positive and negative influence in the campaign. He was critical in fostering introductions for Ignatieff among senior Ottawa players but he was also seen by the grassroots as one of the "old boys" they wanted to replace. But on balance he came through, as godfathers always do.

"I knew that no one would outwork us," Davey recalls, "since the party was overrun with chiefs and we were mostly all Indians. Michael felt it was all coming to him. He never showed much interest in the campaign itself and how it was assembled. He would just show up at engagements and wax poetic on sundry subjects and was pretty good at doing so. You could help channel his message some of the time, but he was very headstrong and sure of himself."

The whole effort rubbed a number of long-time senior Liberals the wrong way. They felt Ignatieff had been away too long to become an effective leader and dismissed him as a queue jumper. Many were also dubious as to why a progressive such as Ian Davey was involved with a "right winger" like Ignatieff, so hawkish on Iraq. Bob Rae, Ignatieff's leadership rival and old friend, approached Ian's mother, Dorothy Davey, and told her he assumed that she was supporting Ignatieff only because her son was on his team.

LOOKING BACK ON that astonishing time, it seems a bit giddy, to be kind, for a political neophyte to launch his political life by reaching straight for the top. From his comments about how he was blessed with the nomination, and the very real accomplishment of winning his parliamentary seat on his first try, it must have looked to Ignatieff as if everything was coming up Moses— the prophet who never asked for directions (a trait the Harvard import shared).

The facts of the situation were not rosy at all. Paul Martin, who had boasted of his prime ministerial qualifications since the invention of moving type, had just been ignominiously beaten. He lost to Stephen Harper, whose party at that point was a creaky coalition of political trail mix that had been given little chance of victory. It was a cold, hard fact that Ignatieff's arrival in Ottawa coincided—to the day—with the last time that Canada was ruled by a Liberal government.

It was easy enough to criticize him for assuming that he needed no apprenticeship, but none of his other incarnations required such training. During the previous two decades he had left the academic sanctuary for the meadows and mountain ranges of the former Yugoslavia, being not merely a journalist and TV star, but a political presence. What exactly these horrifying civil wars had to do with improving Canada's gross domestic product or raising employment in Hamilton, Ontario (where Canada's troubled signature steel company, Stelco, had been bought by U.S. Steel, which then broke its employment pledges), wasn't clear. But the die was cast, and the Ignatieff leadership campaign went into orbit.

The Ottawa where Ignatieff landed as the Liberals' dauphin was a far cry from the city his father knew, and exuded a troubled, furtive atmosphere far from the old, much more relaxed, devil-may-care attitude that treated politics as a game instead of a cult.

At the start of his political stint, Ignatieff would address his remarks to the square of people directly facing him—an imaginary classroom in which he would go on about whichever lesser evil was at the top of his agenda at any given nanosecond. He clutched his lectern, seldom moving a muscle. By the end of his time in Ottawa, he had abandoned his written speeches, and launched into a remarkable "anything goes" period, touring the country—no script, no rigid timetable—answering the people's questions, and in the process demonstrating the stretch and scope of his mind.

Leaping ahead briefly in the chronology, we know he lost this first leadership bid, that his promise stalled and that the man his party elected in 2006 was "anyone but" Ignatieff—a backhanded compliment if there ever was one. The loss changed him. He thought he had lost the leadership because of his team or that he had made too many mistakes. While that no doubt contributed, he was really stopped because he was an outsider, and because he had supported George Bush on the invasion of Iraq while the Liberal Party of Canada had not. Human nature dictated the solution: next time he would run as an insider, a politician. That was a shame, since his most attractive quality had been that he wasn't a professional.

PART TWO

THE LIBERAL CENTURY

5. How the Liberal Ascendancy Transformed the Nation

They were much more than a political party.
They formed a mighty, self-perpetuating cult
that fed on itself and reigned longer over
Canada than Russia's Communists ruled Russia.

HISTORY IS THE SUM OF ascertainable facts, as written by the winners. A loose federation of settlements and regions on the cold periphery of civilization, Canada always has had trouble organizing itself to deal with the crises threatening its integrity; as an immature giant, it was first tied to the apron strings of Great Britain, and later dependent on the not always tender mercies of an aggressive America. Certainly the country had a great deal more geography than history. But the citizens of the large land that poet Al Purdy magnificently described as being "North of summer" shared a distinctive mentality, a combination of creative deference and cautiously progressive pragmatism that eventually became a way of life—and the root of its Liberal belief system. And the like-minded settlers on the windy side of the forty-ninth parallel eventually turned North America's attic into a nation.

It was politics that transformed this set of loose attitudes and ideas (ideology is too strong a description; philosophy too pretentious) into the binding force that held together this often makeshift country. We were different from our aggressively egalitarian neighbours to the south. The Canadian experience flowed from the principles of allegiance rather than social contract and was founded on the organic evolution of tradition instead of the assertion of revolutionary will. Though (as Richard Gwyn pointed out in the first volume of his estimable biography of Sir John A. Macdonald, *John A.: The Man Who Made Us*), those five significant words in the British North America Act, "Peace, Order and Good Government," were only boilerplate, they became our eleventh commandment. They contrasted dramatically with the more florid, more promising and vastly more individualistic American motto: "Life, Liberty and the Pursuit of Happiness."

Dutiful or at least quiescent, for the most part we have left the sculpting of the Canadian soul to our politicians. Which came first, our profound sense of inferiority or intimidation by Brits, Yanks, Mother Nature or our roots as a protected colony? Colonies are fragments of their mother societies (in our case, England and France). The ties with France were breached early, but disentangling ourselves from the apron strings of Britain took a little longer, what with needing Britain for a time to keep us from not being swept up in the United States' manifest destiny, then two world wars in which more was at stake than our maturity as a country. Liberal Prime Minister Louis St. Laurent's 1956 decision not to enter the Suez Canal conflict on the British side was an important marker of our maturity—and the subsequent award of the Nobel Peace prize to his external affairs minister, Lester Pearson, an appropriate reward. It was two Liberal prime ministers, Pearson (with his flag) and Trudeau (with his Charter and the patriation of the BNA) who cut the umbilical cord to Britain.

THE NOTION OF LIBERALISM grew out of the dawning belief that the individual is the unit of supreme value in any society. It was British philosopher John Locke, who died in 1704 and is considered the father of liberalism, who turned the idea into a creed, arguing that individuals had innate rights to life, liberty and property, and that citizens have a right to protect those rights through revolution.

Liberalism was brought into Canada by the United Empire Loyalists, escaping the American Revolutionary War in the mid- and late 1780s. They combined their opposition to American-style republicanism with support for individual liberty to forge a new approach that was much closer to Liberal values than Tory beliefs. Liberalism as a creed prospered in the Canadian West during its great land rush at the start of the last century, then spread into the urban centres and rural Atlantic provinces. By the end of the twentieth century, liberalism was the country's state religion, since the party that expressed its tenants most clearly, the Liberal Party of Canada, had been in charge most often.

During the Second World War when Canadian business executives came to Ottawa as dollar-a-year men to spearhead the defence effort, most of them were full of ginger and ambition. Their professional lives were no longer muted by the colonial mentality that still prevailed in parts of the Dominion. What happened to them politically during that sojourn was just as important as the contacts they made for postwar business deals. For six exciting years—the duration of the war—they came under the authority of Clarence Decatur Howe, the Minister of Everything who was second in command of the government and of the Liberal party. (More of this in the next chapter.) C. D. Howe acted as chief party fundraiser; he was the executive charged with deciding which companies would be granted the most lucrative cost-plus defence contracts; and he maintained a direct link into the Liberal high command. These executives, who became known as C. D.'s boys and who became members of the Liberal party, had not known one another before the war. Suddenly they were living and working together at the Chateau Laurier hotel. There began to develop a clublike atmosphere that eventually became the Canadian Establishment, which lasted for the next quarter century. C. D. Howe had shown them how private and public enterprise can work together for big bucks. After the war, his boys became the party's bagmen, high-level organizers and, of course, eventually senators. The Tories—who by philosophy and inclination automatically considered big business executives their natural recruits—were deprived of a generation or two of the best of the best. And that was how the Liberals became "the Natural Government Party."

Granted, every now and then, the Conservatives took over, like a farm team that doesn't really know how to play in the big leagues. In the past, Tories tended to regard Canada as fragile and in need of protecting, which had much truth to it; Sir John A. Macdonald, the greatest of Tory-minded prime ministers, had always inclined toward caution. Macdonald was a genuine Red Tory, the first of what is now a scarcer breed than dragons. That said, from the CPR to the CBC, the Tories undertook audacious projects, essential to nation building.

The Grits were different in temperament and world view: they possessed a generally more optimistic outlook for Canada's future; they were determined that Canada should appear prominently on the world stage; and they were never shy to leverage the power of our overwhelming neighbour, the United States, to our advantage. They tended to invest more in genuine pluralism (social equality and ethnic diversity) than fearful Tories were inclined to do.

Canada has benefited from a creative yin-yang between the two stances, with the CCF (later NDP) and the farmers' protest parties of the early twentieth century playing their part, mostly by goading the young Mackenzie King into reluctant action.

In a very real way, William Lyon Mackenzie King epitomizes the dichotomy of Canadian caution and audacity. A pseudo-socialist in his early years, King was perceived even by his own caucus in the later stages of his eternal stewardship of the Liberal party—notably by an impatient young Paul Martin Sr.—as the arch-conservative, who "did nothing by halves he could do by quarters." (My favourite fact about this fastidious bachelor was that whenever he traveled he always took along several extra pairs of shoelaces.)

Canada was a country determined to punch above its weight, and we did: from Sir Arthur Currie's pioneering of coordinated artillery and infantry attacks in the Great War, turning the Canadian Corps into "the sharp point" of the Allied spear; to the invention of stem-cell research at Sick Kids Hospital in 1964; to the spearheading of Third World peacekeeping; to the Mulroney-led anti-apartheid drive by the Commonwealth countries; to the establishment of the International Criminal Court at the Hague; to Lloyd Axworthy's Land Mines Treaty (finally, a "worthwhile Canadian initiative," as the dismissive American joke went); and the bravery in a lost cause of our troops on the dusty streets and battlefields of Afghanistan.

As part of Canadian nation-building, the Liberals—in power for all except three decades of the twentieth century—insisted on competence in the public service, which became a sort of boot camp for future cabinet ministers, with twenty-nine of them making the switch during Pearson's tenure alone, including the prime minister himself. (Ignatieff's father, George, was a representative of our exemplary civil service and diplomatic corps and provided a role model for his eldest son.) We had to prove to ourselves, over and over, that we could partake in the great affairs of the evolving international scene, as we did when our Liberal leaders became founding members of the United Nations and NATO.

But the seeds of the Liberal party's destruction were also planted long ago, and can be traced back to Mackenzie King's repeated outwitting of Arthur Meighen, Lord Byng and other adversaries, as well his astonishing benediction of Adolf Hitler's early efforts during a visit to Berlin. Pierre Trudeau stared down the reactionary forces in his own party that were objecting first to bilingualism, and then to multiculturalism (the first made the second possible), which has become one of our greatest strengths. But that success was partly responsible for relegating George Drew, Robert Stanfield, Joe Clark and their successors to irrelevance. The Liberals' success bred arrogance. That is an inevitable curse for those long in power and short on transparency. Christina and Stephen Clarkson's definitive volumes on the Liberal party reveal that the seeds of self-destruction were there—deep and pervasive—in an arrogance based on the possession of power rather than on any superior accomplishments.

The real story is how long the Grits managed, despite their inevitable sense of entitlement, not to have succumbed to these character flaws. One reason can be found in Trudeau's dismissive but wonderful response to critics: "Consider the alternatives." We did. (Joe Clark, Preston Manning, Kim Campbell, Stockwell Day.) And voted Liberal. Until Stephen Harper took over and doggedly assaulted the ramparts of Liberal power.

WHAT WAS SO REMARKABLE about the Liberal party was not its championing of innovative ideas or its sure grasp of what was important for Canada but the mood of self-confidence that pervaded its gatherings. The delegates, however far they may have strayed from their original ideals, believed with good reason that they had made Canada what it has become. They sold us out to the Americans (in order to retrieve us from the British) and put in place a humane, progressive society. Their unshakable trust in the reasonableness of man—that as rational beings we could see who had our best interests at heart—held the Liberal party together, and allowed its members to transform the country.

It is not out of place to mourn the fate of the vanishing Liberals. After all, they were much more than a political party. They formed a mighty, self-perpetuating cult that fed on itself and reigned longer over the country of its birth and flowering than the Communists ruled Russia. They were an extended family that, like the Mafia, mainly killed off its own to make room for each new wave of Grits hot off the grittle, promising they would fulfill every whim of every Canadian voter from erection to resurrection, and to hell with the cost.

6. Why the Grits Became the Natural Government Party

At the same time that they were forming a significant community
of interest between themselves and the public service,
business leaders were being co-opted into the Liberal party.

DURING THE MERRY MONTH OF MAY 1945, peace came to
the European battlefields on little cat feet, bringing with it an epic
shift in self-image for most Canadians. Suddenly we felt the surge
of confidence that comes to late adolescents not yet daunted by
the hesitations of maturity. What this meant to the returning
veterans was the chance to buy a suburban bungalow, a Chevy, an
electric refrigerator (instead of the ice box they had left behind), a
bedroom radio in a cream-coloured case and the right to their
unassailable dreams. What it meant for the hundred-odd earnest
Canadian business leaders who had served their wartime shift as
Ottawa dollar-a-year men, was the birth of a postwar network of
connections and interconnections between business and government that fathered a new economy, its tentacles (and dynasties)
spreading into every form of commercial enterprise across the
country. Thus, almost by default—because Liberal party membership came with C. D. Howe's invitation to serve the country—
the Liberals were anointed as Canada's political power barons.

Canada's industrialists didn't agree to serve the war effort in order to be absorbed by a political party, but that was precisely what happened—although it has never been clear who was absorbing whom. The distinction didn't really matter because the Canadian economy at that point was being micro- and macro-managed by C. D. Howe. Certainly nobody realized— not even the participants themselves—that there had formed in the capital city during the war years a cadre of unusually talented bigwigs who would dominate the nation's business and politics into the 1970s.

Most of them were well-educated WASPs at a time when a university degree was still a privilege, who had already found places in the country's cautious, penny-pinching business firms or in the middle reaches of Ottawa's tiny public service. They were set on performing daily miracles in the service of their country, not burdened with the inner conflicts people who grew up much earlier or much later had to endure. They grew up with the feeling that this country was small time, a place where nothing important ever had happened or ever was likely to happen. They had been taught that history was made across the sea, that business acumen and manufacturing know-how existed below the border, and that the best we could manage here was an imitation. But their wartime service, the fact that they were the architects of the free world's third-largest navy, a fearsome air force and conquering armies, absolved them of that insecurity. They had nothing to feel inferior about.

As they began to leave Ottawa in 1945, they allowed themselves to feel nostalgic about the hothouse atmosphere they'd endured, which had been confusing, frustrating, occasionally absurd, but unmistakably exciting enough to feed the memories of its participants for the rest of their lives. When he was into his seventies,

E. P. Taylor, who would become the leading postwar industrialist and beer baron, could vividly recall the afternoon of his first day in Ottawa, when he walked into the cramped office of Henry Borden, the Toronto lawyer turned dollar-a-year man. Borden was on the telephone. He gestured for Taylor to sit down and continued his conversation with what turned out to be the sales manager of North American Aviation Incorporated in northwestern California.

"Yes! Yes!" Borden was shouting into the phone's mouthpiece. "Yes, we damn well need those trainers or we can't get our air force going. We'll buy them from you. Cash on the barrelhead. We've got the money. . . . Of course, I know about your Neutrality Act. But I've got this scheme. You deliver the planes to North Dakota, right by the Saskatchewan boundary line. Have your men taxi them right up to the border. We'll have our fellows on the Canadian side throw ropes across . . . Yes, *ropes*. You just attach them to the undercarriages and we'll pull them into Canada. Got it? Thanks. It's a pleasure doing business with you. . . ."

FOR THE DOLLAR-A-YEAR MEN, the war was the most creative season of their professional lives. Their innovative talents flourished as they learned to extend the boundaries of self-reliance, to manage the world at large without having to copy or feel inferior to the British or the Americans. The man who set the style for the members of this select group, who became their deity, was Howe, the shrewd Yankee trader from Port Arthur, Ontario (out of Waltham, Massachusetts), who taught them that knowledge is power—and how to use it.

Howe's proteges deliberately set out to learn where all the important pieces were; who counted and who didn't; how to deal with each other, with cabinet ministers and with the political system. At the same time that they were forming a significant community of interest between themselves and the upper echelons of the public service, they were being co-opted into the Liberal party. No pressure applied; just the joining of compatible appetites for winning the Second World War and defence contracts.

When the dollar-a-year men fanned out at the close of the war to run the nation they had helped to create, the attitudes, the working methods and the business ethic they took with them determined the country's economic and political course.

They had come to Ottawa as politically disinterested individuals; they left as a Liberal elite.

A MEASURE OF THIS remarkable group's accomplishments was the dramatic speed with which they managed to convert the rustic, dormant Canadian economy of 1939 into a powerful industrial state. At the start of the war, Canada counted barely eleven million people. A decade had elapsed since the onset of the Great Depression, but 600,000 people were still out of work; only 658,000 Canadians had jobs in manufacturing. Ottawa resembled a sleepy colonial outpost, and Canada's diplomatic representation abroad was limited to missions in Washington, Paris, Tokyo and London.

Many start-up problems during the war's early days were complicated by the "mother knows best" attitude of the beleaguered British. On October 15, 1939, when the first official UK delegation arrived in Ottawa to set up the Commonwealth Air Training Plan, Arnold Heeney, then secretary to the Cabinet, and Clifford Clark, the deputy minister of finance, went to welcome the delegates in their suite at the Chateau Laurier. Just before the talks got under way, Sir Arthur Balfour, a Sheffield industrialist who was the chief British negotiator, drew the two Canadians aside and patronizingly presented each of them with a tissue-wrapped penknife, as if they were boy scouts being awarded a new badge.

A more intriguing game was being played at the offices of the hastily set up Foreign Exchange Control Board, charged with controlling export and import currency transactions. Walter Gordon, a Liberal who later became Pearson's minister of finance, recalled one telling incident. "As soon as I got back to Ottawa from New York," he remembered, "I saw people lined up outside the FEC Board's offices and nobody was doing much for them, so I started to deal with their problems on an ad hoc basis. I'd been the auditor at Falconbridge Nickel, and recognized the company's executive treasurer in the lineup. I asked him what his problem was, and he said he had a ship full of nickel ore bound for the company's refinery in Norway being held up by red tape in Montreal. So I sent a wire to the director of customs ordering him to release the vessel, and signed it FOREIGN EXCHANGE CONTROL BOARD. A few days later we started to get urgent internal communications from the minister and deputy minister of customs trying to find out who'd sent the wire that had released the ship. I just put all the memos in a wastebasket and never told Gordon Towers, the central banker who was in charge, what I'd done until the day I left. He said: 'Why didn't you let me know?'

"I told him, 'You would have had to fire me, and then who the hell would have organized this thing for you?'"

THE DOLLAR-A-YEAR MEN who spent the war in Ottawa considered themselves grossly overworked, but what came out of their mutual experience was a great sense of comradeship, a spirit-lifting knotting together of people who had made common cause and, above all, had got to *know and trust* one another. Real well. Seeing the same people for six years at work, at lunch, at dinner, and into the wee small hours produced a consensus about the kind of country they wanted after the war, the sort of business practices they believed in, and early glimmerings that Toronto and Montreal were not the only commercial centres in Canada that mattered. They began to exchange confidences, to sponsor one another for club memberships, to share perceptions and ambitions. It was an enduring trust, and no badge of honour carried more prestige than the phrase: "I put in time under C. D."*

It was a happy time, but they frequently found their efforts hampered by the bureaucratic framework in which they had to operate, despite the urgency of the ad hoc decisions they were daily forced to make. The most delicate problem handled by the Wartime Prices and Trade Board, which was run with high good humour by Donald Gordon, the former deputy governor of the Bank of Canada, concerned a Hamilton housewife's application for a thousand dollars in U.S. funds so that she could spend a week in New York to have herself artificially inseminated. Because of Canada's shortage of U.S. currency, regulations limited American visits to business trips, with very few pleasure jaunts allowed. For weeks the lady's application circulated around WPTB offices, with some raunchy comments penciled in the margin. Gordon finally settled the matter by scribbling across her papers: "OBVIOUSLY NOT FOR PLEASURE PURPOSES — APPROVED."

The Liberals unashamedly used the awarding of defence contracts to help fill party coffers. "Howe was the greatest bagman the Grits ever had," Tory Senator Grattan O'Leary complained. "There

---

* *The most senior and highest paid ($4,500 a year) woman in wartime Ottawa was Mrs. Phyllis Turner, who was chief of the Oil and Fats Administration branch in the Wartime Prices and Trade Board. Frank Ross, her husband-to-be, was director-general of naval armaments production in the Department of Munitions and Supply. She lived in the Sandy Hill area of Ottawa and when her teenaged son, John (yes, that John), walked the family dog, he would often meet and converse with Mackenzie King.*

were some fifteen hundred war contracts out in 1944, and everybody the Tories went to for election expenses would say they'd
already given to the Liberals. We found out that whenever the
Liberal bagman arrived, he'd casually remark that C. D. had told
him: 'Be sure to tell Charlie (or Ed or Bill) I was asking about him.'
The clear implication was that C. D. would be told the size of the
contributor's donation." (Wallace R. Campbell, a former president
of the Ford Motor Company of Canada who served as chairman of
the War Supply Board, resigned because of political pressure to put
through a contract for $100,000 in excess of its value, with the
balance going to the Grit treasury.)

Although Canadian companies were subject throughout the war
to fairly severe excess-profits taxes, Howe allowed manufacturers to
write off their capital investments more or less as they saw fit. The
system of accelerated depreciation provisions was first suggested to
Howe by his friend R. E. "Rip" Powell, president of Aluminum
Company of Canada, whose firm also became one of the scheme's
chief beneficiaries. Alcan was able to write off the cost of its entire
$193-million ingot and hydro development at Shipshaw, Quebec,
in three years. (As soon as he retired from politics, Howe was named
a director of Aluminum Ltd., parent company of Aluminum
Company of Canada.) Between September 1939, and August 1945,
some $3.5 billion was invested in new manufacturing facilities in
Canada, and at least half of the sum was financed through special
Ottawa tax credits and allowances.

A grand total of $28 billion was spent on the war effort, and the
Canadian economy was forever altered in the process.

WHILE C. D. HOWE became the founder of modern, industrialized
Canada, he also laid the foundations of the country's Americanization.
He was very different from the members of the old WASP elites who

79

ruled Toronto and Montreal, were British (and French) in their orientation, and turned to such symbols of British rule as the Governor General, the British Empire and the Crown for guidance. Howe was middle class and self-made, a tough, American get-up-and-go engineering type. The dollar-a-year men who came to aid the war effort had grown up with Hollywood movies, the first generation to do so. They were in love with the American style of easygoing brashness, the "get things done without a lot of stuffy nonsense" attitude that Howe so perfectly epitomized.

Howe's most enduring political legacy was to lend some measure of credibility to the myth that the Liberal party itself was an expression of the national will. During his time in Ottawa, the Liberal party became, in Jack Pickersgill's immortal phrase: "the *natural government* party," and everybody else was left on the sidelines. "The unreflecting acceptance of this belief," wrote Denis Smith, of Trent University, "smoothed the way for the integration of senior civil servants and businessmen into the Liberal national system."

It is not easy now to realize the great influence Howe was able to exercise over national initiatives during his twenty-two years in public service. Most of his policies—at least, until the midfifties— were regarded as something close to scripture. A curious combination of simplicity and directness on the one hand, and susceptibility to wealth and prestige on the other, Howe gloried in the company of the powerful and felt himself to be their equal. He liked nothing better than to visit London and dine with Lord Beaverbrook. But in his own household, he lived simply and didn't bother with ostentatious trappings. When he was congratulated on getting an honorary doctorate from the Massachusetts Institute of Technology, he shrugged and said, "It's not that I gave a damn for the degree, it's the impression it'll make on my wife's Boston relatives that I care about."

His New England heritage as a doer with a hardrock belief in himself and his capacities remained the dominant strain in both Howe's character and the business/Liberal axis. Born at Waltham, Massachusetts, in 1886, Howe graduated from MIT in 1907 and stayed on as an engineering instructor for a few months until his professor recommended him for a full-fledged lectureship at Dalhousie University. After five years in Halifax, he moved to the Lakehead as chief engineer with the Board of Grain Commissioners and three years later, during the First World War, he established his own engineering firm. (He did not serve in the war.) During the next decade and a half, Howe built grain storage facilities worth $125 million in harbours from Canada to Argentina, including the Port Arthur Saskatchewan Pool Seven, the world's largest grain elevator.

The Depression cut into his business, and although Howe's previous political activity had been limited to a brief term on the Port Arthur Board of Education, he now began to move into the highest circles of the Liberal party, which had been temporarily put out of office by R. B. Bennett in 1930. He figured the Liberals would soon be back in office as the Conservatives weren't up to the challenge of dealing with the Depression, and he and Mackenzie King had met and were impressed with each other. One of his best friends was Norman Lambert, a former secretary of the Canadian Council of Agriculture, who had recently been named the party's national organizer. During the winter of 1933, Lambert invited Howe to dine at the Chateau Laurier with Vincent Massey, then president of the National Liberal Federation. Persuaded by the two men that he should stand for the Port Arthur seat in the next election, Howe set one condition: if elected, he would immediately be taken into the Cabinet. Mackenzie King promptly invited him to Laurier House and enthusiastically endorsed both his candidacy and the pledge of a portfolio. In the 1935 election, Howe won by a comfortable margin, and he was named minister of Railways and Canals. He set his pattern of influence early, helping to establish the CBC and Trans-Canada Air Lines (later Air Canada), which were neither railways nor waterways. He never paid much attention to such niggling details.

Howe's critics, both in government and in business, kept trying to find a suitable ideological label to pin him down, to determine some pattern in the welter of policies he sponsored. John Deutsch, who was certainly the most practical of the great Ottawa mandarins, watched Howe operate at close quarters for more than two decades. "The fact is," concluded Deutsch, "C. D. didn't know a policy when he saw one. He knew how to run a railroad, how to make things go—but *why* you had a railroad, that is a question he did not ask. He never had any decisive input in general policy matters. Someone responsible told him, 'This is what we need,' and he went and did it. He was an operating executive—one of the greatest this country has ever had."

Howe hated inaction. He couldn't stand being in the company of external affairs types who, he figured, thought up a problem and then entertained themselves by discussing it endlessly. His method of running men and departments was wholly unbureaucratic. He was given to issuing terse oral instructions and was the first important Canadian politician who preferred the telephone to writing letters and memoranda. For him, a fifteen-page memo, no matter how beautifully worded or reasoned, was simply an indication that the writer didn't know what was wanted. (Handed a bulky report, he'd grin at its author and ask, "What's it say?") Howe had no patience with written documents of any kind. At the Rideau Club where he lunched, members were expected to write out their orders on a pad brought by the waitresses. One of his luncheon companions remembered glancing at Howe's fast, phonetic scribble, and reading: "Plane omelet & rasin pie." He became exasperated with underlings who protested that what he wanted to do was administratively impossible. "Nothing is administratively impossible," he would say, and when they explained that the department's legal adviser said it couldn't be done, Howe would shoot back: "Then get me a legal adviser who says it *can* be done."

Howe's rapport with businessmen was based on something more than his own decisiveness. He implanted in them the gift of self-confidence. He taught them that a $50-million decision is not necessarily more difficult than one involving $50,000. To make nine important decisions a day—even if only five of them turned out right—was far better than making no decisions at all. When a fledgling dollar-a-year man once breathlessly asked Howe (almost saluting as he did), "What are your instructions, C. D.?" Howe calmly replied: "I never give instructions. I just give responsibilities." That wasn't strictly true, but he did give tremendous leeway to his subordinates and he respected their recommendations.

THE GROUP OF remarkable public servants (including George Ignatieff) who held sway in Ottawa between the midthirties and the midsixties fashioned the policies that kept the Liberals in power for most of those thirty years, but there was little doubt that the most powerful Ottawa presence during that time (next to the prime minister himself) was Howe. He had curiously different relationships with the prime ministers he served. He was Mackenzie King's appointee, and King was the boss of everybody in his Cabinet. "King could usually control his willful colleague," Bruce Hutchison, the ace journalist of his generation, wrote. "Once, returning to Ottawa and finding that Howe had dared to call the Cabinet together in his absence, King lectured him as if he were a school-boy. Howe accepted the chastisement and sheepishly told his friends that he deserved it." On one occasion when King unexpectedly walked into the privy council chamber, Howe stuffed his lit pipe into a hip pocket and burned himself because the prime minister didn't allow smoking during meetings.

Howe's relations with Louis St. Laurent were very different. Early in 1948, when King announced his resignation and the lawyer from Quebec City was being urged by his family not to remain in politics, one of the main arguments that persuaded him to run for the Liberal leadership was Howe's threat that *he* would get out of public life unless St. Laurent stayed. Although Howe was never formally designated as St. Laurent's "lieutenant from English Canada," Howe had far more power than the Quebec lieutenant of any English-speaking prime minister. Under St. Laurent, Howe became more assertive in Cabinet, grew testy with his colleagues, and tried to turn the Liberal business-government axis into a closed corporation with himself as chief executive officer. Mitchell Sharp, who always managed to find a comfortable berth as required in politics and business, remarked of this period that "Howe knew every important businessman in Canada. They seemed to make a practice of talking to C. D. whether they wanted anything from Ottawa or not. Being a loyal and generous Liberal contributor became the passport into C. D.'s inner circle."

"He had business interests of a very wide kind," said Doug Fisher, the history teacher and CCF candidate who defeated Howe in 1957. "He had a very close relationship with men like Sir James Dunn of Algoma Steel and R. S. McLaughlin of General Motors, with the American steel interests through the Hanna company and George Humphrey, who became Eisenhower's secretary of the treasury. He consorted with these people. Now that's kind of a twisty word, 'consort,' but he was very, very close to them and he found this kind of man much more attractive and interesting than his political colleagues. Where did the boundary line come between these private business interests of his and government business? There isn't really any answer. All we know is that he moved with, if you want to use a loaded word, the tycoons of North American, and to a degree he was responsible for setting up and creating them."

HOWE MADE THE NATION'S businessmen feel like they shared in the great experiences of their times. Twice a year, usually in June and December, a select group of Canadian executives was shown draft forecasts on the state of the Canadian economy *before* those forecasts were sent on to government agencies for appropriate policy formulation. These secret, all-day briefings, which included six senior economic advisers from both the private and the public sectors, were held in a large Trade and Commerce conference hall, with time off for lunch in one of the Rideau Club's private dining rooms.

The outbreak of the Korean War in 1950 gave Howe a chance to reactivate at least part of his wartime coalition by bringing a few of his favourite dollar-a-year men back to Ottawa and reviving his accelerated writeoff provisions for industrial expansion. While the Trade and Commerce minister (who had by now also taken on the Defence Production portfolio) seemed to be at the top of his form, in fact Howe's political position was being undermined—by no one more effectively than himself. He had been exercising his enormous influence on Ottawa and the country for twenty years. A succession of emergencies—dragging Canada out of the Depression, waging war, heading the drive for reconstruction, rearming for the Korean War—had allowed him to operate without much, if any, regard for Parliament. He enjoyed politics, up to a point. Politics to him was like a sport he might watch once a year on a rainy afternoon when he had nothing better to do. He paid amazingly little attention to what went on in the House of Commons or in Cabinet that didn't directly concern his departments. "He'd come into the Rideau Club at noon," Grattan O'Leary recalled, "and he'd sit at the members' open table and talk with complete candour about what was going on in Cabinet. He had a sort of relish for crises. Like a strong man being asked to lift a weight, he'd flex the muscles of his personality and bull right ahead."

By this time the Liberal government had grown secure in office: not a single serving cabinet minister had been through the chastening experience of time put in on the Opposition benches. Hugh MacLennan, the dean of Canadian novelists, wrote in *Maclean's*: "They treat the national mind much as the officials of a trust company treat the mind of a rich widow whose funds they have been hired to manage. To keep the widow from asking too many questions is always wise. Treat her with courtesy, of course. Talk to her with an occasional sally of ponderous avuncular humour, ply her with accurate reports couched in a jargon she cannot possibly understand, but whatever you do, don't let her get too inquisitive about what goes on behind the doors of the company." And in this period, Howe behaved as if he were determined to provide suitable fodder for his enemies. On May 21, 1951, during a House debate on trade agreements, Howard Green, a Conservative from Vancouver, expressed concern over a government action, charging that it was trying to escape previous commitments. "Who would stop us?" Howe replied, matter-of-factly. "Don't take yourself too seriously. If we wanted to get away with it—who would stop us?"

The answer was nobody. Except themselves.

THE CONSERVATIVES, under George Drew's leadership, first managed to demonstrate the full measure of Howe's contempt for the Commons to the country at large during the Defence Production Act debates in the summer of 1955. The government had moved an innocent-sounding motion, entitled "An Act to Amend the Defence Production Act," which included the clause: "Section 41 of the said Act is repealed." Section 41 happened to be a provision that stated that the entire act, passed during the Korean War, was to expire on July 31, 1956. In other words, Howe was demanding that the extraordinary powers he had wielded during a national emergency should become a permanent part of the law. Under the provisions of the act, the minister of Defence Production had, among other things, the right to compel anyone owning facilities suitable to defence work to accept contracts "on terms and conditions which the Minister deems to be fair and reasonable." It also gave the minister the right to put a controller into a business to direct all its operations, if in his judgment it wasn't performing efficiently enough. The controversial bill was brought up for second reading on June 7, and the fifty-one Conservatives in the Commons talked it into a standstill until July 11. J. M. Macdonnell, the principled Tory who led the onslaught, declared that it represented "an affront to a free parliament."

Howe had turned down a suggestion that the extraordinary power he was demanding be limited to a three-year term, declaring that, "this would mean coming back to Parliament in three years, and I've more to do than spend my time amusing Parliament." This was how Grattan O'Leary, then publisher of the *Ottawa Journal*, recalled the succession of events that led to the final Defence Production Act compromise: "I was having lunch at the Rideau Club when George Drew the Conservative leader, told me that an astonishing thing had happened. St. Laurent had called him and said, 'George, we have to settle this thing. I'll write a memo to you listing my concessions, and then I'm going home for the weekend to St. Patrice. I'll call you at Stornoway on Monday at noon, and we'll fix it up.' Drew said that he wanted me to be there when the PM called but that he wouldn't tell his caucus, because they wouldn't believe him. I remember that C. D. was away in Sept-Iles on a fishing trip. I sat beside Drew on the Monday, and when he asked for one more concession, St. Laurent accepted it without changing a comma. For me, that telephone call marked the end of the Liberals' hold on power."

Then in May and June of 1956, during the great pipeline debate, the Liberals rode roughshod over the rights of Parliament, trying to force closure every step of the way on debate over Howe's bill to mandate a private syndicate of American and Canadian businessmen to build a pipeline to carry natural gas from Alberta to the east. Although Jack Pickersgill had planned the government's ruinous tactics in the debate, it was C. D. Howe who got most of the blame for the Grits' shoddy, dictatorial behaviour. Howe even threatened to resign if the bill was not pushed through the House in the required time and St. Laurent made it clear that if Howe stepped down, he also would leave. In the end they pushed through the bill over the howls of the Opposition, but their tactics showed Canadian voters how arrogant they had become. It rose to haunt them in their next election campaign.

WHEN THE 1957 GENERAL ELECTION WAS CALLED, the Progressive Conservative party wasn't in great shape. Its new leader, John Diefenbaker, was well aware that his party, which hadn't held office for twenty-two years, was a declining force in Canadian politics. Diefenbaker had won the leadership contest largely because other contenders didn't think the prize was worth the effort, and he knew he couldn't win office unless he could attract uncommitted voters and enlist them in his cause, not necessarily in his party. And so Diefenbaker ignored the issues and launched an emotional appeal to voters, ideally suited to his evangelical-style oratory. "Underlying a good deal of what Diefenbaker said," wrote John Meisel, a Queen's University political scientist, "was the assumption that Canada was on the threshold of greatness, if it could only get rid of its old and inadequate government. Each voter could, so Mr. Diefenbaker seemed to say, participate in an effort which could make his own dreams come true." Instead of stumping for the Conservative party, the Tory leader merely instructed his growing crowds of listeners to keep their "date with destiny" and vote against the Liberals.

Though the Grits had taken a beating in Parliament and the court of public opinion, they were still overconfident, an attitude best exemplified by the fact that they went into the campaign without filling sixteen vacancies in the Senate. St. Laurent, the first prime minister since Macdonald to campaign past his seventy-fifth birthday, spent the election gazing out of his black limousine with a look of disengaged wisdom; he seemed quite unaware of what was going on around him. At a rally in Chatham, Ontario, the prime minister shook hands with each member of his accompanying press corps, apparently thinking they were local voters.

C. D. Howe remained in character, attacking a heckler who had criticized him at a gathering by telling him to organize his own meeting. The heckler angrily marched up to the platform and identified himself as Bruce Mackenzie, the head of the local Liberal riding association. Not to be squelched, C. D. told him to go away and vote for the party of his second choice. He couldn't resist adding, "In fact, why don't you just go away." Mackenzie did, and so did the majority of Canadian voters. Diefenbaker won the election by seven seats (and a year later won an overwhelming majority).

On election night, informed he'd just been turned out of office by the socialist candidate Douglas Fisher, Howe delivered himself of the opinion that the country was being swept by some strange disease and that *he* was going to bed. C. D. was defeated, but he was not destroyed. The following week Howe returned to Ottawa to arrange his affairs. In an oddly silent office, the Minister of Everything listlessly leafed through his appointment book. Nobody would want to see him now. He shrugged and phoned his broker to order him to sell his stocks because he didn't trust this new bunch. He hung up and went home.

After his defeat, he got angry only once, when an underling came pussyfooting into his office to say how sorry he was that Mr. Howe had to retire from politics. "Retire! Hell!" Howe shouted. "I was beat."

7. Grits Forever—No More

"The Liberals aimed at operating noiselessly like a
respectable, mammoth business corporation which
fears nothing more than making people aware it is there."
— PAUL FOX, political scientist

CANADA'S LIBERAL PARTY was in power longer than any other democratic political movement anywhere—for sixty-nine years of the twentieth century and all but half a decade since. The tenure of Canada's first Liberal prime minister, the almost forgotten Sarnia stonemason Alexander Mackenzie, was five years. The Liberal opposition leader was asked by the Governor General to form a government in 1873 after Sir John A. Macdonald and his Tories fell over the Pacific Scandal. In 1874, he and his Liberals won a majority, but then lost again to the Tories in 1878 in one of our first squabbles over protectionism: Mackenzie had negotiated a free trade deal with the United States as a way to overcome an economic depression, but the depression only deepened, and the Tories were carried back into office under the banner of imposing tariffs. Mackenzie resigned two years later because of a threatened internal Liberal revolt.

The Liberals only returned to power after Macdonald died, but they did it with a vengeance under the charismatic Sir Wilfrid Laurier, who ruled the roost from 1896 to 1911, during Canada's initial period of economic prosperity. It was Macdonald who set the coordinates of nationhood with his building of the CPR, his manoeuvring to ensure that Canada stretched from sea to sea, and his National Policy on tariffs, but it was Laurier who turned a struggling, barely self-governing colony into a nation by filling up our West with European settlers before the Americans filled it up with themselves, effectively annexing it.

Soon after the First World War, the Liberals returned to power, and except for Meighen's eleven-month second go-round in office and R. B. Bennett's Depression-plagued term during the Dirty Thirties, they stayed in power until 1957 and the onset of John Diefenbaker's stormy tenure. In the early 1960s, Pearson inaugurated another two-decade Grit cycle that included fifteen years of Pierre Trudeau, whose tempestuous but transformational stewardship, I would argue, altered the character of Canada as a nation (no matter the nine-month interregnum of the Tories' Joe Clark).

Trudeau was followed by John Turner, whose unhappy stewardship was dominated by enemy fire from within. There followed an activist political decade under Brian Mulroney, the last Progressive Conservative, in spirit as well as in name. The Grits then returned to the throne for another thirteen years, with Jean Chrétien and Paul Martin sharing both the honours and the Liberal party's worst scandal. During their era, the party broke up into warring tribes, arguably the most relevant indicator of its looming demise. (John A. had a point when he once told an audience in British Columbia, "I do not say that all Grits are horse thieves; but I feel quite sure that all horse thieves are Grits.")

I remember ending my review of Pearson's *Memoirs* by

commenting on the Liberal party's amazing ability to be all things to all men—and women. "Holy Mackenzie King," I wrote. "It's perfect: the Liberal Gavotte—you take two steps left and two steps right while moving sideways into the future. And that, my fellow Canadians, is how we got social security without Socialism and biculturalism without having to learn French."

SEVEN LIBERAL CHIEFS led the Natural Government Party during the twentieth century; in the first decade of this one, four have been elected or dragooned into taking charge. They have been picked according to two iron rules. First, the Liberals recognized the country's dominant cultural roots by alternating between French and English leaders—from Laurier, the first francophone PM, to King, to St. Laurent, to Pearson, to Trudeau, to Turner, to Chrétien, to Martin, to Dion, to Ignatieff. That was not negotiable. (Though Bob Rae is in charge now, he is only an "interim leader.")

The second rule—more obscure but almost as durable—when selecting new leaders was to pass over worthy party veterans and instead choose fresh standard bearers who were not strongly associated with the *ancien régime*. Instead of having to defend his Grit predecessor's corruption, patronage and other forms of skullduggery, the freshly minted leader could innocently protest, "Who me? I was never part of the Old Gang. This is *moi*, a new guy with new ideas."

Discontinuity ruled. The formula usually worked—though not with Turner, Dion or Ignatieff—or back in Mackenzie's time, with the lawyer Edward Blake, the other member of the trio of Liberal leaders who never became prime minister. By recruiting politically unsoiled "outsiders," the Liberals endured Depression and recessions, world wars, conscription crises, Quebec separation referenda, constitutional shootouts, party revolts and scandals that shook their world—and ours. Their record was impressive. No matter how cynical it may have appeared to be, or how opportunistic it actually was, for most of a century the Liberal machine operated silently and with machine-tool efficiency. The Grits' rules of the road were best described by the late University of Toronto political scientist, Paul Fox: "The Liberals aimed at operating noiselessly like a respectable, mammoth business corporation which fears nothing more than making people aware it is there."

THE PATTERN BEGAN with William Lyon Mackenzie King, who turned Liberalism into Canada's state religion. At the 1919 leadership contest, the Liberals' first open convention, King's main opponent was William Stevens Fielding, who rose from being a lowly clerk at the *Halifax Morning Chronicle* to become the newspaper's managing editor; by 1884 he had been elected premier of Nova Scotia. Fielding went federal, becoming a successful minister of finance in Laurier's 1896 Cabinet, and he remained so vitally active in Liberal politics that after Laurier— who was Liberal leader an astonishing thirty-one years—died of a stroke, he was considered a shoo-in as Laurier's successor. Instead, the Grit delegates opted for new political blood. Mackenzie King had been elected to Parliament in 1908, and briefly sat as a Liberal cabinet minister. After he lost his seat in the 1911 election, he'd left the country to work for the Rockefeller Foundation in New York and came back to Canada to run in the "conscription" election of 1917. He lost again, and worked as an independent labour consultant, until he stood for the Liberal leadership. Regarded by historians as Canada's most effective PM, to many of us he is most memorable for his weirder aspects, including his secret seances with his long-dead mother and his unusual attachment to his dogs, all but one of them named Pat. Despite his clear aversion to risk, he laid down the original matrix for the Liberal ascendancy.

Chosen on the fifth ballot, he led the Liberals into office two years later in 1921, and served as Canada's defining prime minister for a total of twenty-two years, becoming best known for all that he *didn't* do.*

In 1948, King decided it was time for him to step down, and for his party to hold its first convention since the one that had elected him leader in 1919. The party's powerful regional power barons, Agriculture Minister Jimmy Gardiner and Chubby Power, then the popular Quebec pro-consul (who had broken with King over the Quebec conscription crisis), were regarded as the pick of the party regulars who deserved the brass ring. Instead, King had earlier gone outside his circle to recruit St. Laurent, a Quebec City corporate lawyer, first naming him justice minister in his wartime Cabinet, then secretary of state for external affairs and then manipulated the 1948 Liberal leadership convention to assure another outsider's victory. (Mackenzie King joined his spiritual guides in 1950, dying two years after stepping down as prime minister.)

Ten years later, in 1958, Paul Martin Sr. was the obvious insiders' choice to replace St. Laurent, having long served the party in Cabinet posts of ascending importance. Instead the delegates selected Lester Bowles Pearson, who had been a lifelong public servant till he was plucked from the diplomatic corps by St. Laurent to fill the external affairs post.

---

* *King once took aside a young Paul Martin Sr., the radical progressive in his Cabinet, and told him that a PM's job was mainly to prevent bad ideas from becoming policy.*

THE NEXT TRANSITION displayed the outsider theory with a vengeance. In 1968, when Pearson felt ready to retire, nine candidates ran to succeed him, including the inevitable Martin Sr. The most formidable contender was Robert Winters, a suave M.I.T. graduate, who acted and looked like the perfect prototype of an executive. He had served with distinction in the St. Laurent Cabinet, then gone on to become one of Canada's most powerful corporate bigwigs. Not only would his selection have disrupted the English-French alternation, but the Liberals were determined to renew themselves in bold fashion. Passing over Winters and other highly qualified political veterans, the delegates opted for Pierre Elliott Trudeau, who only months before he'd become justice minister in the Pearson government had been an NDP sympathizer, attacking the Liberals for their nuclear-friendly defence policies.

To this point the Liberal strategy of picking relative outsiders was really effective. King won his first election, St. Laurent won the biggest Liberal majority ever, and Trudeau won too, after a campaign in which "Trudeaumania" was coined to describe his effect on the crowds that gathered to touch the hem of his garment. If people had become sick of the Liberals, these leaders were like a heavenly reincarnation, as the party machine hummed quietly in the background.

JOHN TURNER, who succeeded Trudeau, met both of the party's qualifying conditions, as an *Anglais* at the right time in the sequence and as a "born-again" outsider. Raised in Vancouver, he had served the Liberal party in senior portfolios and was regarded as Trudeau's natural successor. But in 1975 Turner suddenly resigned from the Trudeau cabinet, perhaps, as some say, because he didn't want to implement the government's wage and price controls, but likely also because he was fed up with labouring in Trudeau's shadow. He practiced law on Bay Street for much of the next decade, deliberately exiling himself from party involvement at the same time as he was regarded by a faction of the party, certainly by himself, as Canada's next prime-minister-in-waiting.

So glamorous as a precocious young man who had made a better-than-expected showing as a leadership candidate in 1968, Turner was rusty and gaffe-prone when he returned to the political wars in 1984. He reminded me of a jazz musician who hadn't played his instrument in public for most of a decade and had lost the spontaneity of impulse, empathy and rapport with audiences that inspire great performances. It was as if Turner had buried himself in a studio instead of playing for live audiences and had lost his groove—and the ability to improvise that fuels every jazz line. Mingling with the crowd at public events, Turner acted as if he were attending a defensive-driving course, peeking over the shoulder of the person he was talking to, to check out whether there was a better listener in another lane.* His locker-room expletives, his 1950s lingo, his foot-long cigars, and his habit of patting female Liberal party officials on the bum reduced him to being a leader who, in Jeffrey Simpson's phrase, "promises us all a better yesterday."

---

* *Most of the time Turner was civil and entertaining but he could be insensitive. When the Victoria journalist Bruce Hutchison—the ace political commentator of his generation and a friend of Turner—became seriously ill, the* Maclean's *columnist, Allan Fotheringham, paid him a visit. Fotheringham then told Turner that he better visit Hutchison as soon as he could. Turner got right on the phone to call Hutchison. "Bruce!" Turner bellowed when his friend picked up, "Foth tells me you're dying. Wanna come out and see ya." Hutchison, who was indeed failing rapidly, gathered up his considerable dignity and shot back: "Fotheringham isn't going to tell me when to die. I will decide that."*

By the time of the Grit leadership convention in June 1984, other Liberal contenders would arguably have better filled Trudeau's shoes: for instance, the other front-runner, Jean Chrétien, who had been a high-profile Liberal for twenty years, holding nine cabinet posts including that of first francophone federal finance minister. But a Chrétien succession to Trudeau would have broken the francophone-anglophone rotation. So, following the received wisdom of the party, Turner won, becoming prime minister on June 30. Since he didn't have a seat, and apparently didn't want to get into the House by running in a safe by-election, he took the party into a national campaign. No one among the party brass seemed to notice that Canadians had grown weary of Grit rule, which, with the brief 1979–80 interregnum of Joe Clark, had lasted at that point twenty years.

Before the writ dropped, though, Turner implemented scores of patronage appointments requested by the departing Trudeau, an act that had deadly political consequences. Who doesn't remember Turner's exchange with his Tory rival Brian Mulroney in the leaders' debate? And Mulroney was right: Turner really did have a choice. Instead of taking advantage of his period in the political wilderness to break with the Trudeau record, he was the dutiful party man.

Though he was fluently bilingual and his accomplishments were many—at least before he became prime minister—Turner led the Grits to what was at that point the worst defeat they'd ever suffered, winning only forty seats. (Ignatieff would break that record, winning only thirty-four.) At the same time, Mulroney, promising "Jobs, jobs, jobs!" in recessionary times, racked up one of the biggest majorities in Canadian history. Turner was considered the prime minister in waiting for nine years, but actually held the office for only seventy-nine days, a dream-to-reality ratio of forty-two to one.

Ominously for the Liberals, Mulroney, an Anglophone raised in a francophone Quebec mill town where his closest chums had French as their mother tongue, won his big majority by shattering the Grit stronghold of Quebec, taking most of the seats in Canada's second-largest province. (From that point on, the Liberals have never taken more than thirty-six seats—or less than half the ridings in Quebec—becoming also-rans in a province they had owned since Laurier's time.) Taken together with Trudeau's lasting alienation of Western voters, the post-election 1984 Grits were reduced to a southern Ontario stronghold centered on Toronto and were still competitive in Atlantic Canada, but beyond that were *party non grata*.

They had sold themselves a bill of goods with Turner, self-destructively mesmerized by the wrong leader in very much the same way they would be more than two decades later with Michael Ignatieff, another prospect whose glamorous CV exceeded his political reach. Turner, in the end, was a bit player in the drama of Liberal power, but had an impact like the iceberg in the saga of the *Titanic*. Despite quitting Trudeau's cabinet over not wanting to be the fall guy for Liberal policies, he wore the Liberal record, including Trudeau's patronage bonanza, into the campaign and as a result never had a chance.

8. Last Gasp: The Chrétien and Martin Regimes

*"I blame Paul Martin's thugs for launching the decline
of the party. Paul always did what they told him to do.
I coined the term Earnscliffe Man to describe them,
as throwbacks to Neanderthal Man."*
— RAYMOND HEARD, Liberal power broker

JOHN TURNER LED the Liberals for six more years, all of them
in opposition. The 1988 campaign's big issue was Mulroney's
introduction of free trade and the Tories went into the election
dogged by a number of corruption scandals; for a brief moment it
looked liked the Liberals might win. But all Turner managed to
do was to trim the Tory majority and double his own seat total to
eighty-three. The stage was now set for his old rival, Jean Chrétien,
to assume the position. And Chrétien took a Turner-like path to
the leadership in 1990 but with his own twist.

In 1985, while serving in opposition, Chrétien endeared
himself to the public at large with his shrewd act of autobiog-
raphy, *Straight from the Heart*, an instant bestseller that for eter-
nity enshrined him as the little guy from Shawinigan who spoke
his mind for all Canadians, even if he was not exactly eloquent
in either official language. A year after the book came out,

Chrétien resigned from the Commons, clearly unhappy with playing second fiddle to Turner, and he become a temporary outsider in the chasms of Bay Street as a successful legal adviser and corporate director. When he emerged from the political wilderness again, he was the party's natural choice, a quasi-outsider francophone replacing the anglophone Turner. Chrétien won the leadership in one ballot, dominating the runner-up, Paul Martin Jr.

JEAN CHRÉTIEN dominated the years between Brian Mulroney's drastic 1993 fall from power and the rise of Stephen Harper. It was a time out of joint, a listless March break in which the same issues seemed to come around again and again, like unclaimed baggage on an airport carousel. Nothing was resolved but the deficit (largely Paul Martin's doing); less was settled.

But as prime minister, Chrétien made history for four good reasons:

- reinforcing an essential concept of national unity with legislation;
- waking a spectacular international decision;
- setting a record at how long a politician could delay his resignation, once announced;
- being the first Liberal prime minister ejected by his party while still in power.

Chrétien's essential piece of legislation was the Clarity Act that at last set sensible boundaries on Quebec's right to separate. His stellar international decision was something he refused to do: President George W. Bush personally pressed the PM to enlist Canada in the Coalition of the Willing to help fight the war against

Iraq. Chrétien's reply was a clear "No way, José" and Canadians rightly applauded him.

After announcing that he would step down, he persuaded Paul Martin, his impatient successor, to cool his heels while he extended his term in power by an astounding eighteen months. In the process of prolonging his reign, Chrétien had to abandon his favoured stance as an elected dictator to something more like a constitutional monarch. That a three-term prime minister who won majorities lost the confidence of his party takes a little more explaining.

CHRÉTIEN FIRST WAS elected to the House of Commons in 1963. That was the last year John F. Kennedy and his Camelot road company occupied the White House; Fats Domino recorded *I'm Walking to New Orleans*; the Beatles' first album came out; Farley Mowat's *Never Cry Wolf* was published; the *Front de Libération du Québec* set off its first bomb; the average suburban house in Canada sold for $12,650.

During the three decades before he became prime minister in 1993, Chrétien was at the centre of the political action, occupying increasingly significant portfolios in the Pearson and Trudeau governments. He became a floating trouble-shooter and was good at it, though his most stellar quality, according to his long-time boss, Pierre Trudeau, was that "he recognized his limitations."

Chrétien's path swerved when he ceased to do that, and ran for leader of the party. He missed it the first time, losing to John Turner, but a little walk in the woods of Bay Street and some canny manoeuvring, and the party gave him the mandate he believed he deserved, which he immediately turned into the crushing defeat of the Tories in the 1993 election. That win and the two successful campaigns that followed would turn out to be the last gasp of the Liberal party. They were genuine majority victories—preceding one minority (Martin) and to this point two nasty defeats, each more brutal than the last.

It was only when you measure Chrétien's triumphs against the stature of his opponents that they take on a less gilded aspect. First time out, he ran against the hapless Kim Campbell, who spent most of the campaign proving that she had an unerring instinct for her own jugular. She ended up with an unprecedented slide from 151 Progressive Conservative seats to a deuce—neither of the two her own. Chrétien next took on Preston Manning and his Reformers (sounds like a religious rock group), who did well enough to form the Opposition. In his third campaign Chrétien called the election early so he could face off against Stockwell Day, who was so new in his leadership role he hadn't had time to get his act together.

But *le petit gars de Shawinigan* took the results seriously. No other politician in my experience changed character so abruptly after assuming power. The charming politician I had interviewed frequently during his Cabinet days transformed himself into a sub-Arctic Noriega. Prime Minister Chrétien was not the man I had first met on July, 22, 1965, the day he was picked out of the Liberal backbenches to become parliamentary secretary to Prime Minister Lester Pearson. It was a time of unexpected North American fiscal emergencies that preoccupied senior Canadian cabinet ministers, and Chrétien in his new role sat in on all the briefings. At the end of the sessions, Finance Minister Mitchell Sharp leaned over and warned him never to reveal what had been discussed. "Don't worry, Mitchell," Chrétien replied, "I didn't understand a word of it."

In those days homespun humility, self-deprecating humour and upfront decency were Chrétien's dominant characteristics. I remember thinking that he was one of those rare politicians who didn't need adoring crowds or genuflecting flunkies to feed his sense of self. Whenever I asked him a question, he would hesitate like a dutiful child who wanted to get it right, and then give me an honest answer.

But politics, he believed, is "a game of friends." And so it was, once he got into power. No other Canadian prime minister, including Brian Mulroney, was so cynically personal in his distribution of patronage jobs. His appointments required only one qualification: blood-oath loyalty to Jean Chrétien. (Being a faithful Liberal was no longer enough.) He turned out to be one tough mother, unable or unwilling to demonstrate grace under pressure, or in any other circumstances. He treated his parliamentary caucus like a retinue instead of the source of his power; it was Paul Martin's recognition of that difference that allowed him to steal the party from under its leader.

I saw Chrétien several times when he ventured to the West Coast where I was living in the nineties, and I tried to read what had changed in him. There was no more music in the man I had so long admired. His grin now had more to do with cheek muscles than inner mirth; the twinkle in his gaze had been one of his identifying characteristics, but now no light danced in his eyes. Instead of the self-deprecating humour he had projected, he gave off a distant, lunar chill.

THE 1997 ELECTION may have been the dullest campaign on record, but the significance of the June 2 results were electrifying. The election turned out to be a contest in which the verities of the past meant very little and the risks of the future meant everything. In the eleven hours it took thirteen million Canadians to cast their ballots, something profoundly significant happened. Canadians re-elected the Liberals but without the comfortable majority that would allow them to govern as they chose. The voters' obvious disillusionment with the natural government party was due in large measure to the fact that Jean Chrétien sleepwalked through the campaign. Its two defining moments did involve the prime minister, though, and they were both downers.

The first came on opening day. Asked why he had called the election long before his term was up, Chrétien had to consult his notes in order to come up with an inadequate answer. Of course even Chrétien realized he couldn't be blunt about his real reason, which was to perpetuate his power while his opponents were weak: Lucien Bouchard had stepped down as leader of the Bloc and the official opposition, and Gilles Duceppe didn't prove to be as effective an opponent.

The other defining moment, as far as I am concerned, came on May 22 in Halifax, where he opened the country's first commercial virtual-reality laboratory by cutting a virtual "ribbon" using a computer mouse. Chrétien had trouble working the tiny instrument and later confided to reporters that he had never used one. Now, prime ministers aren't supposed to be hackers, but his incompetence was a symbol of how distant Chrétien was from the mental space where most Canadians now lived and work.

In past elections, the winning political leader offered a vision, or at least a plan—some sense of movement toward a better tomorrow. In 1997, the Liberals offered nothing and asked Canadians simply to vote for what they already had. That the voters responded with enough ballots to grant them a slim majority seemed more a reflection of the fact that the alternatives—Reform, the Bloc, the NDP, and the Tories under Jean Charest—were not yet ready for prime time and someone had to govern.

It was one of the great ironies of the campaign that Chrétien, so devoted to retaining his mandate and relatively fresh out of a

Quebec referendum campaign he almost lost, had nothing new or interesting to say about national unity. As prime minister before and after June 2, 1997, he ought to have made that his lead priority. Instead, the future of Canada rested on the shoulders of a man who had panicked in the referendum and had almost lost the country.

Preston Manning's showing was well-earned and surprisingly impressive. Alone of the leaders he ran a tough, policy-oriented campaign, and stuck to his divisive, anti-Quebec songbook throughout. His shock troops were humbled everywhere except in B.C. and Alberta, so that the party seemed to be sliding back to where it had come from. Still, his new prominence as opposition leader became his great test: could he turn himself into a statesman or would Reform remain a populist protest movement with a preacher as leader and limited appeal? The fact that Manning's cause won such strong support in British Columbia and Alberta helped the West to be heard more loudly in the Golden Triangle that still ruled the country, but Reform remained a regional phenomenon. (And the "unite the right" movement was born.)

The Liberals ignored the warning implicit in Manning's western sweep. The overwhelming support for his hardrock platform was no accident. It accurately reflected western Canada's state of mind. The 1997 election results ought to have taught the Liberals a lesson. No group of democratic politicians should aim at governing "comfortably." That Canada's voters allowed the Grits to remain in office but not securely in power was a triumph of collective public will. The fact the Liberals ignored that shot across their bows foretold the disaster that was headed their way. Faced with unpalatable or dreary alternatives, Canadians still elected the Liberals but stripped them of the "comfortable" majority to which they had become accustomed.

THE LONGER CHRÉTIEN STAYED IN OFFICE, the more confidence in him to capably manage a modern corporate state declined. His idea of enforcing the laws of the land was to grab a protestor by the scruff of his scruffy neck until his victim was rescued by the attending Mounties. This stranglehold manoeuvre was an effective instrument of state control, but there was a repellent quality to it.

Chrétien was at his most insensitive in dealing with University of British Columbia students when they protested the 1997 visit to Vancouver of the Indonesian dictator Suharto, who was soon afterwards overthrown by his own people and charged with massive corruption. Subsequent investigations documented that the RCMP had acted on direct orders from the PMO to protect the visiting despot, not just from harm but from embarrassment. When student demonstrators were crudely pepper-sprayed into painful silence, Chrétien ridiculed them by joking that he used pepper only when he was munching steaks.

Chrétien's approach to whatever was ailing this giant slice of the earth that had been placed in his custody was simple, or maybe that should be simplistic: whatever he lacked in proof to support a course of action, he made up for in self-confidence. His belief in himself was based in part on his having achieved a bewilderingly successful career after a less than prosaic start and on being the head of the Liberal party when that still meant something.

I'm not being entirely flip when I say it was also hard to stay mad at a prime minister when you didn't know what in hell he was trying to tell you. At one point, I remember him replying to a female Vancouver high school student who was advocating athletic scholarships, "I tend to incline with you."

In reality, Chrétien didn't need to bother himself with heavy policy matters, since his predecessors largely had taken care of them. By the year 2000, the required reclamation of the federal budget was successfully achieved by his finance minister and the books were back in balance. I would argue that other than his worry about Quebec separation he wasn't much interested in ideas or issues. During Chrétien's time the once strong and enthusiastic bedrock of Liberal free thinkers and mandarins with a sense of duty about public service was eroded by a group of Ottawa insiders: professionals who took over the party because it became their business to run the party. They rose through the ranks, joined ministers' offices then left those ministers' offices to become lobbyists, consultants and power brokers. What characterized them was a vested interest in the status quo—*their* status quo. Whoever they were, they dedicated themselves to no longer sharing internal influence with any volunteers they couldn't control. The Liberal party ceased being a democratic or even innovative institution. It was transmogrified (a word from Conrad Black's vocabulary I have searched for an opportunity to use) into a power-preservation vehicle for its insiders.

As Chrétien's time finally expired, it became clear that his stewardship was devoid of a defining legacy. Lawrence Martin's *Iron Man: The Defiant Reign of Jean Chrétien* remains the definitive study of the period. "He was born not with a silver spoon in his mouth, but rather a cement mixer," Martin concluded. "His instincts were wonderfully at one with the country's broad wash of citizenry and their values. His problem was a failure of words. While having that great gut instinct, he had no intellect with which to clothe it."

THE MARTIN/CHRÉTIEN RIVALRY was fairly senseless: despite his firm grasp on power, the Shawinigan politician never intended to be prime minister for life and Paul Martin was the only logical candidate to succeed him. It was all a matter of timing.

Determined to have the turn at bat that had been denied his father, Martin Jr.'s greatest accomplishment was to balance the federal budget. Turned from a dithering numbers cruncher into a dithering avenging angel, he chose a praetorian guard whose open-ended *coup d'etat* against the incumbent Chrétien regime offended all but the least savoury of Ottawa's politicians and guaranteed Martin a short lease on power. Their putsch may have turned Chrétien into the first Liberal PM to be overthrown by his own party while still in office, but what's happened to the Liberals since is also testimony to the Shawinigan politician's effectiveness. He may not have had a way with words, but he had a nose for how to retain power; the Liberals have been sliding out of contention ever since his departure.

Martin dropped in on me once when Chrétien was still in office to chat about his prospects. I questioned him about his retinue, loyal Martinets all, who kept pushing the envelope to get their man ensconced in the catbird seat, using increasingly crude tactics. I vividly recall his reply to my criticism of his feisty retinue: "These are the people who have grown grey in my service, and I don't intend to abandon them now. . . ." This was hardly a recommendation.

Many otherwise calm and collected Liberals grew increasingly upset about the Liberal family feud as the Chrétien years wore on, especially as Martin's attempt to unseat his own leader gathered steam after the party's poor showing in the 1997 election. Influential Martinets infiltrated the party machinery, eventually controlling it, and also gathering under the Ottawa-based Earnscliffe lobbying firm's umbrella; Earnscliffe had been the beneficiary of major contracts from the Finance Department when Martin was the minister. Led by David Herle (a lawyer from

Saskatchewan and longtime Liberal who became a partner at Earnscliffe, where he worked on the messaging for Martin's deficit-busting budgets) and his common-law wife, Terrie O'Leary (Martin's straight-shooting and loyal executive assistant), the avid Martin camp included Scott Reid, a lobbyist, Mike Robinson, another long-time Martin adviser who worked for Earnscliffe, Mark Resnick, a founding partner of the Rothwell Group, and the Carlton University journalism professor Elly Alboim, a former CBC executive.

During a Liberal party annual meeting in March 2000 when Chrétien was seriously preparing to quit, the Martin retinue staged a "secret" conclave at a low-rent hotel near the Toronto airport to launch yet another assault to dislodge him. When Chrétien's wife, Aline, read about it in the morning paper, she persuaded her husband to run for one more term. The Martinets achieved the very opposite to what they wanted.

AFTER THE PARTY'S 2003 policy convention, specifically held to anoint Paul Martin's leadership, and Martin's first national campaign as leader in 2004, Jim Coutts (who had been a key senior adviser in Trudeau's PMO), reported in *Policy Options* that "a collection of federal lobbyists, paid Ottawa ministerial staff, professional organizers and wealthy businessmen had spent ten years and over $25 million to mount a more or less hostile takeover, as the party's electoral apparatus was systematically closed to all but one candidate: Paul Martin. It was a sad chapter for the same Liberal party which in 1919 had introduced democratic leadership balloting to Canada."

The Martin takeover, and then his two electoral campaigns, engineered by the same gang of advisers, went so far as to alter Liberal electoral signage to distance itself from the Chrétien regime. Liberal identifiers were painted over with Team Martin logos, since, as Coutts noted, the new guys thought that "the Liberal brand was no longer useful—many in the party returned the compliments by sitting on their hands, or publicly complaining about the Martin team." The advisers to whom Martin was so loyal helped him barely snatch a Liberal minority in the 2004 election.

Still, with their mentor finally ensconced in the highest political office, they had dreams of grandeur. But it was not to be.

The Sicilian blood feud between Chrétien and Martin went to the marrow of why the Grits were losing their place as Canada's Natural Government Party. The transition between the party's leaders had once been so smooth that any bickering was conducted behind closed doors. Incumbents did their best to soften their successors' path to power. Lester Pearson and Pierre Trudeau, for example, were very different men: one the son of the Protestant manse in rural Ontario, the other, an urban Quebec radical. And yet Pearson set up Trudeau's 1968 triumph by carefully mentoring him for the position—and his wife, Maryon, had to be physically restrained from rushing on to the convention floor wearing a big Trudeau button. With the Chrétien/Martin vendetta never at less than full Monty, the Liberals were confirming what was once the most heretical of notions: that they were no longer fit to govern a country that thrived on unity.

PAUL MARTIN'S IRREDEEMABLE error during the shaky start of his campaign in the January 2006 election was to treat Stephen Harper as just another western populist that the Liberal party machine would quickly reduce to roadkill. In doing so, the Liberal prime minister and his advisers hanged themselves from a gallows of stale and false intelligence. Anyone who has even vaguely followed Harper's impressive career recognized him as a different breed of political cat: he may not have been charismatic enough to offer us persuasive terms of endearment, but he was a perfectly legitimate alternative to an expired potboiler like Jean Chrétien, and even the enlightened and ambitious Monsieur Martin.

Unfortunately for Martin, after taking office (one hesitates to say "power" since he so seldom exercised it) he continued to rely on the stalwarts who had formed an ideal commando unit for his endless mission to dislodge Jean Chrétien. But winning elections (at least some of the time) is about winning peoples' hearts and minds, not carrying on a vendetta to nuke the other guy.

The Martin team's early campaign tactics urged Canadian voters to take a good look at Harper, presuming that if they did they would discover an evangelical clone of Stockwell Day with a hidden agenda. (They forgot that Day's problem was not that he had a hidden agenda, but that he didn't keep his agenda hidden, allowing voters to reject his off-centre views on original sin, capital punishment, abortion, immigration and dinosaur petting zoos.) One aspect that voters may have warmed to in Harper was that (except for the revolving door incumbencies of John Turner, Joe Clark and Kim Campbell), he would be Canada's first elected prime minister in thirty-five years who wasn't a Quebec-based millionaire lawyer.

So far, Harper's main achievement had been to unite the Conservatives, or most of them, under one banner. That was no mean achievement. I remember cornering Progressive Conservative Leader Joe Clark aboard his campaign bus during the 2000 election and asking him why he was so adamantly opposed to any coalition with the Canadian Alliance, then led by Day. "The Alliance party is fundamentally offensive," he told me. "It's an alliance of people who don't like other people, the very opposite of the inclusion that characterizes our party. In those parts of the country that are a base for us, any kind of association with Reform/Alliance would give those seats to the Liberals." (That, of course, was exactly what happened anyway. The increase in Tory support throughout rural Ontario split the anti-Liberal vote, allowing Chrétien to snatch yet another Ontario-based majority.)

NONE OF MARTIN'S good intentions went unpunished. Instead of mobilizing his forces after his narrow victory at the polls, he squandered his political honeymoon by immersing himself in the swamp of the sponsorship scandals and alienated the veteran campaigners and strategists who had produced a trio of Liberal victories at the polls. The Liberals' problem was trust. Martin kept emphasizing that values were more important than policies. Of course they are. But it was no longer enough for campaigning politicians to exude a tranquilizing mood when voters knew that politics was really about trading favours in back rooms. Paul Martin's only chance was to persuade the voters that he genuinely wanted to jettison the gutter tactics practiced by some of his predecessors—and his own loyal cadre.

While Canadians generally run from radical reformers at the federal level, they were demanding change and wanted some hint of vision from their leaders, especially the Liberals who once provided precisely that.

But Adscam was the ethical tsunami that completely destroyed the Liberal brand in Quebec. Following the menacingly close 1995 referendum, Chrétien had secretly decided to finance a massive, pro-federal advertising campaign in the province. Instead of spending the assigned funds to buy balloons and Canadian flags (which would, of course, have been totally ineffective), the patriotic advertising executives stuffed most of the federal funds (estimated at

$100 million) into their jeans. The subsequent reports of the Gomery Inquiry and from Canada's Auditor General, Sheila Fraser, documented the pattern of theft; a handful of those involved went to jail—protesting their patriotism if not their innocence.

Chrétien had generously offered to hang in for yet a few more months before stepping down so that Martin would not have to take the heat from the scandal. But Herle and his hit squad persuaded Martin to decline this offer. The awkward way that Martin and his gang chose to handle the Adscam affair turned the Quebec wound into fatal damage for the Grits. Having rejected Chrétien's first offer, they also rejected his sensible and politically astute suggestion to defuse the issue by turning the whole matter over to the RCMP. Instead, Martin's go-for-the-throat advisers persuaded him to launch a public inquiry, as they tried to blame Chrétien personally for the scandal. I guess they figured that blaming Chrétien would distance their guy from the disaster, forgetting that in the minds of most voters Chrétien's long-term minister of finance (from Quebec, to boot) should have known where the dollars had gone.

"I blame Paul Martin's thugs for launching the decline of the party," Raymond Heard, the Liberal media and communications guru and Toronto-based power broker, told me after the Grits' free fall became pronounced in mid-decade. "Paul always did what they told him to do. I coined the term Earnscliffe Man to describe them, as throwbacks to Neanderthal Man." Born in South Africa into a family of conscientious objectors to apartheid, Heard first became a journalist on the *Rand Daily Mail,* then attended Harvard (where his professors included Henry Kissinger and John Kenneth Galbraith) and covered the American scene for the London *Observer.* Later he was managing editor of the *Montreal Star* and head of Global Television's news operation, before taking a job as John Turner's communications director. (He's now in his midseventies, a consultant and head of Heard-Cosgrove Communications.)

"When people ask me what the chief Martin adviser, David Herle, is like, I tell them what happened to me at the Ottawa airport once," Heard says. "As I was leaving the Air Canada flight, a big, burly man yelled at me: 'You are a fucking idiot, Ray Heard. You were the worst communications director we ever had.' (In fact when I was in the leader's office, John Turner doubled his seat numbers, whereas Herle & Company took Martin from an inherited majority to a minority and, in the following campaign, to defeat.) I looked at this guy, and said, 'Who on earth are you? Whoever you are, you are very rude. I don't believe we have met?'

"'You know who I am. I'm David Herle,' he said, then approached me with a threatening grimace. Though smaller than Herle, I braced myself for a fight, but he backed off and walked away. Next day, Jane Taber wrote a piece in the paper saying Liberal strategists had almost come to blows at the Ottawa airport. And it was true."

Martin had many more ideas than his predecessor, and his government managed to pass the progressive same-sex marriage law, and came to a historic deal with Canada's First Nations (undone when he lost in 2006). But he was so marked by his long battle with Chrétien, and his party so torn and undermined, that he couldn't survive the political game being played by a newly united Conservative party under Stephen Harper. The machine was not operating silently and efficiently any more, but lurching from crisis to crisis, and Martin couldn't heal the chasms caused by the way he came to power.

THE LIBERAL PARTY'S OPERATIONAL CODE once had been simplicity itself: to govern Canada by striking the most marketable balance between elitism and egalitarianism. Sedate populism with an extended shelf life.

Past leaders have described the process without necessarily appreciating the ramifications of what they were really saying. The closest Jean Chrétien ever came to defining his political philosophy was on June 23, 1997, when he blurted out at a press conference that he stood squarely for *"de* radical centre." Nobody understood what that meant, and the prime minister's rare attempt to venture into lucidity went for naught. Liberals reacted with an almost gravitational pull to compromise, conciliation and the notion that the political ideal is to do as little as possible but as much as necessary.

The price the Liberals paid for their long succession game was that the politically untested leaders—Turner, Martin, Dion and Ignatieff—were beaten by Brian Mulroney and, in the last three instances, by Stephen Harper. Over the Liberal century, Canadian voters had grudgingly accepted the Natural Government Party's tendency to swing between complacence and noblesse oblige. But when their arrogance became unbearable, as it did in 1957, 1984, 2004 and 2006, the party dug its own grave. In the drubbings of 2008 and 2011, for reasons that seem to still mystify Liberals, their belief that they had been punished enough and should return to their natural governing status was not shared by Canadian voters.

But the 2011 election was a loss of a different magnitude. For the first time ever, the Grits were pushed into third place, where the also-rans usually shudder and hide. Once again, the rational-izers came forward. After all, this was Canada, and why does a Canadian chicken cross the road? To get to the middle, of course, and look smug. *Nah.* These new-breed chicks are *free range.* They went wherever they wanted, even flew down to Vegas for a fling during an election campaign. The Big Red Tent that Michael

Ignatieff so graciously invited Canadian voters to share, collapsed like an underdone soufflé.

I first became aware of the Liberals' institutionalized arrogance when I was Ottawa columnist for *Maclean's* in the mid-1960s and found myself researching a profile of Jack Pickersgill, then a senior minister and father confessor in the Pearson government. "It is not merely for the wellbeing of Canadians, but for the good of mankind in general that the present Liberal government should remain in office," he told me with a straight face, though he was a history graduate from the University of Manitoba and from Oxford, and some learning ought to have rubbed off on him. I realized then that Pickersgill and his peers viewed the Liberal party, not as an organ of the people, but as an organ of the state. They genuinely believed that by accepting the burdens of office, they were bestowing a benefaction on the nation at large, and viewed the slightest criticism as an unpatriotic act.

When I reminded Pickersgill that there was, after all, another national party then in active contention for government, he could not bring himself to entertain such a heretical notion. "Conservative governments are like the mumps," he harrumphed, voicing the comment that would be quoted often from then on. "They're something you have to endure once in your lifetime, but when it's over, you don't want it again."

Being a good Liberal, Pickersgill went to his just reward. As transport minister he had sponsored the establishment of the Canadian Transport Commission, whose chairman's retirement age was set at seventy; Pickersgill was approaching the official retirement age of 65 at the time. The newly created position was never advertised by the Civil Service Commission—and guess what? The founding chairman of the Canadian Transport Commission became none other than "Sailor" Jack (the nickname his constituents gave him because he toured his coastal riding in Newfoundland aboard a chartered yacht).

That was the formula for Liberal longevity: they took good care of their own.

Arrogance is as arrogance does. But the first rule of the Grits' presumed superiority used to be act humble—never brag, bluff or bluster in public. That was certainly true for the Liberal party under Mackenzie King, Louis St. Laurent and Mike Pearson. It was less true under Pierre Trudeau and Paul Martin, but Jean Chrétien broke that mold entirely when he was in charge. With *le petit gars de Shawinigan* as their overlord, the Liberals couldn't be bothered to hide their arrogance. For ten years they operated the only federal government available.

Familiarity ought not to breed consent and the advent of new prime ministers ought not, as the British sexologist and essayist Havelock Ellis once complained, "merely be the exchange of one nuisance for another." The problems caused by the Liberals' twin succession rules were considerable and grew worse. In Quebec, the French vote was no longer Liberal by default. The contest for that key constituency was among Grits, the Bloc Québécois and the Tories, who in 1984 under the leadership of a charming quasi-francophone stole Quebec only to have it stolen from them a couple of elections later by the Bloc. (And then Jack Layton and the NDP stole it from the Bloc . . .) At the same time, the glamorous outsider rule had also cost the Grits the west. First lost to Diefenbaker, the west's antipathy to the Liberals was cemented by the Trudeau government's National Energy edicts.

Canada's most serious dilemma during this extended term of Liberal dominance was not the issues grumpy people could list on their fingers: the decline in our health-care system, pension insecurity, the environment, the underfunding and overstretching of our armed forces, our tax structure, national unity or even the price of gasoline. It was the growing and almost universal belief among ordinary Canadians that political action could not achieve any permanently significant effect on the nation's problems.

That has been the deadly legacy of the Liberal regimes. Liberals would never admit such a heresy, but their near monopoly on federal power eventually undermined the efficacy of Canada's democratic system.

The decline and fall of the Grits resembled the near-bankruptcy of General Motors. Instead of plugging into changing consumer ethics, they went on playing the game that had won them dominance half a century earlier. Losing large voting blocs over the past decades—Quebec, the immigrant vote, western Canada, and even urban Ontario, save for the last redoubt of Toronto—resulted in no discernable adjustment in Liberal policies or initiatives. In the aftermath of Paul Martin first losing Chrétien's Grit majority and then being defeated outright— followed by the catastrophic losses of Dion and Ignatieff—what passes for the Grit brains trust still tends to view these tectonic jolts as isolated setbacks. They don't ask the obvious question: If you had the chance to launch the Liberal party today, would you? The answer has to be a resounding "NO!" because there no longer seems to be the need for one.

The major political event of the past decade, rightly celebrated by political watchers—and participants—is the remarkable rise of Stephen Harper and his right-wing coalition. Harper's astute management of Canada's Conservatives has resulted in his party displacing the Grits as Canada's Natural Government Party. There, I said it, and even if I felt the earth shudder, it's still true: the Liberals have finally met their Armageddon. Get used to it.

PART THREE

SEIZING THE DREAM

9. From Tantric Sex to Irrelevance

The pursuit of the party leadership grew into a compulsion
for Ignatieff. Although he was still a newcomer to stump politics
and a newly reborn native son, he was a man on a mission to
save Canada by restoring the Liberal party to its proper place.

THOUGH THE STAKES WERE HIGH—since as far as Liberal and progressive Canada was concerned, Stephen Harper was their worst nightmare—the contest to replace Paul Martin as Liberal leader had an air of the surreal from day one. In late March 2006, Ashley MacIsaac, the badass hillbilly fiddler from Cape Breton, announced that he intended to be a leadership contender, claiming in the Halifax *Daily News* that he was running to save national unity and to "end the continuous mockery of the Liberals." If his mock intentions couldn't bring the flailing Grits to their senses, nothing would. How could the Liberals, who not so long ago had had a stranglehold on federal power, have become such a deserving target of MacIsaac's satirical jabs? The Pooh-Bahs of the country's Natural Government Party were milliseconds away from becoming the butt of every stand-up comedian in the country, if they weren't already there.

But all of the Grit favourites to replace Martin—Frank McKenna, Allan Rock, Brian Tobin, John Manley (again) and

Martin Cauchon—had lists of impressive past achievements to their credit but not much in the way of future political possibilities. If they could even be persuaded to run. Most of the other available alternatives were variously self-deluded entities who heard the clarion call to lead the party out of its self-inflicted wilderness, without realizing that call was an echo of their own voices. What the Liberals should have been seeking was not merely a return to the comforts of power, but a new populist mandate that could become a revolutionary instrument. In order to refresh their mandate, a new leader needed to bring passion, commitment and integrity to the political wars, not a bloody audit of their opponents' alleged follies and potential hidden agenda.

IN LATE MARCH 2006, I showed up with *Maclean's* chief photographer Peter Bregg to record my first interview with Michael Ignatieff at his nondescript riding office in Etobicoke. By the time the piece ran in *Maclean's* April 10 issue, he had officially announced that he was running for leader, and he had already staked out his claim to being the cool dude among the posse of his down-market rivals—never mind that his surprising emergence as the candidate to beat was based on the dropping out of the top "name" contenders, such as McKenna, Rock, Tobin and Manley. Stéphane Dion, the only francophone in the race, was barely a second choice for most potential delegates though choosing him would fulfill the traditional Liberal pattern; Ignatieff's old friend Bob Rae, who declared he was running on April 24, carried so much baggage from his time as NDP premier of Ontario that even the backing of some of Chrétien's power players was unlikely to carry him into the job.

Ignatieff was looking like the man to beat. His candidacy had just received surprising support from columnist Peter Worthington, the most thoughtful of the neo-cons, writing on the *Canoe* network: "What sets Ignatieff off from the rest is not only more common sense and an understanding of how the world works, but a certain amount of courage to say things that are unpopular with the Liberals. He ain't Pierre Trudeau, and that may be why he's the best candidate in a weak field."

And the candidate was taking this new challenge with deep seriousness. Even when answering the irreverent queries of an itinerant journalist like me, Ignatieff winced with concentration.

"So, what have you learned about politics," I asked, "that you haven't already taught or written a book about?"

"What I have learned running for political office is that my fellow citizens want truth, they want the straight goods," he responded. "They don't want you to come to the door with a policy that's half-baked or just consists of sound bites. There is a tension between truth and power but I just passionately believe you can't hold power for very long unless you tell the truth."

Speaking of truth I reminded him that while he was lecturing at Harvard, he referred to himself as an American, a comment that was not yet the fodder for a million attack ads. "I shouldn't have used the word 'we' or 'us' in describing myself,'" he replied. "I'm not and have never been and will never be an American citizen, so I shouldn't have done that. Sometimes you want to increase your influence over your audience by appropriating their voice. It was a mistake. Every single one of the students from eighty-five countries who took my courses at Harvard knew one thing about me: I was that funny Canadian." (During his voluntary exile he never assumed dual citizenship, nor while in the U.S. did he apply for a Green Card.)

Ignatieff had already attracted an eager herd of young followers, but as far as I could make out he had few discernable policies to fanfare across the land. "Being elected a democratic politician is very humbling because you trade in hope, you trade in dreams," he rhymed off to me. "People come to you because they think that you can change their lives—from getting their families reunited, India to Toronto, to much bigger things like revision of the rules that govern the whole country. You come into democratic politics and you immediately take on a great burden of expectation. It's the thing that worries me most about political life. Because if the expectations can't be met, they produce violent disillusion that I quite understand: 'You played with our dreams, you played with our hopes, and let us down . . . ' Every politician in a leadership position can ride up the roller coaster of hope, and then will ride it down as people discover they can't deliver. I'd like to be the public figure who promised little but delivers what he promised, [so that] people would say, 'Well, I didn't like that guy very much, but he did what he said.'"

I reminded him—or perhaps it was news to him—that the Liberal party's success had traditionally been based on policies that fell somewhere between demure elitism and reluctant egalitarianism, something I described to him (trying to rise to his rhetorical level) as a particular form of sedate populism with an extended shelf life. I asked if following that tradition would come easily to him.

"Liberals have tried to make that balance, but one of the challenges for the future is to sustain the egalitarian promise of Liberalism in the face of our competitive challenge in the global economy," he replied. "The entire Canadian social model—health care, pensions, income security—depends critically on having an economy that is world-class, and we're slipping. I don't want to lead a country in sedate decline. I want to lead a country that is dynamic and growing. I don't know whether the country needs healing, but the party—this party I love—certainly does. We've fought each other much too much. We can't aspire to lead the country, unless we heal, unless we unite, unless we decide that our tribal warfare is over, truly over. So the idea is not so much healing as it is creating a space within the party, and then within the country, in which we can explore our differences, peacefully and civilly. Healing is the wrong word. It's the peaceful management of discord that seems to be the art of politics."

He was lofty and impressive, and at the time I didn't think overmuch about the ease with which he had identified himself with the "we" of the Liberal party. Trying to follow his reasoning from step to logical step, I commented that he was the only politician I had ever heard talk in complete sentences—even paragraphs—instead of sound bites. "Will this be a major handicap?" I ventured.

"It could be fatal, Peter!" he replied and burst out laughing.

As we left his office, I nudged Bregg and asked him how he sized up the new politician we had just met. "Nice change," he said. "Good to meet somebody whose heart is attached to his brain."

IN THE MONTHS that followed, the front-running Ignatieff was definitely the most newsworthy of the candidates. Not always in the ways he intended. His campaign had an echo-chamber quality: first his original statement on some issue of the day or initiative he wanted to pursue—and then the next day, his correction or tortuous explanation of what he really meant to say.

The beginning of the race had been auspicious. Led by his campaign manager, Ian Davey, Ignatieff's team included deputy chief of staff Sachin Aggarwal, Mark Sakamoto, Alexis Levine and Leslie Church. Bright-eyed, bushy-tailed and single-minded, they became the leaders of Ignatieff's Praetorian guard.

In the three days after April 7, 2006, when the Ignatieff campaign first went live so many people responded to his call for volunteers on his website they briefly crashed it. The recruits were mostly university grads or post-grads, nearly all under thirty and with few exceptions new to Canadian politics. As Ian Davey noted, they were responding to a leadership hopeful unsullied by the party's recent past, who seemed to speak in a different way about politics and who seemed to be the polar opposite of the country's new prime minister, Stephen Harper.

But he wasn't playing so well inside the party. Many members of the Liberals' hierarchical power structure perceived Ignatieff's sudden intrusion as a threat. "The party structure is composed of people who fear change and feared Michael, who came to represent that momentum for change because he was someone who actually listened to people," Davey told me. "Those who don't know the man saw him as being very lone-wolfish, in many ways, like Trudeau. He can seem aloof, can seem distant, but he listens intently to every person he encounters. This was where his notion of backing Québec as a nation came from. He went into the Gaspésie, toured those parts of the province where you can be shot for being a Liberal and listened carefully to everyone he met. He decided that the idea of Quebec as a nation within the Canadian state was important in terms of the province's self-respect. It was Harper who got Parliament to do this very thing."

(Having one of his ideas ripped off by Harper didn't win Ignatieff many points with the party's power elite, either.)

Out among the delegates and the communities of interest he was courting, Ignatieff was getting mixed reviews. Even his untutored new Grit *apparatchiks*, who thought that *Charisma* was a new French perfume, recognized that his appeal was based on personal intensity rather than crowd-pleasing magnetism, and that voters might take a very long time to warm up to the man. Ignatieff's frequent blunders aside, he was sometimes so intense that in mid-speech his shoulders would hunch as if he was standing under a leaky roof on a rainy day. His eyebrows would narrow into a perfect triangle, a living manifestation of Pythagoras's theorem. Charisma is a rare natural gift, like perfect pitch in singers; if you don't have it there's no point taking charisma lessons.

Ignatieff's mission was also profoundly damaged by his advocacy of new constitutional initiatives that most Canadians identified as quagmires: he had mused on reopening the constitution in order to deal with Quebec's nationhood (whereas Harper did it by un-threatening parliamentary motion). And his meandering comments on the Israeli Defense Forces' bungled assault on Hezbollah in Lebanon, which mostly achieved civilian Lebanese deaths, enraged people on both sides of the Middle East debate: first, he confessed that he wasn't "losing any sleep" over the civilian deaths (odd for the former head of Harvard's Carr Center on human rights) caused by the Israeli attacks on Hezbollah guerillas near the Lebanese village of Qana; later he called it an "act of war" by the Jewish state. And there went his Jewish support in Montreal and Toronto. Even if he thrived on being a rebel, Trudeau would never have been so impolitic. But Trudeau had his intellectual act together in the political forum, and Ignatieff didn't. He had the professorial habit of playing with and testing ideas — out loud — a virtue in the academy, but disastrous in public life.

The Liberal folk memory of Lucky Pierre is that he miraculously appeared as the instant Prime Minister of Our Dreams. In fact, he was first elected in 1965, sat as an ordinary backbencher for a year, benefited from an apprenticeship that had included a stint in Ottawa's privy council office, serving as the prime minister's parliamentary secretary, spending a session at the

United Nations, and then, back in Ottawa, two years as an action-oriented cabinet minister. It was as justice minister, announcing Pearson's decriminalization of divorce and the abolishment of Canada's sodomy laws, that Trudeau both captured the spirit of the times and won enduring acclaim for saying, "The state has no business in the bedrooms of the nation." This all was accomplished before he declared his intention to run for the Liberal crown. His apprenticeship provided an invaluable transition from the narrow confines of his academic background to the hurly-burly of political life.

Ignatieff, on the other hand, declared his bid for the Liberal leadership barely a week after taking his seat in the House of Commons—and it showed. In essence he stepped off his Boston-Toronto flight straight into the contest to become prime minister-in-waiting of his so recently rediscovered home country.

His recruiters thought they'd landed the perfect action-intellectual, but at universities, words and ideas are used as discussion points. In politics, words are bullets—every syllable and nuance becomes a weapon. What hampered Ignatieff in his first attempt to lead the party was that the majority of Liberal delegates felt the chill of his intellectual arrogance without being swept away by his ideas. There were too many gaps between what he thought and what he said (or the other way around); he constantly had to contradict his contradictions. It seemed to me that he woke up each morning wondering, "Which beehive do I poke today?" The miracle is that throughout the leadership race, he did manage to stay the front-runner.

IGNATIEFF'S OLD FRIEND Bob Rae was not having an easy time of it, either. He made enemies effortlessly, mostly on account of Liberal delegates not being able to stomach his time as the only socialist premier in Ontario's history. Following Rae's assumption of the premiership on October 1, 1990, the province's business community had panicked at the thought of the largely neophyte red horde descending on Queen's Park. Toronto's business class was overtly contemptuous of a Rae cabinet stocked with first-time MPPs who were not their kind of people—farmers, country doctors, former chairs of obscure school boards, and the president of a police union local. There was barely a pin-striper to be seen, though Rae's cabinet arguably was more representative of every-day Ontarians than any before it.

Matters did not improve when CITY-TV's political reporter Colin Vaughan asked the new Ontario Treasurer, Floyd Laughren (better known as Pink Floyd), when his government had lost its grip on reality. The minister thought for a minute then replied, "It's hard to pin down precise dates on these things." And laughed.

A vintage story that went the rounds at the time involved three unhappy heavy hitters from Bay Street who couldn't figure out how to get next to the Rae government. When they met to plan a strategy, one of them tentatively suggested that he might be able to arrange just the right contact, since his wife had had her picture taken with a guy who knew a guy who worked at Queen's Park. His friend had a better idea: he had once gone to summer camp with somebody who cut Rae's hair. "Oh hell!" the third man exclaimed. "Let's use my cleaning lady. She's in his cabinet."

One of the stranger events on Bob Rae's watch as Ontario's NDP premier was when one of his cabinet ministers, Shelley Martel, became involved in a slagging match over Northern Ontario health-care costs with a municipal councilor from Thunder Bay. As her parting salvo, Martell revealed that her government was about to discipline a Sudbury doctor for excessive billing, claiming that she'd actually read the confidential government file on the doctor.

The councilor immediately took the story to the media, accusing Martel of slandering a medical professional and having illegal access to privileged information. In her own defence, Martel insisted that she had lied about the case against the doctor out of anger and had never seen any secret files.

Who to believe? Only one solution: Martel underwent a lie detector test. She passed, without cracking a smile. A 1992 commission of inquiry verified the second version of her story. Rae kept her in his cabinet. There is no record of him asking her, "What were you thinking?"

Rae never admitted making any mistakes while in power, except one: "I didn't listen well enough." Still, he managed to alienate leaders of Canada's business heartland—the inevitable consequence of inheriting an economic downturn worse than anything since the Depression—and the NDP base of organized labour, which balked at his "Rae Days," a pay cut to close a yawning budget deficit in the form of an enforced unpaid day off once a month for public servants. The premier imagined that Rae Days would go over better than layoffs. He was wrong.

Ontario survived the NDP interregnum, emerging with a crumpled credit rating, a King-Kong-size deficit and the halt of industrial expansion. After losing the 1995 election to Mike Harris, Rae quit the legislature and joined the Toronto Jewish establishment law firm of Goodmans; he was welcomed in circles of influence as a wit, an occasional barroom pianist and reformed sinner who was a great guy at a party. Indeed, Rae's post-premiership proved far more successful than his tenure at Queen's Park. He helped rescue the Toronto Symphony Orchestra, beloved of the city's Establishment, from near bankruptcy in 1999. He mediated in the Red Cross tainted-blood scandal, and his reputation as an honest broker had him refereeing constitutional talks between a warring

Sri Lanka government and Tamil Tigers dissidents. It was Rae who undertook, at the Martin government's request, a study on whether there should be a federal inquiry into the 1985 Air India tragedy. (He recommended that the feds should go ahead with the inquiry in November 2005; and Stephen Harper did call one the following March, after the Liberals were defeated.)

But though he did not renew his party membership in 1997, so he could take on some of these jobs, and broke with the NDP publicly in 2002—accusing it of a perceived bias against Israel, a refusal to embrace the consensualism of Tony Blair and Bill Clinton's "Third Way" style of politics, and naïveté in its futile railing against the inevitability of globalization—as he ran for the Liberals' highest office, he was having a hard time shaking his political past.

AND THEN THERE WAS HIS PAST with the front-runner in the race. The relationship between Rae and Ignatieff was a part of their inheritance. Michael's father, George, and Rae's father, Saul, were buddies—and rivals—in the External Affairs Department, in the postwar era, Ottawa's most prestigious posting. As quintessential diplomat-politicians they were always more concerned with the consequences of failure than the rewards of success; they were both dedicated to civilizing the international *status quo*. They both applied for Rhodes scholarships, but only Ignatieff won—a generation later Bob Rae would reverse the families' Rhodes fortunes. Afterwards, they moved up the ladder together into senior ambassadorial postings, but Ignatieff was always the aristocrat while Saul Rae had to scramble.

Saul's father had been a gambler and wastrel, while his mother, Nell, fed her three children by enlisting them in a successful vaudeville act called the Three Little Raes of Sunshine. The family denied its Jewish origins until the late 1960s. At the 1968 Liberal leadership convention, Pierre Trudeau introduced himself to Bob's sister, Jennifer, by whispering, "Will you go out with me?" She said yes, and became the radiant woman in his busy new life as the Sun King of Canada; there was serious talk of an imminent engagement. Fearing that they would be outed by a publicity blitz, Saul Rae called his family together to tell them that his name was really Cohen and that they were all Cohens, not Raes—they were Jewish, not Anglican, the religion in which the children had been raised. The revelation hit twenty-year-old Bob the hardest, in the sense that he treated the news not as change of religion but as a change of life. From then on, he made a point of eating at Jewish restaurants, went out with Jewish girls, and married one, the magnificent Arlene Perly, a journalist and prominent advocate for the arts, literacy and women's and children's welfare. She and Bob soon became a power couple; it was her husband, the precocious parliamentarian, who in 1980 introduced the Commons motion that brought down the short-lived government of Joe Clark.

Michael and Bob became friends at the University of Toronto, and spent a year as roommates in a flat above a shoe store near the campus. They both graduated in 1969, and both applied for the Rhodes scholarship like their fathers before them; this time, Rae received it and Ignatieff didn't. And thereby hangs a tale. The third mutual best friend of their college days was Jeff Rose (who later became president of the Canadian Union of Public Employees). He told me that so profound was the friendship between the two young men that Ignatieff stepped aside in favour of Rae. Since Rhodes scholarships are non-transferable, what must have happened was that either Ignatieff chose not to apply, improving Rae's shot at the few spots allotted to Canada per year, or that Ignatieff did apply but dropped out for the same reason. Ignatieff went to Harvard instead, which was not without cachet, but at the time the Rhodes was the top prize. When I asked Ignatieff about it, he confirmed his intent but wouldn't discuss the details.

During his time at Oxford in the early seventies, Rae fell into a deep depression. "Conversation was an effort," he confessed in his first book, *From Protest to Power*. "I couldn't read or write without feeling completely inadequate; my self-esteem was at zero." That bout of extreme anxiety lasted for eighteen months, six of which Rae spent hiding out in Ignatieff's Boston apartment, being consoled by his best friend.

That friendship is now a closed topic as far as Ignatieff is concerned, but Rae persists (for instance, in an e-mail to Jane Taber of the *Globe*) in professing that "life is too short to go through it with one fewer friend," that their friendship "is an enduring one," and that they speak every couple of weeks. I also know that at one point, Rae sent Ignatieff this message: "We've got to find a way through this so we don't blow ourselves up."

But during the 2006 leadership campaign that desire to make nice was missing on both sides. At the Toronto candidates' debate on October 15—the last public confrontation before the convention—Ignatieff attempted to hold Rae's toes to the fire over the Afghanistan mission by saying, "I actually don't know where you stand on this issue." Talk about being the straight man: Ignatieff didn't seem to realize that he'd just opened himself up for an easy shot, given that only days before he had caused controversy with his comment that the Israeli bombing of the Lebanese civilians of Qana during the recent confrontation was a "war crime." Rae looked at his friend with a gleam in his eyes. "You certainly do," he replied, followed by two beats of silence. "For a guy who changed his mind three times in a week with respect to the Middle East . . ."

Ignatieff was left rather woundedly insisting that he had been taken out of context in his earlier comment about not losing any sleep, and that based on forty years of friendship, Rae should know him better. But there could have been an easy comeback from Ignatieff in that Rae was even more of a neophyte in the Liberal party than he was. Back in 1968, Rae had been arguably as mesmerized by Trudeau as his sister, and had actively campaigned for him, but he didn't take out a Liberal membership card. For that he waited until April 5, 2006, just nineteen days before he declared his bid for the party leadership.

Since then, the two best friends had been on a collision course. "As the race shaped up, 80 percent of the attacks against Bob had come from Michael's team, and 80 percent of the attacks against the Ignatieff camp originated with Rae's commandos," Sachin Aggarwal told me. "So you had this situation where two old friends and two teams of people, who should have naturally had some synergy, had opposite objectives. Setting up any conversations between them was absolutely impossible, especially towards the end. There never was any agreement." The deputations exchanged mainly poison darts.

ASHLEY MACISAAC had withdrawn his satirical candidacy in June, though I was wishing he hadn't as I watched the legitimate candidates in their last debate at Roy Thomson Hall. It seemed to me that the contenders, and the party as a whole, were blind to the long-term consequences of choosing the wrong leader: I was certain a bad choice could bring about the destruction of Canada's once invincible Liberal party. Or more precisely, what was left of it.

As I sat listening to the procession of innocuous, drawn-out, self-congratulatory speeches, it occurred to me that this exercise was the political equivalent of tantric sex, a form of prolonged lovemaking that channels rather than dissipates orgasmic energies, transforming sexuality from the plane of *doing* to a place of *being*. It may be stretching the analogy, but there certainly was more *being* than *doing* going in this final debate of the campaign to choose a new Liberal leader. The candidates said nothing that made anyone quiver, as they pronounced what amounted to loyalty oaths in tones of skin-deep sincerity.

Bored with the words, I shifted my focus, instead, to comparing the culinary offerings the various camps were distributing to the swarm of Liberal delegates in attendance. Michael Ignatieff's hospitality shack featured duck crepes and sushi while Bob Rae was handing out tiny bundles of trail mix. Telling choices. The most sought-after prize that night was dinner with Belinda Stronach (who refused to enter the race after she discovered there was nowhere left for her to defect).

The contestants seemed as bored as the audience, and the evening wore on and on. I searched in vain for the first result of tantric sex. No such luck. There was no wakening here of the psychic energies through which adepts can enter into higher states of consciousness.

MOST POLITICAL CONVENTIONS resemble unclaimed baggage on airport carousels. The same issues keep coming around, again and again. The Liberals' talk-a-thon at Montreal's Palais des congrès in late November and the first three days of December in 2006 was no exception, involving 5,800 delegates and a press corps well north of cynical. The building exuded all the charm of an abandoned railway station, which turned out to be symbolic of what was about to happen. Given the chance to modernize and re-energize itself, Canada's Liberal party settled instead on Stéphane Dion to lead them into the new century. Their choice seemed bizarre—at the time and later. What were they thinking?

Perhaps they were adhering to the proud Grit tradition of standing up to Quebec nationalists—rather than playing footsie with them, as Mulroney and Harper had done—since Dion's main claim to fame was drafting the Clarity Act, designed to ensure that both the question that framed a independence referendum, and the results, were "clear" (with that clarity being defined by Ottawa). In Quebec, Dion was hated even by the supposed federalists. Choosing him as leader was no way to win back the disaffected Quebec vote, and was a win by any measure for the separatists.

Jean Chrétien viewed the act as his brightest legacy because for the first time, boundaries had been set to separatists' demands. As a result, Paul Martin had fired Dion from cabinet. Martin's people rightly saw Dion as a Chrétien favourite and mandated a whack against Dion purely as revenge. A chagrined Martin later realized Dion's great usefulness as a goad to the PQ, which never could marshal coherent responses to his federalist assertions, and brought Dion back into the fold. Dion was, and was perceived to be, the Grits' chief antagonist of Quebec nationalists, and as such commanded great respect in the party nationally.

He also was the party's sole credible voice on environmental progress, at a time when all things green had captured the public's imagination. The Grits under Chrétien and Martin had been correctly excoriated at home and abroad for not even bothering to pay lip service to the Kyoto Accord on global warming, which Canada had signed.

THE WINNERS at political conventions are usually picked out before the votes are counted by television camera operators. They pick the candidates most likely to triumph then bathe them in klieg lights until they give off their own, reflected voltage—which in turn, boosts their chances. In 1968, for example, eight camera crews and countless klieg lights were constantly trained on Pierre Trudeau, crowning him in brightness, marking him as a beacon of hope— the man to beat. Not this time. The TV directors hedged their bets and shared their camera crews equally among the top contenders.

Watching Dion perform at that convention, I noticed how his features materialized slowly like a developing Polaroid. A loner cursed by the forbidding manner of a political scientist with a Cartesian mindset, he projected no definable presence. It seemed weird: at press conferences, he was articulate (in at least one of Canada's official languages) even if his illusions of political adequacy knew no bounds. His platform manner suffered from the fact that his lips didn't move when he talked, rendering him expressionless. His body language, at best stiff, shut down when he spoke. Many Quebec delegates walked out when he started to speak.

(I only talked to Stéphane Dion once, half way into the 2008 election campaign. I joked that he could win handily if he'd only change his first name. That made him so nervous that his incoherence in English went into orbit. "What you mean? What you talk about?" he blurted. With an exaggerated smirk, so that he would realize I was trying to be funny, I said, "All you have to do is change your first name to *Celine!* You'll win by a landslide." He responded with a puzzled silence, then gingerly stepped around me to join a protest rally intending to dump

Alberta-based carbons into Boston Harbor, his sense of humour slumbering undisturbed.*)

The applause for Dion at the convention, according to Paul Wells of *Maclean's*, "might well have been designed to illustrate the term 'smattering.'" His campaign ran on a miniscule budget. His nearby hotel headquarters offered visitors a free drink provided they allowed their right hand to be swabbed by a red felt pen, so they couldn't claim a refill. His platform concentrated on "economic prosperity, social justice" and something called "a new third pillar of environmental sustainability." No one knew what that meant but his youth delegates interpreted it their way by freely handing out condoms labeled "For Your Third Pillar."

Dion delivered a motherhood statement on the environment that sounded as stilted as if he was lip-synching the operating instructions for some complicated Japanese toy. Then, instead of speeding up as he approached his rhetorical climax, he slowed down. His words seem to hang in the air like skywriting. He began waving at his wife, Janine Krieber, a political science professor at the St. Jean-sur-Richelieu Military College, like the guy with the paddles at the airport who guides in the 747s—maybe encouraging her to land near him and soothe his nerves. He patted his Prince Hal haircut and pushed up his glasses. Finally she waved

---

* He wasn't entirely without lightness. He once blamed his conversion from being a youthful separatist to mature federalist on an incident when he was going from door to door on behalf of the Parti Québécois: "I was invited in by a federalist whose wife kept bringing us rum-and-Cokes. I came at five and left at ten, completely drunk, and said to him, 'Maybe you're right.' I don't know how I found my way home but I went to sleep right away. Since then I've never been active for the separatist cause—and I've never drank rum-and-Coke again. It was a double healing."

back and gave what looked to be a Trudeau shrug. He smiled then, and carried on.

But it turned out that Glen Pearson, Dion's introducer, had appropriated so much of the time that Dion couldn't complete his rehearsed address. When his mike was cut off, he kept going, in pantomime—delivering the balance of his message, even if nobody could hear it.

NEXT UP was Gerard Kennedy who billed himself as the farthest-out party outrider, although he had been a Liberal since he was seven, when he carried the local candidate's briefcase during an election campaign in The Pas, Manitoba, where he was born. A former Ontario Minister of Education, Kennedy gave a masterful speech, sensible and free of cant, peppered with a clever collage of relevant images. His was an exemplary presentation but there was little echo of the firebrand who had so frightened the delegates at the 1996 Ontario Liberal leadership convention that they chose the more conventional Dalton McGuinty over Kennedy.

Scott Brison, a former Progressive Conservative leadership candidate, was persuasive, his address heartfelt. He is a man of restless grace, his speech marked by the friendly slurring of vowels that marks so many Haligonians. His time will come.

As Joe Volpe—the token Italian candidate—began to speak, I watched the delegates' mouths tighten and eyebrows rise in puzzlement and then growing disdain. He sounded too hungry, too intense to be believable. He wanted to lead the party with every nerve-end in his body, and clearly thought it was only his due, but he sounded too desperate, and talked too fast.

Ken Dryden was the hockey star expected to score with his speech. And he did. He took the chance of foregoing the usual political verities and instead threw out mesmerizing images—giving the convention a tone poem glorifying Canada, which was, after all, the loving object of all this fuss and bother. It was the convention's best speech but his delegate count didn't even break five percent. If he didn't exactly score, well, that's not what great goalies are supposed to do. He sauntered back to his seat, sat down and seemed to go to sleep with his eyes wide open.

MICHAEL IGNATIEFF was piped into the Liberal leadership convention by Bedouin Soundclash, an alternative pop band from Kingston, Ontario, and he delivered a speech that dealt with awakening dreams of Canada's unlimited future. It was not a "this will be my shining hour" presentation, but the speech did articulate his plans for a creative nation destined to rise above the jarring echoes of political bickering.

If I'd had to mark his performance, I would have given him a B-minus. It didn't fit the occasion. The delegates weren't in the mood for a lecture. This was the moment for a whoop-up—for the audience to go wacky, to wave their arms and pound their feet in an offbeat tattoo. Instead they were asked to hum along to elevator music. The Grit burghers who had flown many weary miles to get there stood around, looking at each other, applauding occasionally with the listlessness that greets runners-up at British dart tournaments. I saw not a single high-five exchanged. Though, at the end of his presentation, his troops erupted in noisy approval, the followers of all the other camps resolutely sat on their hands.

Rae went for a presentation as far as he could get from Ignatieff's style, orating to the crowd as he strolled the stage: I thought that if he couldn't make a go of politics, he had a good shot at becoming an afternoon TV game show host. The truth was that none of the candidates were able to deliver one of those crowd-igniting game-changers; the night stumbled along its erratic course, proving only that the Liberals were no longer capable of truly exciting themselves.

EVEN AS HE HAD BEGUN to speak, Ignatieff knew that while he would lead on the first ballot, he didn't have the reserves to take him over the top. Unless Bob Rae could be persuaded to climb aboard, Ignatieff would be the convention's runner up. He longed to ignite an economic and social renaissance but his pre-convention fugitive thoughts had betrayed him once too often — prompting those overnight changes of views to become his brand. He had ignored his own axiom: that the central theme of history is not what's taking place, but how people perceive and feel about what's happening. His only chance was to win more than 30 percent of the crucial first ballot, which was supposed to trigger Scott Brison's support, which in turn might have panicked prospective cabinet ministers into Ignatieff's fold. (The theory being "I better go with this guy so I can be on the gravy train if he gets elected.")

Ignatieff had come temptingly close to upsetting the party's crusty old boys' network. The actual agents of change were the impressive members of his Children's Crusade—the youthful newcomers on his staff, bound together by their loyalty to Michael and their determination to shake the party's smug foundations. They had spent seven months with him on the road, exhausted their psyches somewhere between Trois Rivières and Moncton, and now were facing the frosty realization that there would be no triumphs for them here. The issue was cruelly simple: victory would be claimed by the candidate who lost more slowly than the others, and the required growth in ballot strength for Ignatieff on successive votes simply wasn't there.

At the time, to most Canadians—and a little over half of Liberal delegates, who ended up voting for Dion—Ignatieff was just another import. To those of Russian descent, he was Michael Georgevitch—his father George's eldest son, whose antecedents stretched back to the dazzling imperial court of Tsar Alexander III. His folk memory extended back to his ancestors watching the Bolsheviks ravaging their family home in St. Petersburg, stealing the 100-room mansion, uprooting their majestic gardens, and transforming the Ignatieff dynasty into a congregation of ghosts. That's a tough legacy to live down, as you're hustling for votes in a small-town Canada that worshipped Rita MacNeil and Stompin' Tom Conners.

ON THE FIRST BALLOT, 82 percent of the delegates had voted for candidates other than Dion. Yet within hours, Dion would be declared the winner, even though he had given the worst of the candidates' speeches, made no startling pronouncements, and except for dressing up his core delegates in green scarves took no discernable action. What happened was that the other candidates and their delegates concentrated on eliminating one another instead of trying to stop Dion. His victory wasn't entirely won by inadvertence, but nearly.

On the first ballot, as expected, Ignatieff received 29.3 percent of the votes (not enough to trigger the deal with Brison); Rae, 20.3 percent; Kennedy 17.7 percent; and Dion 17.8 percent—ahead of Kennedy by two votes. In the second ballot, the gap widened between Dion and Kennedy, 974 to 884, which was enough to kick in the pre-arranged agreement between Dion and Kennedy that on the next ballot, whichever candidate received the lower number would throw his support to the winner. Kennedy was able to bring along 91 percent of his followers to Dion, giving the Stéphane camp its momentum. (That was highly honourable, but it deprived the Liberals of a highly capable leader in Kennedy.)

On the third ballot, Dion leaped ahead to first place with

37 percent, though Ignatieff and Rae together retained 63 percent of the votes and could easily have won together. Had the former Ontario premier gone over to Ignatieff's camp after he dropped out, enough of his delegates would have followed him to change the outcome and give Ignatieff the prize. At the time, Denis Coderre, Ignatieff's national campaign co-chair, advanced this suggestion to the former Ontario premier, who declined even to discuss the possibility. Several other emissaries also attempted to negotiate an agreement. Rae had to decide: would he saunter over to Michael's enclosure and shake his friend's hand—signalling that his troops should follow. Or would he walk away, releasing his delegates, jettisoning his friendship, and sending out the message: "If I can't win, neither will Michael." He released his delegates.

But intriguingly Ignatieff got to the point where he was considering taking his support to Rae. "Michael asked if there was even a remote chance that we could win at that point. He suggested that it might be better for the party and for the country if we dropped out before the ballot results were known [which would force Rae off the next ballot] to support Rae and forestall a Dion victory," recalled one of the participants in that huddle. "We began contemplating what it might look like and whether we could take enough people over to Bob to make it happen but we ran out of time." Along with Ignatieff and Zsuzsanna, the participants in the huddle were Davey, Aggarwal, Jill Fairbrother, Mark Sakamoto, Senator David Smith, Elvio DelZotto, Doug Richardson (the other co-chair of the Ignatieff campaign) and Abe Schwartz, one of Ignatieff's original backers. Had Rae made himself accessible to this group, the convention might have ended quite differently.

When Rae released his delegates, 424 more did go to Ignatieff on the fourth and final ballot but it was too late. Dion picked up 750, and so he was the new king.

"Let's show these people what unity means!" Ignatieff shouted at the winner, then walked over to him and raised his hand. The crowd roared. In the end, Dion won the race by remaining aloof from yet another polarizing Liberal feud.

After he was knocked out of the race, Rae told reporters, "I've had a lot of fun, but this is not life—this is politics."

Ignatieff's attitude was precisely the reverse. For him, this wasn't "fun," it was the redemption for a career spent as an observer when he longed to be in the centre of the action. Now he was, and it was hell. "I'm here to be serious," he maintained. "This is the only place I can be a participant, not a spectator. Now I'm in the boat, fishing." But his net was empty.

DION, the former University of Montreal political science professor, would lead the party for the next two years—mostly into the ground. His was a tarnished crown from the start. His win was as much a protest against the professor from Harvard as a vote for the professor from Montreal. Dion triumphed primarily because he wasn't Ignatieff, who had triggered a wave of hostility that felt almost palpable in the unused train station where the convention gathered. The resentment was not based on any ideological differences, nor was it connected to Ignatieff managing to skip roughly three decades of Canadian winters, nor any of the other weighty issues that surrounded his candidacy. It was the old-fashioned sin of queue jumping that brought him down. He hadn't earned his turn.*

"Who does he think he is?" was a common complaint. "I've been in the trenches for thirty years, working on elections,

---

* The same charge could have been made against Bob Rae.

building this goddamn party from scratch. What right has this intruder from Harvard got to take it over?"

Apart from not being Ignatieff, the other reason Dion unexpectedly triumphed was that, like Joe Clark, who had walked away with the Tory leadership in 1976, he counted the smallest number of enemies in the hall. Many delegates parked their votes in his camp, never imagining they might be electing Dion as their leader. Just like "Joe Who?," "Stéphane Who?" brought little glamour to the job. He was a compromise pick, the least disliked of the choices available. The Clark comparison was apt: both men shared serious intentions and commendable courage under fire but they possessed only a tiny dollop of *mojo*.

After it was all over, few Liberals could figure out how they would deal with such an oddball for a leader. Here was the fate of a newly fragile political movement thrust into the hands of an almost comically awkward Quebecker whose wife summed him up as a klutz. "Stéphane can't be trusted to change a light bulb — particularly if it's a halogen," she observed.*

The fundamental flaw of the convention — apart from picking the wrong candidate — was that there was no mention, let alone discussion, of how terminally exhausted the Canadian brand of liberalism had become — or how it might be fixed. The convention deteriorated into directionless pandemonium that felt like nothing so much as an approaching avalanche.

At the Ignatieff campaign HQ at the Delta Hotel, Stefan Hoffman, a McGill University law student who had spent months as a volunteer on the campaign trail, was so upset that when Ignatieff came in to thank the troops, Hoffman burst into tears. "I didn't want

---

* *A bit of a tradition among Canadian leaders. Sheila Martin once mused that her husband's culinary skills were limited to making toast.*

him to see me crying," he said. "I particularly recalled one evening in Sherbrooke when he was answering somebody's question, and the audience interrupted by starting to clap. He shushed them because he wanted to hear exactly what the questioner wanted to ask. I thought that was a rare quality among politicians. "

Back on the convention floor, Monsieur Dion put on a green scarf, gave an awkward Victory sign with the wrong fingers, slipped on his backpack, and left the building.

AFTER ASSIMILATING HIS LOSS, the pursuit of the party leadership grew into a compulsion for Ignatieff. Although he was still a newcomer to stump politics and a newly reborn native son, in the aftermath of his failed attempt to become leader, he was a man who was slowly perceiving his mission. Under the iron fist of Stephen Harper, the transactions of state were becoming hidden behind so many layers of partisan armour that no simple truth was ever offered or available to the public or to Parliament. It was that reality that Ignatieff became determined to change, and in order to do it, he needed to return the Liberal party to its rightful place.

10. Canonizing Trudeau

Trudeau appealed to the one sentiment that united
Canadian voters: the need not so much for a new leader
as for a new kind of politics that would fulfill their longing
for a role model and create a faith worth following.

THE DAY BEFORE THE LIBERALS' 1968 leadership convention, I found myself at Ottawa's Chateau Laurier hotel, standing
beside a middle-aged farm couple from deep in the heart of
Manitoba. As Pierre Trudeau, the candidate to beat, made his way
towards them, the wife visibly panicked. Flushed with excitement,
she clutched her huge block of a side-burned husband, and asked,
"What if I faint when I see him—what should I do?" He cut a look
of dismissive disgust her way, and said, "Ah, don't be silly, he's just
another goddamn politician."

Then, suddenly, Trudeau stood there facing the couple. He gave
the farmer a look half way between meaningful and cursory,
shrugged when there was no response and moved on. The farmer
had not been able to say a word. Just stood there, transfixed. Then he
quietly began to cry, hugged his wife and they moved away together,
arm in arm. Watching that silent exchange, I knew the race was
over. We had ourselves a new prime minister and a new politics.

THE LEADERSHIP CONVENTION that followed in Ottawa's new Civic Centre was the most exhilarating political event I have witnessed. It is relevant to reconstitute it now, because this style of event was exactly what Ignatieff ought to have staged for his own inaugural convention. The 1968 convention signalled the death of one kind of politics and the birth of another, the shift from Old Canada to the New. Exactly what Ignatieff needed to signal and wasn't able to.

This was Canada's Liberal party at its apogee. Trudeau had faced down the professional machinations of his opponents in one of those rare contests when a movement that seemed airy and idealistic assumed political substance and defeated the respectable but pedestrian contenders. Trudeau appealed to the one sentiment that united Canadian voters: the need not so much for a new leader as for a new kind of politics that would fulfill their longing for a role model and create a faith worth following.

WHEN TRUDEAU FIRST appeared in Ottawa after the 1965 election as a Montreal MP, he was already an imposing presence, having been awarded degrees in law, economics and political science from universities in Montreal, London, Paris and Harvard—a record not dissimilar to Ignatieff's. He had written half as many books as Ignatieff but he had solid academic credentials. His ideas weren't revolutionary, but his style was fresh and intriguing: the turtleneck sweaters, the eloquent shrugs, his two Mercedes convertibles, the stunning girlfriends, and the lingo he used, which was impressive in all three official languages—Parisian French, Boston drawl and Westmount *anglais*. He had a Jesuit-trained discipline allied with a highly evocative, original mind—a potent combination.

I was one of the few English-speaking journalists he knew in the capital city before he arrived. We met for monthly lunches: he, to probe me about the national press corps, who not to trust and who not to trust absolutely; me, to do my job, which was to search for the most fascinating people and news in Ottawa. After he was named justice minister, I published leaks about his legislative plans that he floated to me so he could test public opinion by the degrees of outrage prompted by my stories. This was his "the state-has-no-place-in-the-nation's-bedrooms" period, so there was much to write about.

My wife, Christina McCall, and I had Trudeau to our house several times with Madeleine Gobeil, a stunning Carleton professor who Christina later described as "the most enduring romantic relationship of Trudeau's life." They were a fun couple, hugging on our sofa, enjoying one another's closeness. (I later published a political memoir that contained several documents judged to have broken the Official Secrets Act. When the issue came up in cabinet, Trudeau who was by then prime minister, ruled that it was not me but the public servant who gave me the documents who ought to be charged; I, of course, did not divulge his name. Still, I often wondered whether Trudeau's impulse to deflect the heat from me was driven by his belief in the freedom of the press or by remembering those loving moments in our living room).

Most memorably, in the late sixties we once entertained Beland Honderich, then the publisher of the *Toronto Star*, who had asked us to invite the Liberal leadership candidates so he could look them over. They all did their *Star* turn, preening for him and promising that if elected they would follow the paper's editorial commandments. Christina later recalled watching Trudeau, standing alone in the hall, observing his rivals sucking the editorial teat, carefully sipping his sherry. At last he remarked to her that the guest of honour seemed to be fully occupied and slipped away into the night. "I was left trying to decipher the emotion reflected in his glittering blue eyes when he took in the antics of the office seekers," she wrote in *Saturday Night*. "Probably he was being coldly intelligent. Reason would tell him there was nothing to be gained at our party, and reason would be correct. Trudeau's predilection for denying feelings in favour of the rational over emotional was his one constant."

I had been the first Ottawa columnist to place Trudeau's name publicly into leadership contention, recognizing in him a necessary antidote to the Diefenbaker-Pearson feud that had polluted our politics for most of a decade. The idea was widely dismissed as a bad joke. The denizens of Ottawa's Rideau Club, which was where the powerful met for lunch, told and retold the story about how Trudeau had turned up on a Saturday morning at the Privy Council Office dressed in desert boots and a boiler suit. He was minister of justice by then but the commissionaire on duty, convinced he was a plumber with a botched work sheet, had turned him away.

Whenever his name was casually mentioned in the early speculation about candidates, the talk inevitably came around to the way he wore his hair. ("How could anybody who combed his hair forward and wore bangs like Julius Caesar become a *Canadian* prime minister?") Ottawa was still a nineteenth-century burg with Sunday school values and politicians who thought it was daring to ski on Sundays. Few of the establishment players could be bothered to parse Trudeau's thoughts or realize that his was the voice of the future, despite Prime Minister Pearson's clear regard for him. In the bleak chill of December 1967, just after Pearson resigned, the thought of Trudeau taking over for him seemed far from inevitable; in fact, it was scarcely credible. To most Liberals, his hippy manners, that Roman haircut, the fact he was an untested outsider made him a heretical presence foreign to the collective Liberal party mentality.

IN RETROSPECT, Trudeau's conquest of the Liberal party appears predestined, with the other leadership contenders serving as mere spear carriers in the dramatic elevation of a once and future king. But that was not how it was. Not at all. It was television that made the difference. From the moment he entered the race, everywhere Trudeau went he was followed by TV crews, recording his shrugs, wisecracks, dance steps and swan dives into hotel pools. Throughout the convention, eight camera crews clustered around the justice minister, bathing him in the beams of hand-held klieg lights, endowing his presence with an incandescent glow that transformed him into a star.

Trudeau in turn provided the cameras with some dramatic scenes. When he arrived for the convention in Ottawa by train girls threw wedding rice at him, squealing in delight as he approached. The whole crowd surged toward him like an ocean wave, gathering as it rolled in his direction, finally bursting police barriers. Later in the evening, at the Chaudière Golf and Country Club, Newfoundland Premier Joey Smallwood, an early and loud supporter, elbowed his way to the bandstand and in his customary understated way declared: "Pierre is better than Medicare—the lame have only to touch his garments to walk again."

There was about him an indefinable intensity, a suggestion of pent-up power and hidden dimensions that fascinated the nation's television viewers, impressed the delegates and frightened his opponents. Barry Callaghan, literary editor of the Toronto *Telegram*, best caught the intruder's essence. "In his own way, he is a true believer in his intellect. This transformed Trudeau into a potentially great man. It also turned him into a potentially dangerous presence; for in his refusal to recognize emotional responses, in the belief that one was always bound to be acting rationally, he played with the danger of self-deception."

Riding a chartered jet and wearing his signature leather coat, Trudeau went campaigning for the leadership crown. His every appearance brought standing ovations. In Victoria, where the monarchy was still an important issue, local Liberals questioned Trudeau on the topic. He won the crowd over with the comment: "I was in Saskatoon last night and crowned a very lovely queen, so I feel very warm toward the monarchy."

At his sessions with delegates, I could sense the moment they switched from being merely titillated by his presence to joining his cause. They came prepared to be scandalized by a wild man in sandals spouting socialist slogans. Instead, they found an immaculately turned out professor delivering proposals that *sounded* exciting but would not have been out of place in any undergraduate classroom. "The truth," my mentor Paul Fox, the University of Toronto political scientist, told me, "is that beneath his dashing image Pierre Trudeau is conservative. His attitude on many matters is cautious and conventional. That is the source of his appeal to many English Canadians. They especially like his conservative, hard line on Quebec."

Unable to classify him as a man of either the political right or the political left, most of Trudeau's audiences simply regarded him as a man of the future, which was exactly how he wanted it to be. "Trudeau won because, if Expo 67 [held the previous summer] had been a person, that person would have been Trudeau," wisely observed Richard Gwyn in the *Toronto Star*.

All the carefully planned demonstrations by fellow candidates were suddenly made to look old-fashioned and contrived when Trudeau "crept into the arena like Jesus Christ," as Frank Walker, editor of the *Montreal Star*, put it, slipping unheralded into his seat followed by his moon maidens holding home-made banners aloft. Trudeau's cadre of young women had other inadvertent ways to captivate the male journalists covering the convention, along with the delegates: the "walkie-talkies" of the time were bulky and awkward to carry. Instead of being connected by way of demure, tiny ear plugs, as they would be now, the Trudeau women had to stuff their walkie-talkies into their blouses somehow, and wandered the floor apparently talking into their brassieres.

The crowd in the convention centre roared when they caught sight of him. His opponents, clustered with their advisers, tried to divine the source of Trudeau's sorcery, suspicious that he had some special trick they just might be able to master. They sent emissaries to observe him, talk to him, perhaps to touch his hem. But the courtiers come back as puzzled as before. Trudeau maintained his inner repose, refusing to lend himself to the gravitational pull of the convention. And the more he held back, the more the crowd wanted a piece of him.

SUDDENLY, THE SIEGE OF PHOTOGRAPHERS, reporters and TV cameramen around his box parted to allow Pierre to saunter to centre stage. As if pulled by a single string, Trudeau signs were silently lifted in every part of the crowded arena. Instead of applauding, the delegates let out a collective "AAAHH," as if he was a daring high-wire trapeze artist doing his star turn. His demonstration had been meticulously planned but *looked* spontaneous, as though the Liberal party had reached a sudden consensus. Trudeau waited in the stands for precisely five minutes as the demonstration unfolded, then slouched as to Bethlehem, slow-walking toward the platform. He did not give a great speech, but the delegates listen in awed silence. "As Liberals," he said, "we rely on that most unlikely bulwark again chaos—you and me, the individual citizen, the young and the old, the famous and the unknown, the Arctic nomad and the suburbanite." This was the sober not the witty Pierre, softly blowing his horn. At the end of his sermon he stood there, smiling, a daffodil in his buttonhole, presuming worship.

Trudeau's victory appeared to be as spontaneous as a 1960s love-in. It was anything but. Two hundred Trudeau workers were constantly patrolling the Civic Centre, carrying lists of delegates and votes by individual voting machines, jabbering into those clumsily concealed walkie-talkies. Every move of every delegate was monitored as these lady persuaders were assigned to bring doubters into line. Watching the balloting, apparently without a care in the world, Trudeau reached over, grabbed a grape from Jean Marchand, threw it in the air and caught it in his mouth. A nearby TV producer who missed the performance demanded a repeat, stuck a microphone into Trudeau's face, and barked, "Let's hear that crunch again, okay?"

As voting on the third ballot began, Trudeau was reading notes. "Is that your acceptance speech?" asked an excited reporter.

"No. It's a love letter."

As the next ballot was announced, nervous Trudeau workers swarmed to round up delegates. The arena erupted into a frenzy of excitement. Mike McCabe, the finance minister's executive assistant, sidled over to tell me, "If Trudeau doesn't win, the entrails of the Liberal party will be left all over this hall."

As the final results were being read the wild chant, "TRU-DEAU, CAN-A-DA!" obliterated thought. Trudeau had 1,203 ballots; Bob Winters, 954; John Turner, 195. It was over. But few remembered that the emotional tide that carried this singular man of reason to victory was no coronation. His margin was 51.1 percent, on the fourth ballot. It was that close.

I emerged from that steaming convention hall into the April night, feeling that I was walking into a new Canada.*

DISSOLUTION OF THE COMMONS triggered the 1968 election that was Trudeau's most spectacular performance. It was a campaign that left those of us in the media shaking our heads in wonderment. This was not the Canada we knew, nor a political event we had ever experienced or would ever witness again. Girls, their long manes of hair streaming like banners in the wind, clutching their machine-autographed pictures, followed Trudeau everywhere, swarming whenever he deigned to kiss one of them. Bemused toddlers were held up on the shoulders of their parents and admonished to "Remember him," as the excitement surged across the country. The press cameras clicked like insects whenever Trudeau alighted from his jet, and as he made his triumphant way from one mobbed shopping plaza to the next.

---

* *From the convention hall, I went to the Civic Hospital where one of my favourite Ottawa characters, Bryce Mackasey, had been hospitalized after suffering a suspected heart attack on the convention floor. A unique apparition among the dauphins and deacons of the Trudeau entourage, Mackasey was a former boxing champion with calloused hands but un-calloused instincts, who was feeling anxious about obtaining a spot in the new regime. When I entered his hushed hospital room he was encased in an oxygen tent, seemingly gasping for his last breath. As soon as he saw me, he threw back the plastic sheet, and urgently whispered: "Tell Trudeau I want Labour!"*

I figured that if there was ever a sacred trust, this was it. Surely I was honour-bound to relay this dying wish from one of the new leader's most pumped-up supporters. When I went back into the corridor, I told the nurse on duty how brave her patient had been to temporarily abandon his oxygen. "Oh, that Mr. Mackasey," she replied, exasperated. "Every time someone comes to visit, he puts on that damn oxygen tent!" I did not relay Bryce's message but somebody did because he spent most of the Trudeau years shaking things up in the Department of Labour.

I recall in particular flying into Halifax. The leader of the federal Progressive Conservatives was Robert Stanfield, a former Nova Scotia premier, and this was wall-to-wall Tory country. But along the route from the airport in Dartmouth into the city, as if on a prearranged signal, people had backed their cars into driveways so that they could flash their headlights in silent tribute to the invisible man in the leather coat, slouched in the passing, darkened limousine.

In Victoria, we couldn't get near Trudeau; he stood on a small hill, alone, prophet-like, overlooking a large park that had turned into a sea of mesmerized faces. This was where he was asked how he felt about the monarchy, and quipped that he felt warmly because he'd crowned a beauty queen the night before in Saskatchewan. Asked by the same frustrated questioner about the future of the Liberals, he replied: "An exciting political party should have both blondes and brunettes." Political leaders weren't supposed to talk like that.

In Winnipeg, to yet another screeching herd of supporters, Trudeau carefully explained that he more or less stood for nothing: "I do not feel myself bound by any doctrine or rigid approaches. I am a pragmatist." The response to this was summed up in the yell of a fellow philosopher-king, who had quaffed too many Molsons: "Yeah, you tell 'em, Pierre-baby!"

THAT WAS JUST OVER 40 years ago. It's hard to imagine any person running for office in this day and age, let alone a Liberal contender for prime minister, being greeting with such a combination of fascination and generosity of spirit. But it's also surprising that the lessons to be learned from Trudeau's canny and charismatic run for the leadership, and the way he organized the subsequent election campaign to intrigue and inspire voters, didn't sink into young Michael Ignatieff's very marrow. He was there, after all, and it was his only previous experience of politics from the inside. But clearly not much of Trudeau's example stuck, except maybe the arrogant assumption that he was the right man for the job. Ignatieff's second leadership vote was not a national firestorm of enthusiasm, but a survival ploy conducted by an enclave of insiders who produced the desired result without a whiff of spontaneity. The covert operation to install Ignatieff as leader was the beginning of the end of the Grits as a political force, and deservedly so.

11. Coalition of the Reluctant

"Ignatieff didn't get to experience the hurly-burly of
a leadership convention that actually would have been helpful
in terms of conditioning and preparing a new leader—it would
have been a rehearsal for the big show, the election to come."

— PETER DONOLO

TO STEP BACK JUST A LITTLE to set the scene, Stephen Harper wasn't going to wait around for a non-confidence vote to bring down his minority government—despite his apparent commitment to fixed election dates. He didn't respect Dion as a leader, and clearly thought he might have a shot at vanquishing the Liberals completely and gaining a majority. Using the excuse that Dion was the person making Parliament unworkable, Harper called an election for October 14, 2008, timing that put the campaign right in the heart of the world economic meltdown. Though the Harper campaign was the farthest thing from brilliant, Dion couldn't recognize how to capitalize on Harper's gaffes in Quebec—or how to emphasize his own party's record at vanquishing a massive deficit during an earlier fiscal downturn—and campaigned incoherently on his ideals. Two days after his defeat— the Liberals reduced to a paltry 77 seats—Dion resigned, but insisted he would leave only after his successor had been chosen at the party's scheduled convention the following May.

Tentative talks about forming an anti-Harper coalition bubbled up as soon as the votes were counted, sparked by the NDP. Senator David Smith became the Liberal go-between, with Brian Topp, a highly literate and acutely sardonic former national campaign chairman acting for the New Democrats. They first met at Toronto's Albany Club on October 21, 2008, but made little progress. Harper then came to their rescue by announcing that he intended to eliminate federal subsidies to political parties in the next budget, which would have left all of the putative coalition partners in dire financial straits. It was that initiative by a Conservative prime minister obsessed with wiping out the Liberal party that breach-birthed the coalition. The political fires were further stoked by Harper in the same November 27 economic statement that threatened his opponents with extinction. He and his finance minister seemed remarkably oblivious to the fact that the Canadian economy needed a little help from its government to weather the economic storm.

Two more mutually respectful and credible coalition negotiators came out of the woodwork: former NDP leader Ed Broadbent and the redoubtable Jean Chrétien. The rumour soon was circulating that Dion would emerge as head of the coalition government by promising to leave in early January, rather than May—thus greeting Santa Claus at Sussex Drive. (His outspoken wife's retort to this bit of absurdity went unrecorded.) The rapid accord, reached with Broadbent's and Chrétien's blessings, and signed by Dion, Jack Layton and the Bloc leader Giles Duceppe, prompted Brian Topp to observe: "The incubus in the Liberal Party was also immediately visible — Michael Ignatieff's revolt against his leader."

Ignatieff thought any coalition was a bad idea, and he wasn't shy about letting Dion know his views. He also had some clout: although he was only the party's deputy leader, he had been performing very well as a fundraiser, always a good sign of political influence. On March 31, 2008, the Toronto dinner for Ignatieff netted an amazing $500,000; and Sachin Aggarwal's efforts had retired Ignatieff's leadership campaign debt.

The backstage machinations grew byzantine. A day after Ignatieff made his opposition to the coalition known, it looked like the Liberals had changed their mind, not saying they wouldn't be part of any coalition, but not saying they would, either. Dion was still negotiating with Layton, who had asked for one-third of the cabinet seats in any new coalition government, including the deputy prime ministership—which given his position inside the official opposition should have gone to Ignatieff. That set off alarm bells in Liberal circles, because in the off chance of something happened to the Liberal leader the acting prime minister of Canada would be Jack Layton. By November 29, the deal had shifted slightly to guaranteeing the NDP only a quarter of Cabinet positions, and Dion was ready to sign and carry forward the agreement and the offer to form a government to the Governor General. All was not happy inside the Liberal camp. The anti-Dion attitude was summed up by one leading Grit, who said: "There is no fucking way that asshole who ruined our party will get any benefit from this."

What was also accelerating Dion's exodus was the activation of the Liberal leadership contest—Dominic LeBlanc, Bob Rae and Michael Ignatieff all had publicly declared their intentions during November—which had thus far been an ever-present but relatively tame undertow. Now Ignatieff began to pick up momentum because he was the only one of them on record as being against the idea of a coalition. Then came the complete public relations disaster of December 3. The PMO announced that Harper would speak to the nation at seven p.m., to be followed by Dion speaking for the coalition. Dion's broadcast was a fiasco in terms of content and presentation: his video looked like it had been put together by a shaky-handed twelve-year-old. In effect, Dion blew his brains out on TV in front of the whole country.

Harper was rallying public support by claiming that the coalition would be the end of Canadian democracy. The official photograph of the Dion, Layton and Duceppe signing their Declaration of Independence, all looking like Cheshire cats who ate the canaries, played right into Harper's hands. That photo made it appear as if the Bloc, which made no secret of its intention to destroy Confederation, would be an equal coalition partner. That was never the case. Gilles Duceppe was a hard-core separatist but he had signed a non-compete clause, excluding him from participating in any coalition decisions for two years. Any sensible public relations person would have excluded him from the photo-op, but there he was in living colour. That picture sealed the coalition's fate, because it seemed to validate Conservative accusations that the nation's business would now be in the hands of people who were pledged to destroy Canada. As one Tory put it, "That photograph saved Stephen's hide."

Dion resigned for real (which meant that he picked up his knapsack and walked out the door, humming *"Il a perdu son epaulettes"*) on December 6, after Senator David Smith read him *le riot act*: polling was showing them that voters would have no confidence in a coalition if it included the Bloc in any way and was led by the man they had voted against in the last election. As the national mood turned against even the idea of a coalition, the only Liberal who looked fit to take over as leader in Dion's wake was the one man who firmly opposed playing the coalition card. The concurrent machinations of the Liberal Leadership contest caused rivers of bad blood to flow between the party's warring factions, turning off its grassroots.

But there were three happy guys at the Toronto island airport on December 9, 2008, nervously fingering their BlackBerries: Sachin Aggarwal, Ignatieff's deputy chief of staff; Mark Sakamoto, the chief political adviser; and Alexis Levine, political director for Ontario, waiting to board the Ottawa flight. They froze as the CTV News anchor read a new flash: "Bob Rae is about to hold a press conference. Stand by." They hugged one another, realizing that this meant the Rae leadership drive was *kaput*. Since the third leadership candidate, New Brunswick's LeBlanc, had folded his tent the previous day, this meant unconditional victory for their guy.

Of the trio of Liberal strategists only Sakamoto was out of his twenties — at thirty, he was the old man on the front line of Ignatieff's electoral hit squad; hailing from Medicine Hat, Alberta, he was one of only two non-Torontonians on staff. (The other was Leslie Church, a Calgarian who was a graduate of the London School of Economics.) They were on their way to the capital to set up their new war room. Before leaving their Toronto headquarters, they had sent two vans brim full of computers, printers and other assorted gear, along with a cadre of supporters aimed firmly at installing their boss, Michael Ignatieff, as leader. Their destination was a dump masquerading as an Ottawa hotel called the Capital Suites, which had been Dion's campaign headquarters.

While one team of Ignatieff negotiators were dealing with the coalition, the pick of Ignatieff's disciples were harvesting votes. At the end of that exercise in enforced volunteerism, they controlled the ballots of 54 of the 77 caucus members (including the vote of Gerard Kennedy, whose original previous support had pushed Dion into the leadership); a slight majority of the national executive; half the Senate votes; and 130 heads of ridings; and Zsuzsanna's ballot—well over the margins required to endorse the Ignatieff leadership.

A CAUCUS VOTE elevated Ignatieff to the Liberal party's interim leadership on December 10. He pledged to stand for confirmation of his position at the party's annual May meeting in Vancouver. Since he was the only candidate—and had not yet reached that level of exasperation with politics in which he might be tempted to vote against himself—his triumph seemed assured.

At the three-day convention, April 30 to May 2, 2009, in a majestic new convention centre on the western shore of Burrard Inlet in downtown Vancouver, Ignatieff ostensibly brought peace to the internal blood feuds that had torn the party apart under the preceding stewardships of John Turner, Jean Chrétien, Paul Martin and Stéphane Dion. But his acceptance speech had little impact for the very good reason that he was the only candidate on the ballot.* It was a coronation, but Ignatieff still used the occasion to accuse Stephen Harper of every possible malfeasance except spreading a leprosy pandemic.

"For three years you have played province against province, group against group, region against region, individual against individual," Ignatieff charged. "When your power was threatened last

---

* Only 97 percent of the registered delegates voted for Ignatieff. That left a puzzling three percent unaccounted for. It was my guess that Laureen Harper's cats were probably the dissenting culprits.

November you unleashed a national unity crisis and saved your-self only by sending Parliament home. Mr. Harper, you have failed us. If you can't unite Canadians, if you can't appeal to the best in us — WE CAN. We Liberals can build a federalism based on co-operation, not on confrontation."

His assignment was clear: to ride herd over the bitch's brew rem-nants of a once-great political movement and frogmarch them into power. That seemed like an impossible assignment. By this time, paid-up membership in the party was down to fifty thousand — from a previous total of half a million. *

The Vancouver gathering of the tribe had been convened as a showcase for Ignatieff's personal policy priorities but the delegates still had to take him on faith. He revealed little about himself and less about his intentions. Of the many Canadian politicians who have flashed like meteors across the northern sky, Ignatieff was the most complex, most puzzling and least transparent. Ignatieff was determined to revolutionize the Liberal party and alter the coun-try's political equations. That it couldn't be done didn't occur to him. Late in middle age, he'd grabbed the chance of returning to his home and native land and struck a Faustian bargain: he would give up his treasured privacy for a fling at a final career during which he would not write but *make* history, becoming the man in full he always wanted to be.

The Count, as he was sometimes called behind his back, was self-contained and protective of his inner core. Guided by his intuitions, and the even sharper instincts of his wife, he was diffi-cult to read. Still, at that time — to his loyal cadre, to the delegates who gave him a free pass, and to some of us in the media — he was

---

* By the time Ignatieff departed, the roll call was closer to 37,000, and dropping.

a star and that was what Canada's political firmament all too obviously lacked. We forget now how recently it was that people were ready to believe in him as the Liberal party's last, best hope. There was a quality about him that raised unreasonably high expectations, which of course, became his biggest problem.

He knew little, if anything, about ordinary Canadian voters, yet he felt that he could read the national and regional moods. He was well aware that the contradictions in the country's character had grown so acute that no simple show of authority could reconcile them, but he believed that such a vacuum might be his greatest opportunity. Canadian politics has always been the art of making the necessary possible, a process that depended on a leader's ability to inspire, to demonstrate superior negotiating skills and to exercise creative urges to heal. Despite all his qualities, Ignatieff was painfully slow in opening himself up so that Canadians could endow him with their shared hopes and fears. He never really managed it.

In the dark days after the stock market crashed and the world slipped into global recession, the party needed a leader willing to move beyond safe boundaries in order to inspire changes of national mood and a sense of common purpose. This became Ignatieff's testing ground. He had come this far by being a cool man in a hot world, by doing his thing. Now, he could no longer afford to remain satisfied with being considered to have great potential, he had to act on it.

THE WHISPERINGS OF HOPE kept this Vancouver gathering of Grits in an expectant state of contained optimism throughout the whole three days of the conclave. The new leader's surname still puzzled some of the older delegates, who referred to their new chief as "That Michael Guy." But he was now clearly in charge.

On a Saturday afternoon in a hall of momentarily happy delegates, the cool dude was consecrated as the party's new twenty-first century leader. The final phase of the first stage in his march to the nation's highest political office had been sanctified. He was exactly in the place he wanted to be. Now it was up to him.

HE WANTED TO TRIGGER an election for June 2009, which he might well have won. But first, the Liberals had to appoint a National Campaign Director, the hands-on person-of-many-talents who would act as field marshal of the campaign. Gordon Ashworth's name appeared on every computer screen searching for a candidate. After all, he had served that function in half a dozen past Liberal campaigns, as recently as the 2008 run by Stéphane Dion—which, come to think about it, was just about the worst template available.

Ashworth was a capable apparatchik, but never a strategist or even a tactician. Some considered him an ambulatory example of the Peter Principle, a functionary operating beyond his competence, who advanced mainly just by being there. His name and reputation had been linked with the Patti Starr scandal of 1989 though he was never charged or even accused of any criminal wrongdoing. As head of Ontario Place, Starr was convicted and jailed for several counts of fraud and misappropriation of charitable funds: in violation of the Elections Finance Act, she had used charitable funds to make donations to political campaigns, predominantly Liberal ones. Ashworth, a senior aide to then Ontario premier David Peterson, was forced to resign after it was revealed he had accepted a free refrigerator from Starr.

Ashworth's private financial deal with Dion was rumoured to be generous, and he was also paid a retainer of $10,000 per month between elections. He was rehired by the Grits for the Ignatieff campaign despite some lively doubts expressed by some of Ignatieff's new-wave advisers. (Ian Davey soon put a full stop to the monthly retainer.) And so it was that when Ignatieff pushed for a June election, Gordon Ashworth, now the campaign chair, persuaded him that the party apparatus wasn't ready for such a contest, and the leader took his word for it.

Peter Donolo, the Chrétien communications guru (destined to later come aboard as Ignatieff's chief of staff, displacing Ian Davey), worried about their chances too, given that the road-testing of Ignatieff before he took over had been minimal: "The manner in which he assumed leadership was atypical because it was an exceptional moment—the whole failure of that ill-fated and ill-considered coalition idea propelled him, made it a necessity for the leadership change, which Dion eventually recognized. But it meant Ignatieff didn't get to experience the hurly-burly of a leadership convention that actually would have been helpful in terms of conditioning and preparing a new leader—it would have been a rehearsal for the big show, the election to come."

Donolo, a lifelong party member, admitted, "The Liberals are terrible in a lot of ways. We've fallen into the habit, as a party, of acting like spoiled children. We look at the toy, we want the toy, we grab it off the shelf and then we want the next one, after we've thrown it away. So we always want our next leader, instead of the one we have. It's not a healthy mind-set. The flaws of the current leader—and every leader has flaws—tend to be magnified. Liberals in opposition feel somehow cheated and uncomfortable and Liberals in opposition in a minority government even more so . . . Being in a perpetual election watch and operating in a minority situation where we did not hold the balance of power made it even worse. There was this constant schizoid pull: on the one hand, to oppose the government, on the other hand, to support them to stave off an election for which we weren't ready. We needed time for the government to accumulate more mistakes and to wear out its welcome—and to recharge so we could get our act together."

But time did not turn out to be Ignatieff's friend, as the Harper attack ads wore away at his reputation and the moment never seemed right to cause the government to fall.

ON MARCH 12, 2010, Senator Art Eggleton spoke for most of the Liberal caucus when he told Liberal MP Alan Tonks, while they were sipping all-shook-up martinis at the Badminton & Racquet Club of Toronto, "You know, we should really have stuck with Stéphane Dion."

Tonks said, "Are you crazy? Why would we want to have done that?"

"Because," replied Eggleton, an undemonstrative guy who periodically erupts into solid common sense, "we would be in power now—heading a coalition government."

Tonks grew very quiet.

Interview Excerpt: **Ignatieff on the coalition**

I had doubts about the coalition from the beginning, for some fundamental reasons. I'm a Liberal. This is not a flag of convenience for me. I've been a Liberal since I was 17. Big capital 'L' and small 'l'. I'm not a Social Democrat. I'm not an NDPer. I see the two as different family traditions. Different traditions, going back to Woodsworth. They're just different beasts. They have questions about capitalism that I don't. They have an attitude about taxation and fiscal responsibility that I don't have. We come from different families. So from the beginning I thought this was a kind of loose union on the left—we're not a party of the left. We're a party of the centre, progressive centre, centre left sometimes, but always in the centre. . . .

I was the last member of my Caucus to sign the coalition agreement, and I did it as an act of party loyalty. My leader gave me a direct, personal order. And that's what it was. On the morning that he signed it, and he did not do me the courtesy as his deputy leader, I'm being very blunt, of informing me the coalition discussions were under way. I learned of it in the press. And I thought that's a hell of a way to bind a party together. We're also a federalist party. A national unity party. And we were making a coalition agreement with a party determined to break up the country. So, in caucus, privately, everyone who was there will know, I had very substantial objections from the beginning. Other members of the party felt differently, and that's where the battle over Dion's succession was played out. Because I said, 'I don't like this. I'm not comfortable with this. Give me some more options. What is this?' And then Dion's leadership basically began to crumble from within, for twenty-seven reasons.

On December 10, when I took over I said, 'Coalition if necessary, but not necessarily coalition,' to buy time, to see if the party would settle down on this. Remember also, I hadn't met with Jack Layton. I wasn't privy to any of the negotiations, so I didn't know what was going on. I then met with Layton, listened to Canadians, talked to people, and my initial feelings that this was the wrong move were re-doubled. I also thought that the fury about the coalition, among people who don't vote for us, was actually a significant issue. You think through what it would be like to vote the budget down on January 29, gamble that in the middle of the worst economic crisis since the Second World War, the Governor General would ask you to form a government. Assumption #1, not sure. Assumption #2, that you *could* form a government, get a vote through the House in a condition of radical economic difficulty, with—this is the kicker—with 40 percent of the country thinking you're illegitimate. In the middle of the worst economic crisis since the Depression?

I felt then, and I feel now, that—look, I could be prime minister right now if I made that [call]—but I just thought . . . I don't want this, because I don't want to re-fight this battle within my own party. I've said some sharp things about Dion, which I feel. But I think it's inappropriate for me to talk about the former leader in a disrespectful way. I disagreed with him. I mean going forward . . . were we to be in a minority situation, of course you work with other parties. You would work with the NDP the same way Trudeau worked with Broadbent. That's not the same as a coalition. You've got to play the hand that the voters give you.

I would go to the voters and say, 'Give me a majority.' If the voters give you a majority, that's one set of hands. If they give you a minority, then you play another set of hands. And I'd play it very differently than Harper. Harper's always doing 'my way or the highway.' I'd sit down with other party leaders and say, 'Okay. I'll put some water in my wine if you'll put some water in yours.' That's the way Trudeau got two years of good government in the 1970s. And then of course he kicked away the ladder.

"But the fundamental point is, I do believe these are two different political families. I say that with respect to the NDP. It's not meant to be a condescending remark. It's just we're not the same political family. We fight each other in the backstreets for 60 years. And we're supposed to forget all that? Other members of my party take a different view of this, but I don't feel it. I just don't get how you're supposed to do this.

PART FOUR

BE CAREFUL WHAT YOU WISH FOR

12. On Redemption

"We're flawed. We came into the world very imperfect.
We make mistakes and sometimes we hurt people.
We've got no excuses, but you do things you wish
you hadn't done, so you want to . . . make amends.
You want to live better."

— MICHAEL IGNATIEFF

IN THE CAPRICIOUS YEAR OF 1979, Prime Minister Pierre
Trudeau suffered a rare out-of-mind experience: being unexpectedly beaten at the polls by Joe Clark, the well intentioned but
awkward Tory who had richly earned his reputation of never
having set the world on fire, except by accident. Clark's tenure
lasted barely nine months, until Lucky Pierre reclaimed his
throne and began the search for a suitable legacy.

The joke that went around the capital in those days was that
part of his quest was to reserve a plot in a cemetery suitable to his
stature. He'd remembered Menachem Begin showing him
around an impressive graveyard during a visit to Israel, and had
phoned him to ask if he could reserve a plot. Begin explained
that this was one of the country's most illustrious burial grounds
and that a grave site would cost a million dollars.

"*C'est trop d'argent*" the thrifty Pierre shot back. "After all . . . I'll only be there for three days . . ."

Of course the joke worked because Trudeau was enjoying an earthly political resurrection, when everything seemed possible. The national mood was reflected in this imaginary dialogue of a pair of Ottawa boulevardiers, greeting one another on the banks of the Rideau River.

"Did you hear about Trudeau's accident?" said the first.

"No," replied his companion. "What happened!"

"Well, Pierre was out for his morning walk . . . when he was hit by a motorboat."

Such miracles faded after Trudeau finally left office—except when he revived his Right Honourable self long enough to defenestrate Brian Mulroney's Meech Lake Accord. That personal crusade of his took root at Le Maison Egg Roll, a Chinese all-you-can-manage-to-swallow joint in Montreal's east end, and spread across the country, the final curtain call of Trudeau's extended grip on the national consciousness.

SIX PRIME MINISTERS LATER, during the first decade of the new century, Ignatieff took over as Liberal leader as if he had stepped out from behind a magician's cloak. He turned out to be a deep one, that stranger from paradise, far removed in style and background from any of his predecessors. He also faced a far different political climate, in that Ottawa, for Liberals, had turned into a poisoned well.

Unlike Trudeau, the only other certified intellectual in our pantheon of political leaders, Ignatieff was never a natural politician. He was, to put it kindly, a puzzlement. I'd been following him closely, talking to him regularly and was in constant contact with his inner circle, and I still had no idea who the man was. He

seemed to know everybody who counted and had done everything that a contemporary man of letters could achieve, but he
was definitely not the sum of all his accomplishments nor of the
significant people he knew.

I had made my career on recognizing and harvesting the best
anecdotes about the people who intrigued me, but Ignatieff was
an anecdote-free zone. Frustrated, I turned for insight to the wisest
individual I knew: Douglas Beardsley, the poet of distinction who
formerly taught at the University of Victoria, and is my best friend.
He pointed me toward the Polish writer Czeslaw Milosz's study,
The Witness of Poetry. The slim volume evocatively described the
changing role of intellectuals in the postmodern world. Once
society's prophets and *agents provocateur,* they now detailed the
agonies of contemporary genocides but did nothing about them.

Michael Ignatieff had roamed the world, bearing witness to
the horrendous human rights abuses inflicted in the name of
ethnicity and patriotism, bravely venturing into many a no-man's
land between blood-feuding antagonists who had slaughtered
innocents on both sides of several former Yugoslav republics.
Then he gathered his notes and returned to his digs in London
to chronicle the massacres in books that satisfied his wallet but
not his conscience.

He was shot at but remained a bystander rather than the
man of action he wanted to be. His Kosovo venture became a
kind of memorial graveyard of twentieth-century Europe, where
cemeteries replaced the noble but impersonal cathedrals of
earlier times as sacred places of worship and remembrance.
Perhaps Ignatieff suffered something similar to the "survivors'
guilt" of those rare and haunted creatures who stumbled out of
the Nazi concentration camps in the closing days of the Second
World War. Except he hadn't really suffered along with the

innocents, and hadn't survived anything except the rigors of the reporting itself.

I asked Beardsley and his friend David Johnston, a Jungian psychologist, to help me analyze Ignatieff's psyche. Their report, based on his published material alone, pinpointed redemption as Ignatieff's most poignant quest. It wasn't that he had done anything bad he needed to be redeemed from, they argued, it was that he hadn't done anything good for human rights either, which, after all, was supposed to be his mandate. Here is an extract of what they wrote:

> His background is essential—a strict, rigid, powerfully ambitious father and family—Ignatieff grows up repressed and stifled by all this pressure. His friendship—perhaps disciple-ship is a better description—with the legendary public intellectual Isaiah Berlin permits Ignatieff to break out by adopting Berlin's "value pluralism," which believes that a liberal society leads to cultural and individual license operating under the guise of freedom. His early writing was focused on world peace—as in the U of T conference he and Bob Rae organized as early as 1967 where U Thant, secretary general of the United Nations, was the plenary speaker.

They agreed that Ignatieff didn't really come into his own until much later when he hosted a series of high-voltage, late evening BBC talk shows that were part of his determination to find purpose and more relevant meaning in his life. At the same time, he began writing the first of his three novels. "That," my experts contended, "was where the search for Redemption becomes a major theme:

> . . . he wants to redeem his life, to do the one good thing, or go down in flames, like the anti-hero of his best novel, *Charlie Johnson*

in the Flames. Trying to square his world vision of peace with the turmoil of his private life increasingly troubles him. Liberal idealists like him have romantic notions and are highly judgmental—they eternally want to redeem the world but, in doing so, neglect their own lives. In the process of writing his novels, Ignatieff discovers the fiction—and the reality—about himself. He creates a world in which his protagonists go in search of Redemption in order to bring peace to their [and his] private turmoil.

While the writing of his books becomes a personal crusade, spiritual and religious answers are denied him because he will not permit himself to be open to receive faith, he cannot take the leap, even though his intuitions and feelings pull him in that direction. He is an idealist yet he depends solely upon reason, which is not a recognized operational code [for an idealist]. The soul knows by feelings, giving access to other, deeper knowledge. George Grant, Ignatieff's uncle and occasional nemesis, must have spoken about this to his nephew. When Ignatieff initially goes with his feeling side, he supports the American invasion of Iraq, based on the massacres of the Kurds that he had witnessed first hand. He later apologizes for his earlier statements—but that was how he really felt. That contest between idealism and politics is never resolved.

That's why he appears publicly to be a whole army of guys, or a dozen defensive personas. And it shows, oh how it shows. The central unresolved conflict is between his true feelings and his defensive postures. He longs to achieve a balanced understanding between these poles but seems incapable of doing so.

Tolkien wrote that "our vocations are an essential part of our identities." But the reverse is also true, namely, that our identities are an essential part of our vocations. Writers attempt to work this out through their prose and that's why Ignatieff's fiction is so essential—that's what he was doing, that's where he was attempting to redeem

himself by creating secondary fictional worlds in his narratives, struggling to integrate his creative feelings into the wholeness of his life.

There's an intense effort by Ignatieff to become a first-class
writer in those novels, and two literary triumphs out of three tries
ain't bad. But like his quest for faith, he's pulled up short. He can't
quite get there. He discovers revealing truths about himself
through writing the books, but the process is not a valid vocation
for him because it's not a world of action. Writing is a contempla-
tive, meditative exercise, and the best work is done in private. He
is writing about action but it's once removed and he remains
unsatisfied. He has always been engaged, yet remained on the
periphery of things. His fights were with his father or his uncle,
George Grant, who always appears [in his novels] as a costumed,
bearded villain, spouting intellectual non sequiturs.

Ignatieff's novels are astonishingly readable—most of all for
what they revealed about him. They are intensely autobiographi-
cal, but because it's the ever-complex Dr. Ignatieff, they reflect the
characters of three authors, not one.

WHETHER REDEMPTION WAS A STEP up or down from
Trudeau's musings about resurrection is a moot point, but as my
friendly analysts pointed out, it was a recurring theme to which
Ignatieff kept returning like a homing pigeon. The Latin origin
of the word "redemption" (*redemptio*) means to "redeem" or
"earn back." But in theological terms, redemption describes a
release from bondage—historically, the deliverance of the Jewish
people from Babylonian exile.

It is a notion defined best by (of all people) that well-known
philosopher, Sylvester Stallone, who described his Rambo films
as being "based on redemption and revenge. Moby Dick was
an example. It's how you get to the conclusion that makes it

interesting." More applicable to Ignatieff's life-path is U.S. presidential candidate Adlai Stevenson's quip: "I believe in the
forgiveness of sin and the redemption of ignorance."

For a secular, humanist, twenty-first century figure such as
Ignatieff, I think redemption signifies an intense quest for the
purification of guilt, whatever its source. I discussed with Ignatieff
his feelings of guilt, real or imagined.

He had said to me, "I guess I just have a deeper sense of my
own weaknesses and failings. I suppose I have a deeper sense of
sin. I don't know where it comes from. Maybe it comes from going
to the Orthodox Church with my father when I was a child.
Maybe it comes from the Old Testament. Maybe it just comes
from something inside myself.

"We're flawed, we came into the world very imperfect. We
make mistakes and sometimes we hurt people. We've got no
excuses, but you do things you wish you hadn't done, so you want
to . . . make amends. You want to live better.

"I love my life. I have a passionate aspect to life, but I think the
desire for redemption comes from that sense of striving to do better,
striving . . . to care about other people, to live in the moment with
them. Some of it may just be masking the fact that I'm an ambitious person and ambition can leave some bodies on the road.

"I had one marriage that failed. I don't carry that around lightly.
She made her mistakes and I made mine; there's no way around
it. There were some mistakes with my kids. I adore my kids. And
I think I have good relations with my kids. There have been some
mistakes with my beloved wife but we have talked through
everything, and I think are more deeply together than ever. The
experience of going into politics has strengthened us.

"There's some guilt, but Zsuzsanna says guilt is the most useless
emotion of all. And it's true. You can't fix stuff that's happened, so

you put the emphasis on redemption—trying to be better next time. It's very primal. My dad died alone in Sherbrook hospital. It wasn't my fault that I wasn't there. But I will always regret it."

At the end of one of our more cathartic exchanges in his Parliamentary office—which had once been occupied by Mackenzie King, and maybe was still haunted by his eccentric spiritual energy—I pulled out of my briefcase a sweatshirt that I had made for him blazoned with the slogan that I felt would resolve his redemptive obsession, as opposed to repentance or contrition, which seem foreign to his nature. Or maybe it's an obsessive suffering from pangs of conscience rather than a redemptive quest, despite what my experts had found.

SCREW GUILT! screamed the fat white letters on the chest of the sweatshirt. He took the garment from me, then moved it from hand to hand as if it was an unexploded hand grenade, and finally shoved it in his desk drawer. Zsuzsanna, who was watching us, laughed so hard her glasses steamed up.

I thought of the moment as a noble transaction, akin to those of my hero, Don Quixote, who never saw a windmill he was afraid to take on. And I thought of Quixote's most memorable declaration, in which he grandly invites us to join him in abandoning "the melancholy burden of sanity"—a sound warning for any Canadian politician. Ignatieff probably just thought I had accepted the Don's invitation.

I, TOO, RE-EXAMINED Ignatieff's novels for clues to his character, rereading them with new appreciation. The first was the saga of Asya, the beautiful young princess who escapes the 1917 revolution in Moscow, flees to Paris to get away from historical events, finds the love of her life twice but loses herself on a continent in turmoil. Even so, it does read like a tale of redemption, not victimhood.

An entirely different context of redemption explodes on the opening page of *Scar Tissue*, a thinly disguised lament for his mother, Alison Grant, who was dying of dementia, which was shortlisted for the Booker Prize in 1993. His narrator wrote, "I still have days when everything she ever was, everything she ever meant to me is entirely erased by the memory of those great agonizing breaths, that frail body wracked with spasms, those lips wet with blood. There must be some way to redeem this, some way to believe that the banal heartlessness of it all was not for nothing."

Finally, *Charlie Johnson in the Flames*, his most personal venture into documentary fiction, recounts the saga of a world-weary foreign correspondent who tries to save a young woman who was set on fire by a deranged local militia colonel. She dies and Charlie is eventually murdered by her assassin. Yet the redemptive theme persists because Charlie, the anti-hero, has witnessed much in a life of reporting and earned at least a tiny sliver of grace. It's a play on Ignatieff's search for order out there in the warring universe, which it later became his self-appointed mission to restore.

These novels were written when Ignatieff was at his literary best. The pivotal characters were seeking some form of purification from their guilt. From 1991 to 2003, during Ignatieff's London period, he was beginning to clear a path in his own life that would lead him into action—a place in the centre of the arena where the brave matador faces the enraged bull (a.k.a. Stephen Harper).

Ignatieff at last discovered that the secret of redemption begins with confession, and extends to discover a route that would lead him to deliverance. Confessing his desire to come home and becoming a politician turned him from observer to passionate participant.

Action exacted its price. Having stepped into the arena, he could no longer bow out of responsibility or escape into theory, but had to obey Norman Mailer's admonition that "there is a law of life, so cruel and so just: that one must grow or else pay more for staying the same." As the prime minister in waiting of a country that occupied such a generous chunk of the earth's land surface and maintained an economy that weathered the economic storms far better that the empire to its south, he was suddenly charged with the possibility that he might have to instill 34 million citizens with visions and aspirations while enforcing harsh rules of survival.

He abandoned the killing fields of Kosovo, the treacherous meadowlands of Croatia, the controversial bombing campaigns on Iraq, and even the trimmed hedges of Harvard to seek redemption on his home turf. He chose to challenge the odds by accepting an assignment potentially equivalent to climbing Everest on a dinner date: the leadership of the Liberal Party, a once-proud luxury liner whose glory days were long gone.

And so, Michael Grant Ignatieff went to war at last, where he expected it least—at home in Canada, where his odyssey had taken him, and where a brand new incarnation of himself played out to its bitter end.

13. Sudbury Madness

"Just win, Michael. Just win.
Otherwise, it will all
have been a waste of time."
— IAN DAVEY, Ignatieff's first chief of staff

OF THE MANY bloopers of judgement authored by Michael Ignatieff, arguably the worst was his unexpected and ill-considered election call in the fall of 2009. On September 1, at a routine party gathering in Sudbury, Ontario, he stood up to speak and without any provocation (I'm tempted to write "without any thought"), he blurted out, "Mr. Harper, your time is up!"

I was half-awake, watching the proceedings on TV, and mistakenly imagined that Ignatieff's challenge was the punch line of a dated *Royal Canadian Air Farce* skit. But no. He was still glaring at me from the screen, eyebrows on guard, trying to look mad as hell. And as his speech wore on, he kept repeating his newly discovered mantra: "Your time is up, Mr. Harper!"

If he was anywhere near his TV set, I imagined Harper must have been as puzzled as any of us, glancing at his watch and calmly disagreeing. That was about as scary as Ignatieff seemed as he issued his stern, completely meaningless warning. It was also disconcerting that as he was repeatedly mouthing this threat, Ignatieff would spot a friendly face in the audience, smile and wave. Once, he even winked. What was going on? Had the former Harvard prof flipped his lid? Or had my TV set gone free range, its electronic guts signalling that they needed to be recalibrated?

AFTER THE FACT, my journalistic colleagues assumed that this unadorned bit of mischief must have been the doing of Ian Davey, Ignatieff's chief of staff. He must have whispered, "We better have an election, boss—and you better tell Harper his time is up." This was par for the course, since Davey at that point was being blamed for most of the many Liberal mistakes.

It hadn't been an easy road for Ignatieff since he'd wangled his way into the leadership. Having pressed the Tories so hard to respond to the economic crisis, Liberals had to grit their teeth when Harper and crew stole a march from the old Liberal playbook and turned their economic stimulus programme into history's longest-playing photo-op, with Conservatives delivering plum after plum to municipal functionaries, ecstatic to have one more gazebo to build. When the Harper Tories described new merry-go-rounds and outdoor privies as being essential to the country's economic prosperity, the Liberal leader found nothing much he could complain about—except the ungenerous terms of the Employment Insurance programme. (That issue turned into a Gong Show as Conservative and Liberal strategists competed for the least practical approach available.) Oh yeah, then there was the absence of a national power grid that no one had noticed—since like Sherlock Holmes' dog, it didn't bark.

Even though he'd been unanimously confirmed as leader only that May, a profound sense of frustration with Ignatieff had been percolating within the Liberal caucus for the whole summer. Its more combative members felt that Ignatieff was giving Harper a free ride, particularly after he appeared to disappear into the manicured pastures of Provence for the summer, and returned to Canada just in time to have his television viewing interrupted by those crude, never-ending "just visiting" negative ads. Funny how they happened to flood the airwaves just as he got off the plane from his extended French leave. Ignaiteff's retort in the *Globe and Mail* that while he'd been in Provence he had been "Thinking Big Thoughts" was a lead balloon from the get-go.

The caucus itself was torn between the tigers with a visceral loathing of Harper's methods—Ujjal Dosanjh, Denis Coderre, Bob Rae and Ralph Goodale, among others—and the lambs, including Martha Hall Findlay, Hedy Fry and Ken Dryden who, with more than a little justification, objected to inflicting another election on a politically exhausted populace. But the Liberals' visceral distaste for Harper's sense that he could exercise unilateral power in a minority meant that Ignatieff was far from alone on this gambit; enormous pressure had built up for the party to stop supporting the Tories in the Commons.

As Davey told me in a later interview. "When September rolled around, Michael said, 'I've got to stand up to Harper . . . I've got to look like I can stand up to him . . . I've got to say, "This isn't a good government, we can no longer support them." We're going to become a real opposition.'"

Davey knew that most of the press corps thought the announcement was his fault. "You accept those things because you've got to protect the leader," Davey confided. "That's the price of entry for the job." But Davey emphatically did not believe it was the right time to threaten Harper with an election. He believed the NDP did not have adequate electoral funds and far too few star candidates and thought they would support Harper in any non-confidence motion, thus preventing an election. Sudbury was his leader's idea.

IN FACT, IGNATIEFF HAD prepared a much more guarded and careful speech. Sachin Aggarwal says, "The objective of that softer speech was to turn the Liberal party once again into the Opposition. Instead of voting with the government, we would go issue by issue and oppose as required. We would no longer default to preventing an election, and we would let the NDP do so if they saw fit."

But then on the day of the speech, Ignatieff had met with the senior caucus members and his strategic advisory group, which included Bob Rae. When Ignatieff told them that he intended to announce that Stephen Harper's days were numbered, Rae responded that that was all well and good, but wondered what Ignatieff was going to say when people then asked him if he was prepared to vote against the government and trigger another election. As one of the Ignatieff advisers in the room remembers it, Rae said, "You've got to do that. Otherwise, the motion to call an election is hollow. You can't be half pregnant."

The room took Rae's comment as an endorsement of Ignatieff's new tough on Harper stance. Davey said, "That comment ran around the room and everybody seemed to think it was a solid idea. Shortly afterwards, Michael was in the main meeting room making his combative speech allegedly based on Bob's advice. It just became a runaway train. For people to think that chiefs of staff tell the leader what to do—and that he's taking their advice— is crazy. He did not. We were set up for September to make a series of speeches on everything from foreign policy to where Canada was going in health care in order to showcase Ignatieff across the country. All of a sudden, we got into this incongruous proposition of 'We've got to bring down the government immediately.' So we headed off on two paths after very careful planning through the summer to do something that now wasn't able to happen. What quickly came to pass was that we were no longer the Liberal party, we became the Election party. And that was to the leader's detriment."

Another one of Ignatieff's advisers, who wasn't in the room to hear Rae's remark, said, "I was told that Rae pushed for a much more aggressive stance, and the senior caucus leadership agreed with him. And hence, the speech was 'punched up.' Another sign of Michael Ignatieff listening to everyone and no one."

Going forward Ignatieff had no choice but to attempt to live up to his fateful Sudbury speech, which contained that threat and promise in the first paragraph. "Earlier today," he claimed, "I met with my caucus and told them what I'm telling you now: Stephen Harper's time is up. At the first opportunity, we will move a motion of non-confidence in this government. We're here because our country is in trouble. We've lost half a million full-time jobs so far this year. And more young people than ever before are starting their working lives in the unemployment lines. . . . Your time is up, Mr. Harper!"

BY THANKSGIVING, Ignatieff was in a tough corner. And Ian Davey got the blame. He said, "I can recall vividly meeting him at Stornoway and he was absolutely snake's belly—really down. I was always pretty good at keeping him loose and feeling optimistic, able to find the good in the worst situation. Not this time. He said, 'If things don't turn around, we'll have to get rid of some staff at Christmas.'

"My response was that we had the best team I had seen in the Liberal party and that if we needed a change it should be me.

That would give you an optical change. Let's see where we are at Christmas and decide then."

After that conversation, Davey prepared an exit strategy but thought he would still be a voice at the table, given that he'd offered himself up as a strategic sacrifice.

It was not to be. Jill Fairbrother, the Grits' gutsy communications chief and Davey's partner, had plotted a reasonable path to enact Davey's exit if he had to go. They both thought everything was under control. "The first time I got wind of something," she remembered, "I had a call from John Geddes, the Ottawa bureau chief of *Maclean's*, asking me if Peter Donolo was coming in as our new chief of staff and Ian was leaving. I wasn't surprised to hear Donolo's name because we had recommended that Michael talk with him. We were aware of the charge that we were too new to Ottawa and needed more experience on the team. So we had been reaching out to bring in more seasoned advisers. Donolo was one of the people we had recommended Michael approach. When Geddes asked me if Ian was out and Peter was in, I said, 'No, we don't have any announcements of that kind to make.' But I told Ian and Sachin that they had better reach Michael and find out what was going on because this rumour was out there. In fact, it was everywhere, all across the press gallery. Michael was in Montreal for the day, so we weren't able to reach him until later but we had word that CBC was going to break the story on its five o'clock newscast. Sachin spoke to him. Michael's response was that he would talk to us when he got back to the office, which wouldn't be until six. During that window, we received private clarification that Michael had indeed talked to Donolo but there wasn't anything to announce. At that point, we just kind of shut down for the night."

Late that afternoon, Davey was heading for a meeting with

Marc Garneau, the Montreal MP (and Canada's first astronaut), but as he walked by a television set, he heard CBC News reporting that Ian Davey has been dumped by the Liberals.

"Garneau looked at me, and I looked at him, and he asked, 'Should we still meet?' I said, 'Yeah. I haven't heard any of this. So, who knows?' We had the meeting and afterward I got Michael on the phone. He was still driving back from Montreal. 'Michael! What's going on?'"

Ignatieff told Davey that they would talk when he got to Ottawa.

Davey wouldn't be put off. He said, "Look, this story's breaking all over the place. Don't you think I deserve to know what's going on? I'm sitting in meetings with members of Parliament. I have a strategic meeting at six with senior caucus. You still want me to go?"

"Oh, yeah," Ignatieff told him. "Go to the meeting."

Ignatieff arrived at his office just before six, met Ian, and blurted out, "I didn't want this to happen this way."

"So what's happened?"

"I've asked Peter Donolo to be my chief of staff. I'd like to find another role for you."

"I want to think about that."

"No, I'd like to find another role."

"I want to think about that," repeated a traumatized Davey, then he turned and walked out. "To say that I was dealt with in an absolutely ridiculous fashion was an understatement. I had been loyal to Michael for five years. No holidays. Available twenty-four/ seven. Politics is one hundred percent a people business, and it runs on loyalty and trust. If you don't have that combination, you do not succeed. It can't be a one-way thing. Sometimes things happen, you have to give people the benefit of the doubt. I always did—I guess, to my detriment . . . It was a shame that things came apart the way they did, a shame for me not to have been given the opportunity to exercise a sensible exit. That was unforgivable. There may be many things I deserved, but I didn't deserve that. Not after five years."

Davey then said, "By chopping off the head of a simple, loyal guy from Toronto, Michael had undone his organization—it just made me want to cry. I thought at the time that somebody else would come along and do [my job], hopefully successfully. But Michael never listened." Not to him, not to Donolo. Not to his own caucus.

IGNATIEFF'S JETTISONING OF DAVEY and Fairbrother was serious enough, but his loss of four other loyalists diminished him further. Though young and previously untested, they had won their spurs at the operational command level, organizing and implementing the takeover of the Liberal party—moving the whole thing into Ignatieff's corner.

Brad Davis, his chief policy adviser, had died of cancer in January 2008, before the deputy leader had morphed into the leader. Davis had been in a class by himself because he was the only one of the crowd who could pierce Ignatieff's mental armour, actually making him change his opinions and reassess his actions. I watched the two of them finishing each other's sentences and found their mind-meld remarkable—especially considering the difference in their ages and backgrounds. A corporate lawyer, Davis arrived in the Ignatieff camp with no political experience or agenda except to lift the Grits from the lowest-common-denominator initiatives still cluttering their policy files. But he died of cancer at thirty-four, leaving his wife and two young children, and a bereft Ignatieff, who spoke at his funeral and was the last to leave his grave.

The three others left with Davey and Fairbrother. Sachin Aggarwal, deputy chief of staff, was one of those rare people who is a natural leader; when he made it clear that he had full confidence in you, you believed more confidently in yourself. At twenty-seven, he held the operation together, with either a smile or a hammer lock—whatever the occasion demanded. Mark Sakamoto's title was Director of Organization West/East, and he'd built provincial organizations out of airport phone books and personal enthusiasm. The other indispensable presence now gone was Alexis Levine, one of whose major roles was to be yelled at by the others (including the leader) for pushing the schedule too hard. Scouting for Ontario delegates in every mouse hole, Chinese restaurant and country club, he was relentless—just like his father, the über-agent Michael Levine. "Ignatieff's key people," Sakamoto pointed out, "all learned their work ethic from their immigrant families. I learned about hard work watching my grandpa Sakamoto sleep in his truck three hours a night during harvest season."

They had been with him from the beginning, and now they were all gone, victims of a misapprehension about who called the disastrous shots in Sudbury, and the resulting inability to follow through on an empty threat.

AND THERE WAS ANOTHER NARRATIVE out of Sudbury that had played into the demise of the key members of Ignatieff's praetorian guard, focused on the party's heavyweight Ontario caucus. They were all on the lamb side of the caucus divide over how to fight Harper, unanimously opposed to the idea of an early election and determined to confront Ignatieff on the issue at the Sudbury meeting. But when they arrived for what they thought would be a private tête-à-tête with the leader, Ignatieff showed up accompanied by a rowdy retinue of reporters and TV camera people, ready to shoot the story of his electoral challenge to Harper.

The stunt produced the most catastrophic fallout possible for a political leader: irretrievable loss of caucus confidence. Between elections, it is the caucus that sanctions the leader's mandate. The Sudbury episode was the turning point in the Harvard exile's terms of political endearment: he lost his own caucus, and never got it back. Nobody said, "Your time is up, Mr. Ignatieff,"—but they sure thought it.

A FEW WEEKS AFTER they'd been dumped, Davey and Fairbrother ran into Ignatieff at a funeral. He looked embarrassed, and said, "I want to look you in the eye, Ian, and apologize. I want to tell you, that if you feel bitter, that's okay."

"Michael, I don't feel bitter. I'm hurt, but I'll get over it," Davey replied.

They saw one another one more time, after there finally was an election call in spring 2011. Davey said to his former boss and former hero: "Get the job done. Just win, Michael. Just win. Otherwise, it will all have been a waste of time."

BY CHRISTMAS 2009, nearly all of the original crew of bushy-tailed enthusiasts who had been attracted to the prospect of a Liberal party recharged and rebuilt by the estimable Ignatieff, were summarily dismissed.

This massacre of the loyalists had a long-term effect that was telling: in a survey of the party's popularity, taken by coincidence on December 10, 2010, exactly two years after the caucus vote that gave Ignatieff the leadership, the Liberals registered exactly the same dismal numbers on the popularity scale—in fact they were a cat-whisker lower. Maybe some statistical genius might have deduced that the problem wasn't the staff. It was the boss.

But in the short term, the mass exodus silenced Ignatieff's critics, who had blamed his pratfalls on poor staff work. Donolo and his new group brought in some impressive Liberal veterans and there certainly was less daily chaos in the leader of the opposition's office. But he was now bereft of his praetorian guard, the term dating back to the private bodyguards recruited by Roman emperors to guard their backsides while they were otherwise employed. Ignatieff's first wave of staffers ranked loyalty to him ahead of being red-blooded Grits.

That couldn't be said of his new team, for better or for worse.

14. The Watch on the Rideau

"For too long, we have experimented with the dark side of excellence. For too long this country has suffered from politics that stresses economic efficiency instead of social fairness — and it's in that direction our party must make its next policy thrust."

— PIERRE TRUDEAU, 1988

WHEN LIBERAL DELEGATES confirmed Ignatieff as leader in May 2009, the one thing they had to have been hoping was that one of Canada's best-known public intellectuals could spearhead a renewal of Liberal policy and ideas.

Party history was rich with ideas translated into action. Despite his minority mandates, Lester Pearson turned the welfare state into Canadian law. Trudeau's major initiatives, of course, were the Charter, with its emphasis on a new balance of state and individual rights, multiculturalism and the fight against separatism. These were the mighty pillars that defined the Liberal party for a generation: attractive, if controversial, ideas road-tested from the grassroots up, then combined with a skilled political operation to see them through

After Trudeau resigned, and the party under John Turner lost the 1984 election, that potent combination of the Pearson-Trudeau era fell apart. The country and the Liberal party became preoccupied with reducing the budgetary deficit, inherited from earlier Liberal governments and built up even more under Brian Mulroney. Instead of positive programs, the issue of the Chrétien years became, "How do we get out of the hole that we're in?"

Granted, in order to do that, Chrétien had to change the party's view of itself and its priorities. In the 1980s and early '90s, many people on the progressive side of the party, did not think the deficit was important. And so Chrétien convened a new ideas conference in Aylmer, Quebec, in 1991, where that issue was firmly debated. As a result, the Liberals changed their traditional position on the deficit from not caring about it very much at all to making it a priority, supporting Chrétien's promise in the 1993 election to target deficit reduction as the major thrust of his government. To his credit, Chrétien did not impose that priority from the top down, but did what he had to do to educate his party to bring them along.

But after Chrétien and Martin rescued Canada's finances, they launched few new initiatives. As I've said, the Clarity Act (crafted by Dion) and his refusal to join the Americans in Iraq were Chrétien's main accomplishments; the sponsorship scandal the major blemish he left the party. After the deficit was beaten, instead of moving on and organizing another thinkers' conference on what the Pearson-Trudeau legacy might mean for the twenty-first century, nothing happened.

Tom Axworthy, a one-man Liberal brains trust, says, "From the days when Mike Pearson asked Mitchell Sharp, Walter Gordon and the volunteer wing of the party to do the thinking about where the party should go next in the 1960s, the 'professional' wing consisted essentially of a group of volunteers — amateurs, with instincts and energy to create a better Canada.

They were not lobbyists, not organizers for anyone, but concerned citizens, searching for new agendas.

"At the same time, there was a group of Ottawa insiders, professionals who ran each of the parties because it was their business. They rose through the ranks, joined ministers' offices, then left to become lobbyists and consultants. It may sound ridiculously romantic of me to say this, but the tenure of the professional eventually pushed aside the voluntarism that had fuelled the Liberal party's great days. Everything was put aside for the interest of the leader's office and the concerns of the professional, political cavalry, whoever they were. This was as true for the Martin interregnum as for the Chrétien decade. The one thing they didn't want to do was to give up any power to volunteers they couldn't control and, I think as a result, neither leader was really interested in a serious policy rethink, because it would mean that the parties' future wouldn't be controlled by them."

This was actually not a new tension. Pearson's caucus and inner circle were vigorously opposed to the Kingston conference (which I'll discuss below). Paul Martin Sr. and Jack Pickersgill, for instance, thought it was a terrible idea because it would reduce their power. But Pearson insisted that the party needed some new thinking to restore its fortunes and also insisted that they ask some new people to do it. That was a great, transformative moment, Axworthy argues. The old guard and the caucus had a huge influence on Pearson, but they didn't run everything; Pearson reached out for volunteer, grassroots input into party renewal and was rewarded. "What a difference between then and the year 2000," Axworthy says, "when the pollsters, the leader and a small inner professional group of three or four advisers decided what to do on every issue. The genius of Pearson was to genuinely open the party up to new ideas and to bring in talented outsiders."

But at the end of the Chrétien era, Axworthy claims, "The power group in the caucus and the leader's office refused to tap the influence of the party volunteers outside of their span of control. The Liberal party is no longer a democratic institution, or an innovative one. It became a power-preservation vehicle for whatever elite happens to be there at the time."

The new guard who brought Ignatieff into the party were trying to fight that status quo. They believed that somebody who had lived by ideas, wrote well and had spent his entire career thinking about politics should have been a natural source of renewal, and that hope spread: thus the eventual coronation of Michael Ignatieff. His problem, once he became leader, was that the voters had no idea—not a clue—what the disintegrating Liberal Party of Canada actually stood for, except as a vehicle for gaining power, by representing the elusive "middle." The party needed much more than little message tweaks and incremental reforms.

Ignatieff inherited a politically disconnected, dissatisfied political movement. His support was based on the not unreasonable assumption that while he may not have been a good politician or a great organizer, he would certainly bring a climate of intellectual ferment to the party. "That would have been the one thing that everybody would have said about him, those who knew him and those who had read his books," Axworthy contends. "Yet it's the one thing that was totally absent. I don't for the life of me begin to understand why or how he didn't bring himself to do that."

Axworthy may be mystified, but others believe that in his precarious time as leader, Ignatieff deliberately kept creative thinkers at a distance, all too aware that his ideas on foreign policy—especially his support for the invasion of Iraq—were opposed by most of the Liberal party. (One well-informed senior Grit estimated that an overwhelming 84 percent of the party was against him on the issue.)

His contradictory stance as a "liberal imperialist" meant that he was willing to impose some form of democracy on rogue states by the use of force. That was certainly an intellectually provocative position, and never a part of the Liberal mindset. Laurier had been on the peace side of conscription; Pearson had helped invent peacekeeping; Trudeau was regularly attacked for being a "peace-nik;" and Ignatieff's own father had proudly called himself a "peace monger." The party instinctively shied away from the military side of issues. "I was at that Montreal convention, where Ignatieff first spoke," Axworthy recalls. "He was in favour of ballistic missile defence for Canada, but the party voted down the resolution supporting the idea so overwhelmingly that its then leader, Paul Martin, who was leaning toward the idea, withdrew the motion. It was Ignatieff in 2009 who was most instrumental in helping the Conservatives extend the mandate for Canadian combat troops to remain in Afghanistan until 2011."

The problem with trying to pin down exactly where Ignatieff landed on the Iraq issue was that the butterfly of indecision never stopped flapping its wings. A serious student bent on being fair to his position would respect the fact that he was caught in a trap of his own devising. Driven by his liberal instincts, he recognized the overthrow of Saddam Hussein as a moral necessity. Yet there he was, following into war a president he didn't respect. Both he and Bush had jumped into the same quagmire, the pretext being that Hussein appeared to be threatening the destruction of civilization as we know it. At the time American leaders were building up an image of Iraq as an evil empire armed with a fantasy arsenal of nuclear weapons, pretend interstellar missiles, pellet pistols that glowed in the dark and other such nonsense.

Following the invasion, the U.S.-led Iraq Survey Group concluded the Iraq had ended its programme of developing weapons
of mass destruction in 1991. It turned out that Hussein's silos
were storing corn, not missiles, and that those suspicious-look-
ing garages that the former head of the Joint Chiefs of Staff,
Colin Powell, had testified at the UN as containing nuclear
whatsits, turned out to be simply garages. Only the White House
propaganda brigade (along with UK prime minister Tony Blair)
continued to regard Hussein as anything but a despicable thug
with less than two independently programmed sensible brain
cells to rub together.

Having flubbed the "disarmament through regime change"
challenge, the invasion still had to be justified, and Ignatieff was
thrown back to complaining about the dictator's "malignancy of
intentions." He was not alone. Intellectual supporters of the Iraq
invasion included the distinguished Canadian author and historian Margaret MacMillan, the British historian Niall Ferguson
and the journalist and intellectual gadfly Christopher Hitchens.
They were all justified in their moral outrage over the Iraqi
regime's brutality. As I mentioned earlier, Ignatieff had been in
Halabja in 1992, and talked to the survivors of the 1988 poisoned
chemical attacks that had killed up to five thousand innocent
Kurds and their children.

Still, Ignatieff was well aware of the risk he ran in supporting
the invasion. "I was in the middle of the largest moral and political gamble of my adult life," he confessed. "Everything I've said
and believed since I was eighteen was on the line over this
war, and I could be very seriously wrong." And so he was, according to his own confessional *mea culpa*—which the *Star*'s Linda
McQuaig described as "rich in *mea* and slim on *culpa*"—
published in the same section of the *New York Times* that had

carried his previous declaration of support for the war. It had been the gravest possible transgression of his once sacrosanct liberal-left orthodoxy, and he paid the price.

Or perhaps not the gravest: his position on torture is a tortured one. Ignatieff has spoken out strongly against torture of any kind. With one exception: Suppose the authorities had captured a terrorist on September 10 and found out that he knew that something catastrophic would happen the next day, but he wouldn't say what. If all else failed, should torture have been used under such circumstances? The choice might be to use a predetermined range of non-lethal tortures or to do nothing. That's the real-world scenario that no one can answer. It's called the "ticking bomb" scenario and Ignatieff has come down on both sides. He did at one point come out for an outright ban of all torture rather than attempting to regulate it—but then softened his position by suggesting that "coercive interrogation" might be all right, adding that "congressional legislation would have to define exactly what constitutes acceptable degrees of coercive interrogation."

David Olive, the thoughtful and well-informed *Toronto Star* columnist, nailed the morass Ignatieff was in. "My principal bias against Ignatieff, with his patina of liberalism and thoughtfulness," he wrote, "was that he provided liberal and human rights cover for the barbarity of the Cheney-run undermining of the U.S. constitution in striving to create an imperial presidency. Far from protecting the Kurds, as it turned out, U.S. forces could not, and did not, protect even the Iraqi museums holding some of Western civilization's most valuable treasures of antiquity."

And so the theory as to why the Liberal party was unable to renew itself on the intellectual level goes like this: Ignatieff was well aware that he had not persuaded his own party of his militaristic point of view, and that he may have lost his first leadership bid in 2006 because many delegates were so uneasy about his original position on Iraq. Maybe he thought it would be better not to bring its members together to talk about such issues, since he might well be repudiated. To change the party's position on foreign policy, he would have had to debate Tom Axworthy's brother Lloyd, for one, who led the party's antimilitaristic wing and brokered a land mines treaty when he was foreign affairs minister under Trudeau.

And that's an interesting aspect of his leadership. He came in with a point of view on something he cared deeply about that was alien to his party but he never debated his own people to see whether he could change their thinking on the issue. Coming in, Ignatieff could have said, "I stand for these things. I'll tell you why. I know that many people don't share this point of view. Let me tell you why it's right. I'm going to debate first my party, and then the country." Instead he kept his intellectual strengths hidden, and refused to engage.

The caucus was not involved in the move to support the extension of Canada's involvement in Afghanistan, which was engineered by Ignatieff and Bob Rae. As a trained polemicist, Ignatieff should have attempted to educate the party to move with him.

THE BEST IGNATIEFF had to offer, finally, was to convene a meeting in Montreal at the end of March 2010 where he invited fifty-three big thinkers to speak to a select crowd of Liberals—all of whom paid $700 for the privilege—about the kind of Canada they wanted to see in the year 2017, Canada's one-hundred-and-fiftieth birthday. The gathering proved a lovely satirical target for Conservatives, especially when the organizers made a point of not inviting the Liberal caucus, either to speak or attend the Montreal venue; instead, they were supposed to take part in free "satellite conferences" linked to the main event by Internet. The price point of the tickets also offered ready ammunition for the charge that the Liberals were following their same old elitist track.

Ignatieff's caucus was miffed. Instead of seeing this as a wonderful opportunity to listen with open minds to what the best had to offer about a way forward for the country, elected members simply . . . griped.

Then there was the timing. The Grits' intellectual grind fell into the same week as Ignatieff's monumentally ill-advised parliamentary motion advocating that the costs of abortion be included in federal foreign aid initiatives supporting women's reproductive health. Just days before the ideas session was to convene, the motion had been defeated by his own party. Three Liberals voted against him, and thirteen others didn't show up for the vote; if all sixteen had toed his line, the motion would have passed. It was a real sign of how alienated the leader was from his own caucus.

The Montreal meeting of brains, designed to spark a lively election platform, seemed jinxed from the start since its presenters' highest priority seemed to be to disowning their hosts by declaring their own political objectivity. Its most relevant contributor was the white-bearded figure of Robert Fowler, formerly one of Ottawa's wisest mandarins and diplomats, and most recently the Special Envoy of the UN Secretary-General to Niger. As the lead-off speaker on the final day, devoted to "Where Will the World Be in 2017," his brief was to talk about Canada and Africa. He took the opportunity to accuse the Liberal party of having "lost its soul" in a mostly vain attempt to incite the crowd into real thought about why they were in the room when all that most of them were trying to do was sleep with their eyes open.

A thirty-seven-year veteran of every posting that counted in the federal civil service and diplomatic corps, Fowler had been kidnapped with a companion while on mission to war-torn Niger to help the African republic to make peace with Tuareg rebels who were claiming a bigger share of uranium mining revenues from their traditional northern lands. His kidnappers were al Qaeda of the Islamic Maghreb, the wild North African branch of the al Qaeda terrorist network. He was unexpectedly set free four months later, following payment of a hefty ransom.

Fowler reminded the delegates in Montreal, by his presence if not in so many words, that there was one other witness to international violence and double-dealing in the hall, namely their leader. A few delegates had already made that connection; for the others it was an interesting sidebar to what turned out to be an inconclusive gathering that offered only a few significant insights. Speaker after speaker grappled with "the big issues facing our country," rattling off many encyclopedias' worth of facts, parading their non-partisanship while attempting to ignore the obvious reality that their hosts were Liberals, starved for marketable ideas with an election in the wind.

Nobody was actually saying it, but the Liberals at the Montreal gathering knew that the options for reviving their party were running out. Ideas they could cull from these fifty-three thinkers provided the last best chance of renewing their mandate, so rudely interrupted four years earlier by the redoubtable Stephen Harper. But it wasn't a pretty picture. The idea cupboard was bare.

PROGRESSIVE PARTIES are usually consumed by policy debates. Since unanimity is impossible, and respect for others' opinions runs high, verbal chaos is the curse of progressives. By contrast, conservative leaders such as Harper and the American neo-cons have a narrower set of policy objectives, and a custom of at least attempting to avoid public debate or disagreement among each other. (The right Republican movement in the United States basically excommunicated prominent writer and thinker David Frum for daring to criticize the party's internal inconsistencies and failings.) In their most enlightened and stable moments, they are guided by President Reagan's Eleventh Commandment: "Thou shall not speak ill of a fellow Republican."

As usual with such high-visibility events as the Montreal Thinkers' Conference, there was a pretty rough back story. In the run-up to the conference, there was infighting over who should speak and who should attend; in the aftermath, there was intense bickering about the value of the whole exercise, told here in e-mails between Alfred Apps, who had become the president of the Liberal party, and Ray Heard. Reading from the bottom of the chain, you'll see the return salvo Apps fired off to Heard after Heard had got it into his head that Tom Axworthy and I should speak in Montreal, and then decided it was a personal insult to himself that we didn't (for Axworthy and me, it was a relief!):

From: Apps_Alfred
To: Ray Heard
Sent: Saturday, April 03, 2010 11:10 AM
Subject: Heard Versus Apps on Who is an Asshole — Continued

My point is this. You called it a gathering of elitists. You hammered the party for charging $700 per person to attend. The fact is that almost 30,000 Canadians participated in a policy conference sponsored by the Liberal party from their desktops and seven satellite locations and most of them participated for free. Nothing like that has ever happened before in Canadian politics. McKenna was invited and attended. Axworthy was invited but was out of town. If Peter [Newman] had wanted to attend, he could have. . . . Your case is just a case of sour grapes and I would rather have you outside the tent pissing in, than inside pissing out, if forced to choose. . . . BTW I did not personally attend the conference as President of the party. I participated with the grassroots at one of the satellite conferences. All of those were wide open to the public. Where were you or are you "above" that sort of engagement.

From: Ray Heard
Sent: Saturday, April 03, 2010 11:00 AM
To: Apps_Alfred
Subject: Heard versus Apps on who is an asshole — Continued

Alfred
Below, you call me an asshole for daring publicly to raise questions about the Thinkers' Conference which, to my mind, was the biggest let-down since Liz Taylor went braless in Cleopatra.

Well, Alfred, you and Donolo made a choice: Have me in the tent pissing out, or outside, pissing in. You opted for the latter.

You will recall that, in a friendly email to you and Peter (who had told me he wanted to reach out) I recommended as conference speakers:

[Frank] McKenna, on jobs (by far the biggest issue), North American security and trade;

Tom Axworthy, former chair of the totally neglected Renewal Commission, on empowering our aboriginal people. . . .

Peter C. Newman, on what really happened at Kingston and what it means to today. . . .

I also offered you my help in staging the conference, given my experience of event management for ten years at RBC, and assisting with the successful Mandela and Stones celebrations.

You emailed me back that very night promising I would get a response within 24 hours. Nothing happened, of course.

Then, after you asked me to try to get Tom Axworthy to attend, you agreed we should meet at your office to mend fences. I postponed a business meeting and showed up at your office. Your secretary said you had other things to do and would not see me. In other words, you stood me up, a rare experience for me to be treated as an interloper on Bay St.

Regarding the thinkers' conference: The choice of Burney, a top Conservative, over McKenna or Tom Axworthy, was dumb. . . . The $700 a seat admission fee was outrageous, a total barrier to Young Liberals attending. AND, WORST, THE ONLY NEW POLICY TO EMERGE, FREEZING CORPORATE TAX CUTS, IS A SURE WAY TO HALT JOB GROWTH SINCE MIDDLE AND SMALL BUSINESS CREATE JOBS WHEN TAXES ARE LOWER.

Anyway, if this makes me a "complete asshole" in your mind, so be it. I am used to being called an asshole: By Herle for daring to insist that Martin should campaign on jobs, jobs, jobs, stupid; by Dion's handlers for daring to say he had to be dumped; by Davey Jnr's friends for demanding (successfully) Ian's dismissal for his Keystone Kops management style—and now by Iggy's new guard.

So, like many others, whose private views I echo publicly, I am retiring to the fence to sit out what remains of the Ignatieff inter-regnum.

RH

From: Apps_Alfred
To: Ray Heard
Sent: Friday, April 02, 2010 11:37 PM
Subject: That was Disgusting

The 'elite' conference had 30,000 participants. You are a complete asshole.

WHENEVER POLICIES were debated among Canadian Liberals, the word "Kingston" was the magic mantra. Caught in a similar quagmire when John Diefenbaker decisively defeated the Grits in 1958 by winning 208 seats (compared to the Liberals' puny rump of 48—which then was considered an incomprehensible disaster), Lester Pearson convened the Study Conference on National Problems at Queen's University in Kingston, Ontario, from September 6 to 10, 1960. It was a historic occasion. I was there and witnessed the magical rebirth of what had become a comatose political movement. Billed as a non-partisan assembly of liberal-minded Canadians, the conference's recommendations moved the party decisively to the left, away from its preoccupation with the gross national product. But the gabfest's main endowment was the new-wave liberals it attracted to switch into Liberals.

After the Pearson government came to power three years later, forty-eight of the conference's 196 delegates claimed senior government appointments. They included Keith Davey, who as national campaign director invented the modern Liberal party; Maurice Sauvé, who became a pivotal reformer of the Quebec wing and whose wife, Jeanne, became governor general; Claude Morin, who authored the Lesage government's social security platform and eventually became a cabinet minister under Premier René Lévesque as well as a paid stool pigeon for the

RCMP.* Along with Richard O'Hagan, the talented PR wizard who became the most credible spokesman for both Pearson and Trudeau. Kingston's most influential presence was the fiercely independent Quebec labour leader Jean Marchand, who eventually led Trudeau and Gérard Pelletier with him into the Liberal fold.

I recall most vividly the impact of the remarks delivered by Tom Kent, a former assistant editor of London's *Economist* and editor of the *Winnipeg Free Press*. His speech, "Towards a Philosophy of Social Security," provided most of the then radical ideas that propelled the Liberals back into office. (In his ninetieth year, Kent remains his party's social conscience, still thundering at the neo-con infidels at every opportunity.)

Professor Frank Underhill, the party's most dazzling political wit, delivered the closing address. He spoke of his dedication to the cause with the effortless erudition of a great classical scholar, then delivered this stinging valedictory. "At times," he confessed that when voting Liberal, "I have had to hold my nose while marking the ballot." He had been a founder of the CCF before becoming a Liberal, and was a serious iconoclast and reformer who was still queasy at betting on the party as the best way to drive social change.

Though just like Ignatieff's version of a thinkers' conference, the meeting had been billed as a nonpartisan event meant to bring together non-Conservative, non-socialist thinkers, its real purpose was to provide the Liberals with some badly needed policy momentum. Pearson, who had been chosen party leader two years previously, had experienced a sour debut in the House

---

* *That became a cause célèbre for a while but the controversy fizzled out when Morin assured his critics that he had paid income tax on his stipends.*

of Commons. Having lost power in 1957 after a twenty-two-year run, party members didn't know how to behave in opposition—and wanted to shed that demeaning label before they learned how to live with it.

(Grits have typically been lousy in opposition, having had so little experience with it. From 1990 to 1993, Chrétien put on a clinic of how *not* to behave like an official opposition—even with the Mulroney government imploding, Chrétien could muster so little interest in the role that Canadians noticed, and the Liberals' standing in the polls nosedived to around 20 percent. Turner should have quit on election night in 1984, since he couldn't control his caucus during the Mulroney era and made history mainly by becoming the victim of so many plots that he had to inspect the name plate on his office door to make sure he was still the leader. Dion and Ignatieff were also catastrophic, and compounding the fact that they were fish out of water and out of power was the lingering Chrétien-Martin wars that so devastated the party, and have not been settled, even now.)

Marchand, then president of the Quebec-based Confederation of National Trade Unions and attending his first Liberal meeting, made some stirring remarks that left their effect on Pearson, who later as prime minister, invited Marchand into his cabinet, granted him almost unprecedented powers and for a time personally pushed him as his successor, before switching his allegiance to Trudeau. (Marchand eliminated himself from contention, mainly because of his lack of fluent English.) Also there was Maurice Lamontagne, a Harvard-trained economist who was Pearson's chief Quebec adviser. "The ultimate objective of economic activity is the maximum common welfare," he stated, going against the economic orthodoxy of his time.

Kingston worked because it gave voice to a new generation of small-l liberals who could be drafted into the party because they had faith that Pearson was the kind of leader who could take their ideas, then march into electoral battle with them and eventually make some of them come true. Ignatieff never engendered that kind of faith from his followers. He could quickly grasp new ideas, but he seldom translated them into action plans.

One idea that came up at the Kingston conference was to revive the old slogan "Tory Times Are Hard Times" in order to undercut Diefenbaker. Prime ministers Louis St. Laurent and William Lyon Mackenzie King had used the phrase to kill Tory chances for a generation. The motto dated back to the time when R. B. Bennett, a hard rock Tory from Calgary, was Canada's prime minister for the worst (1930–1935) of the Depression years. At one election rally, when St. Laurent repeated the slogan, pointing out that Liberal times were good times, a heckler yelled: "It's a coincidence!" St. Laurent, who had earned his nickname Uncle Louis for being kind to political heretics, nodded and replied: "Ah yes, my friend, but which coincidence would you rather have?"

AT A PRIVATE OTTAWA DINNER party on April 6, 1988, held to mark the twentieth anniversary of Pierre Trudeau's assumption of power, the former prime minister laid out a political agenda for the future that contained an interesting catchphrase. "For too long," he proclaimed, "we have experimented with the dark side of excellence. For too long this country has suffered from politics that stresses economic efficiency instead of social fairness—and it's in that direction our party must make its next policy thrust."

"When we talk about 'the dark side of excellence,'" explained Senator Jack Austin, the intellectual godfather of the idea, "our concern is with the loss of tolerance, the absence of compassion and the downgrading of fairness, as expressed in this neo-conservative age. There has been a hard edge in the Conservative's pursuit of national competitiveness and a subsequent dilution of optimism among Canadians. In contrast, Liberal policy for forty years was based on the politics of optimism through the emphasis on equality of opportunity."

Austin, who had been Trudeau's principal secretary and later became his powerful minister of state for social development, carefully differentiated between the Liberal idea of individual, state-guaranteed rights and the collective concepts of the Tories. Conservative ideas, he claimed, depend on benefits trickling down from a process that inevitably strengthens the already strong. "Under the Mulroney government," he charged, "income disparity began to widen and its changes in the tax system reduced the impact of progressive taxation, putting ever more economic power in fewer and fewer hands. Instead, governments must return to the animating idea of fairness. A country is not a business and a government should stand for much more than economic efficiency. It's 'the dark side of excellence' that throws people below the fairness line, because those who have already succeeded maintain a vested psychological interest in the lack of success of others in the system."

Austin and the growing number of influential Liberals who shared his views hoped that future Liberal leadership conventions wouldn't become popularity contests. "I don't believe," he told me at the time, "that to be successful a political leader needs to be personally strident nor make more and more spectacular promises to offer even richer rewards for the self-interest of the already comfortable. People no longer believe that governments can deliver everything. The age of political magic is over. Hard work, fairness and realism—that's what matters now."

While Austin worried about the size of the federal deficit, he firmly opposed any retreat from universality in social programmes. "If we maintain proper standards of fairness, sacrifices as well as benefits will have to be equally distributed," he insisted. "The principle of universality was originally based on the idea that there was a charter of economic rights for all Canadians in which each citizen is entitled to basic support. Those who advocate doing away with universality are basically saying that society will confer special benefits on the needy, which hurts people's pride and sense of optimism."

Austin, whose interests later switched to expanding trade with Asia, became a sort of permanent Liberal think tank, along with Tom Axworthy and Ray Heard. The idea of another major conference became a mythical Watch on the Rideau, with diverse interests anxious to proceed with some sort of master plan but no one sure who would take the first step.

The odds of even fielding another conference with the impact on the party, and the nation, of the Kingston conference were slim, not because of the cost of such an affair, but because the kind of political thinkers who would devote their lives to the party's and Canada's benefit only exist in the Liberals' storied past.

The only concrete suggestion out of the whole Montreal exercise was that the Grits would veto the upcoming Tory cut in corporate taxes and use the proceeds for progressive legislation of some sort. This outcome was a far cry from the Kingston Conference, which fed Liberal policy for a decade or more and actually was responsible for generating ideas that brought the Liberals back to power. It was some sort of sign of the times, and the state of Liberal Canada, that in Montreal, with rare exceptions, the speakers were mostly showing off how much they knew about their areas of expertise and appeared so careful not to appear political that they really said nothing of interest at all.

15. The Bus Ride Where Ignatieff Went Wild

*"I'm up against the most uncivil and ruthless government
in the history of the country."*

—MICHAEL IGNATIEFF, 2010

CANADA'S CULTURE CAN'T be defined by trying to guess how many angels dance on the head of Margaret Atwood. It's best caught at summer bake sales, corn roasts, county fairs, and country music festivals where singers search for their humanity while listeners catch its echoes deep inside themselves.

That was the captivating forty-three-day quest Michael Ignatieff undertook in his summer 2010 cross-country marathon, which saw him and his cavalcade hunkered down in a bus that took them to 130 events in ridings that Donolo and the members of his brains trust categorized as winnable seats.

I joined part of the tour and found Ignatieff in the best frame of mind since he'd dumped his crew and decided to tackle the Harper juggernaut. He described to me the epiphany that marked his summer jaunt: his realization, at long last, that the political game was not really about *him* but about *them*—the voters. Ignatieff spent the rest of summer taking advantage of that shift in perspective, attempting with all his might to imprint his presence on the national conscience at the same time as Stephen Harper remained obsessed with defending innocent citizens against the toxic dangers of filling out census forms.

On the road, I judged Ignatieff's success by applying the umbrella test: when it rained at monsoon strength during his speech he had no choice but to get soaked. The test was how many in the audience expressed their allegiance by closing their own umbrellas in solidarity and acceptance of his message. In the instances I witnessed, there were just enough umbrella-closers to be noticeable, even though they often looked a bit embarrassed as the raindrops kept falling on their heads. To make the point: Canadians are not politically demonstrative, but maybe our pollsters could start measuring the closed umbrella factor—within acceptable margins of error, of course. I watched Ignatieff get drenched at his Brantford, Ont., rally, where it poured as if Noah was about to launch his ark, then swim back to his seat, grinning all the way, and waving at the odd umbrella-closer. The message was clear: Ignatieff's chief opponent—with his meticulous helmet of hair and his distaste for the slightest show of emotion—would never even try to duplicate Ignatieff's aquatic feats.

Back on the bus that day, the Liberal leader sat down beside me and let himself go. It was the best interview he ever gave me, and after the whole debacle was over, I did think that if people could have only heard the way he talked to me on the bus, and if he'd managed to make his actions speak as loud as these words, there might have been a different outcome. Or maybe I'm dreaming in technicolour here, as he really never did seem to realize that most of the people turning out to his rallies weren't the great mass of Canadian voters but the remnants of the country's partisan Liberals.

"THIS THING IS BEGINNING to seep into my bones as never before," he said, as we rolled toward the next stop on the tour. "I live in a world where perception is reality but I don't want to be fooled by appearances. What I saw out there was a deepening distaste for Harper. What's sticking in people's throats is the way he governs—proroguing parliament; failing to show respect to the courts; the census controversy, which makes him appear to believe you can run a government without valid information; the single-source fighter contract, which will cost Canadians $16 billion without *any* public justification. This stuff accumulates. People are connecting with us and feel seriously concerned.

"I'm up against the most uncivil and ruthless government in the history of the country," he declared, his eyebrows in attack mode. "You can't be a centrist on tactics alone. I'm a centrist by temperament and persuasion. That's a core affirmation of where I've been all my life. I want to get rid of all this 'natural party of government' stuff; it's arrogant and speaks of entitlement. We have to earn the right to govern.

"A lot of people feel alarmed by Harper's fundamental contempt for institutions. If you're a party of the centre, one of the things you understand about this country is that there is a set of constraints on prime ministerial power—the courts, the Charter, federalism itself, cabinet, caucus, parliament, independent regulators. Harper has a systematic hostility to all of them, and that's the core issue: that's what people fear and distrust. That's why they won't give him a majority.

"There's been a spine of consistency in the Liberal party that has resulted in a Canada that has a centre of gravity consistently five percent to the left of the United States. And it basically says that the government believes in a market economy, a market society, and in personal responsibility, but nobody's going to let you fall through the cracks. What Harper feeds on is disillusion with how government delivers. The challenge for Liberalism is not merely to champion good government, but to defend the idea of responsive, compassionate, caring service delivery where government meets the people. Harper just preys on the disillusion with politics. Less participation is good for Stephen Harper. More participation is good for us. . . .

"The times I've been happiest in politics, have been sitting on a stool in front of a room full of fellow Canadians and I remember the ones I enjoyed the most, and they weren't necessarily easy. Orillia — 400 people; Edmonton on a Saturday night — 600 people; Brantford — 450, just sitting there with a mike. People come at you. And Mr. Harper doesn't do that. Canadians don't react terribly well to things that are overproduced. Canadians will react well if you just say, 'I'm showing up. Let's talk. Let's talk politics.' It's important that I set up a contrast between the way I do politics and the way he does.

"We're living in a country where half of the aboriginal kids don't finish high school. We're looking at a growing gap between the successive previous generation of immigrants like my dad, and the generation coming in from Africa and Asia. We're looking at infrastructural deficits. You come back from Shanghai and think, 'Holy smoke. Are we dreaming here?' Do we think it's acceptable to have traffic as bad, as snarled, and our infrastructure as behind as it is in Toronto, Montreal? Only Vancouver is getting up to speed. There's a lot of unfinished business in this country that is crucial to us being just, and crucial to us being competitive.

"When I'm wading into the crowd, I'm not just shaking hands — I'm listening, talking," he told me. "There was a woman who had *this* issue. There's another one with *that* issue. You can't do this job unless you make an institutional commitment to listen, not just a personal one. We've got to get some new people in here, young people. There are some stops we made during the tour where you go out there and some of these people have been with the Liberals for forty years. The party hasn't trained their own succession. All institutions have to be in the succession business. We've been too casual, sometimes brutally dismissive, about such lapses. There's a lot of unfinished business in this country that is crucial to us being just, and crucial to us being competitive. You need a nice centrist party that's going to get down there and do those things, one after the other, until they're done. And that's what I'm here to do."

That day he also talked about his power base. "I was born in Toronto, so my political experience comes out of being an Ontario Liberal. I've got family connections in Sherbrooke, Quebec. My entire family on my Russian side is very old. And I've got some serious roots in Maritime Canada, because so many of my people are buried there, in New Brunswick and Nova Scotia. So I feel at home in all those places, and I don't feel I need a particular regional base. That is, when I get up in Atlantic Canada and talk about my grand-ancestors, people understand that I have roots in the Maritimes that are real for me. I've walked the cemeteries, I've got background. When I'm in Quebec and talk about the fact that it was in Quebec that my Russian family started its new life, people connect with that.

"My driving motivation is that I don't want, at the end of my life, to say that I was merely a spectator," he said. "I want to put it all on the line. Our political system and the health of our country, and the health of our democracy require an alternative to this government, and I want to put it together. People say, 'Well, you know, these guys are creating a new normal.' And I think the 'new normal' is imperceptibly moving the country to the right, moving the whole centre of gravity of the country. And I'm trying to say, 'Let's not do that.' Canadians are so insecure about their economic future, so distracted by it, that they're not really listening terribly hard to anybody, and to the degree that I get up and say something, I'm being framed in a climate that's making me difficult to be heard. But I'm very persistent. I know when I'm striking a chord and when I'm not.

"People sniff a basic, partisan ruthlessness in these guys. . . . I don't want to play their game. They're not in the Canadian grain, and I've got to capture that, and express that, and get Canadians angry with the way they've been governed.

"People say, 'He doesn't have any policy.' Well, there's a whole vision of a learning society, and that's not trivial. You have a society where aboriginal kids aren't completing high school. You've got a society where immigrant kids aren't learning English well. You've got a society where people with learning disabilities aren't becoming fully literate either. You've got a society where a lot of kids can't get to post-secondary because they haven't got the money. You've got a society that's not ready for prime time, right? So, owning that space is one piece of the puzzle. Owning a space, owning a life that says, 'You don't have an economic future, unless we get environmentally sustainable and energy efficient.'

"Harper's saying we've got to choose between the economy and the environment. I don't think we'll have an economy unless we become environmentally sustainable, and fast. I've been coast to coast about thirty to forty times. This thing is now seeping into my bones—it wasn't true before. You can't get that vision of where you need to go overnight; you have to do it from the bottom up, not from the top down. It has to come from me listening to a lot of people. And I think a lot of my life prepares me well for all that. I've spent my life as a distiller, condenser and focuser of ideas.

I don't find a special originality, I find I just know how to distil and focus. I've taken a bunch of positions already that have gotten me into hot water, and I've stuck to them. Just the other day, I told my caucus, 'We're going to vote for a harmonized sales tax, because we think it's good public policy.' Well, I'll tell you, Peter, most of that caucus wasn't too happy. I'm aware that being a leader means not walking around following the lowest common denominator, but making choices.

"Now, Christ knows, I've made some mistakes. I'm not on Mars here. But the rap that I can't choose and I can't make up my mind is not the problem. The problem is that this party needs to change, this party has to grow, this party needs to renew, and I need to give it back its sense of confidence, its sense of fight. We've got to be aware that we're not the natural governing party, we're in opposition—we've got a hell of a lot of work to do.

"People underestimate my resilience. I've had a year of unmitigated, negative attacks. And I'm still standing. They've spent $10 million trying to take me apart. There was a period in September when I was watching baseball games at night when I'd come home. I couldn't—literally couldn't—watch an inning of baseball on TSN without seeing my own goddamned face on there saying, 'I'm only in it for myself. I'm only passing through.' But I'm still here. And I feel fine. I feel fine. And am I willing to fight? You betcha.

"Let's get some perspective here. This is—this is what you go through. You've got to earn it. You've got to show you want it, and you've got to show you can take it. You've got to be able to dish it out. I don't think anyone can quite expect it.

"I know I have a reputation for being an arrogant son of a gun, but I didn't actually think the whole world would fall down at my feet, acknowledging my superior virtues. No, this is politics. Never forget, the first political meeting I went to, there were people with placards saying, 'Get the hell out of here.' I fought from the minute I arrived in Canadian politics. I fought ever since. I fought for my right to be heard. I fought for the right to be considered a goddamned Canadian. I've had to fight for everything. Right? The image that I can't fight has been comprehensively disproved by the fact that I'm here, talking to you. And I'll continue to fight because I'm angry. You bet I'm angry. Instead of getting mad, I want to get even."

From that day on, Michael Ignatieff was no longer seeking redemption. Now he wanted revenge.

THE POLITICAL DEEDS AND MISDEEDS that account for the destiny of a candidate for the country's highest political office flow as much from luck and timing as his character and his intentions. So much of the political game is chance, and how you seize those chances.

As a student and teacher of history, Ignatieff took a fatalistic approach to politics, because, despite his inspired talk on the bus, the essential issues would always remain insoluble. All that a sensible man could do was work out his destiny with as little unpleasantness as possible. To shrug and smile sometimes remained the precisely perfect response to the preposterous incongruities of the daily political challenges. To Ignatieff, the British tradition of muddling through struck him as right.

Even when he was subject to deadly daily pummeling by the Harper assassination squad, whose members never allowed truth-in-advertising to influence their TV messages, in private Ignatieff usually complained more in sorrow than in anger. He took shelter in his self-confidence and his past accomplishments. At the same time, he mostly acted within the consciousness of his own limitations and of the voters' awareness of them.

The simple fact was that he had always had trouble dealing with groups—unless they were students in his classroom, where he had a natural advantage. This problem of being unable to communicate political passion confirmed him in the public mind as a curiously disengaged politician with no urgent agenda of his own. So he tried hard to make up for any such perceived short-coming by touring the country like a whirling space cadet.

But (as the polls confirmed) these excursions did little to improve his public image. The sessions did allow ordinary citizens to express their unadorned views, and he answered all their questions. And answered them well. But by not using these occasions to push his own policies, voters complained that he didn't have any.

His negotiable approach to the major issues of the day marked him as a politician drifting with the tide of events. Stephen Harper's tough love didn't provide any solace, but neither did Ignatieff's apparent inability to take a stand that voters felt they could count on.

Though he could describe to me his Canadian bona fides, he really had no base: unlike political lifers he had no root constituency of his own. As the member for Etobicoke (who insisted on living in his condo in Yorkville), he could not claim to represent the aspirations of any particular region or group, except maybe for academics, many of whom had disowned him for his support of George W. Bush during the Iraq war.

Though he applied gobs of goodwill to the task, he could never identify himself with Canada's grassroots politics. His views were intelligent, tolerant and compassionate, but they were held once removed from the passions and complexities of Canadian realities, English or French. Ignatieff's supporters maintained that he was more than credible, that he was an informed, thoughtful and articulate guy who was serious about his mission and his politics.

They also said that he was let down by his own strategists. But wasn't he supposed to be a master at learning from experience?

Harper was actually beating him on that score. Even if the Conservative prime minister wasn't noticeably enlarged by his sojourn at the peak of Canada's political system, and remained the prisoner of an ideology that found few echoes outside the prim, doctrinaire precincts of the neo-cons, Harper was demonstrating the welcome glimmer of genuine pragmatism, while Ignatieff still appeared lost in the clouds.

Harper, owner of the best medieval mind in the Commons, proved himself capable of reaching out to the political centre. (Though I'd argue it's still too early to be sure whether his journey on little cat feet toward the political centre is anything more than a tactical hip-hop, or the real thing.)

One secret of success, as noted by Benjamin Disraeli, the most cunning of British statesmen, is that great politicians must feel comfortable both in themselves and in their times. Though many of us might like to deny it, Harper may in fact be a creature of his times. Ignatieff showed little sign of being able to master the politics of his time and gave little evidence that he was comfortable with himself.

The function of democratic leadership is to respect the past, manage the present and enlarge the future. The incumbent must possess grace under pressure, be aggressive without being contentious, decisive without being arrogant and compassionate without sounding confused. The ideal PM must respect ideas but not substitute ideas for action, fashion resonant political prose but not become intoxicated by the sound of his own voice, be pragmatic but spurn the arithmetic of expediency.

No coalition of political forces can match prime ministerial power, yet the high office's holders find themselves shackled, like latter-day Gullivers, by tendrils of regional disparity, burgeoning social problems, economic dislocations and the iron-lunged complaints of special interest groups who won't take maybe for an answer.

Custom and precedent have vastly multiplied prime ministerial powers: they are able to make major appointments, speak for the country as its chief diplomat, set cabinet agendas, be the final arbiter of ministerial budgets and rally the country in these terrorizing times. Former U.S. president Woodrow Wilson might have been talking about Canadian prime ministers when he described the American presidency as being "so much greater than any man could honestly imagine himself to be, that the most he can do is look self-possessed enough to occupy it."

The longing for a historical legacy afflicts all prime ministers and prompts them to stretch their mandates beyond daily operational demands. Yet most of our recent leaders have lacked any noble cause, beyond clobbering the other guy. What we need is a prime minister who can inspire us to the contemporary equivalent of a national railroad. What we've been getting is the political equivalent of the fakers in the World Wrestling Federation.

TO PERFORM HIS TASK, a prime minister must possess knowledge, power and purpose. Harper has the knowledge and the power but his ultimate purpose remains wrapped in mystery. Ignatieff had the knowledge, never had the power, and failed to define his purpose, beyond replacing the guy with the hair helmet.

While the Tory leader has had no trouble maintaining distance between himself and the people, Ignatieff was unable to create any sense of awe or respect or faith in Canada's voters. Though he could talk the talk, he behaved as if he would rather be himself than a memorable leader.

Interview Excerpt: **Ignatieff on Canada and Harper**

It truly is driven by the land. We were up in Badger Lodge, a boat-plane ride away from Yellowknife, sat out on the porch and looked out into the northern lights. It slowly dawns on you, there is not another human soul in front of you, 180 degrees, for many, many hundreds of miles. That's a primal Canadian thing.

I often have a sense that Canadians know, like maybe the Laplanders do, or the Bushmen of the Kalahari—the survival thing is there, the prudence, the caution, the sense that there aren't enough people. On the positive side, there is the incredible warmth, the quite special warmth of Canadian communities. Because we all know, beyond the city lights, there's nothing.

We've also got a constant struggle to elaborate and sustain a sense of pride next door to this gigantic, self-advertising behemoth to the south.

And the other thing, finally, that has changed every Canadian who does it, is to go from one language to the other in the middle of a sentence. Our political culture is absolutely distinct. It changes the character of the people who live it.

I just don't think Harper understands. He speaks French, and that's to his credit. What he doesn't understand is that this breeds moderation into the national character. We cannot afford to be an ideological community. We cannot afford to be a country in which adversaries are enemies. We cannot afford the luxury of hyper-partisanship. . . .

Something I passionately believe in [though] is that Canada is not fragile; its secret is that nothing is taken for granted here. We have to work at this every day, and we cannot stop trying to understand people with whom we disagree and we cannot banish them. . . . It's just the wrong way to go.

16. How the Grits Lost Their Mojo

The Liberals had $23 million in the kitty but couldn't get at it.
That was why the party failed to launch its own offensive
to challenge Harper's deadly negative ad campaign.

BY THE SPRING OF 2011, Ignatieff was ready to take the greatest of gambles: in April, just as the first buds appeared, he pulled
the trigger that would set off the May 2 election, based on the
Harper Tories having been found guilty of parliamentary contempt, the most severe such condemnation in Canadian history.
Even if the House of Commons had become one of the most
unruly of the democratic assemblies, this had never happened
before. The government had rudely refused to honour the request
of a multi-party committee to reveal the real costs of the Stealth
F-35 Fighter jets, the most expensive military purchase in the
nation's history, and the price tag on the Harper anti-crime bill.

This was accompanied by a truckload of other obfuscations
dating back to the Afghan detainee scandal, International
Cooperation Minister Bev Oda's admission that she had lied to
parliament—and other serious misdeeds that the Conservative
government chose to ignore. On March 9, the speaker of the
House of Commons found there was sufficient evidence of

contempt to send the matters to their respective parliamentary committees for consideration; he committees found the charges to be true in all cases. On March 25, the Commons voted the government guilty of contempt for failing to provide the cost estimates, and thereby launched the 2011 election. Harper's Tories had seldom appeared so vulnerable.

Who could have believed that in the heat of the election these weighty issues were not debated and were only vaguely mentioned. But that was what happened as the party campaigns peaked and dramatically altered Canada's electoral map, wiping out more than half of the Liberal and almost all the Bloc Québécois MPs, boosting the New Democrats to the edge of power and rewarding the Conservatives for their misdeeds with a generous majority. It didn't seem fair, but as President John Kennedy found out when his planned invasion to free Cuba turned into a fiasco: "Nobody promised fair." Certainly the Grits could vouch for that, having been reduced to the indignity of third-party status, a one-way ticket to political purgatory.

IN THE GALAXY OF GLARING ERRORS that caused the Liberals' free fall in the 2011 election was the startling absence in their platform of anything to indicate that they had always been Canada's party of patriotism. That was how they saw themselves and that was how they had campaigned in previous outings. But this time, the Grits surrendered that precious territory—gave it away without even a whimper of explanation—and substituted no ready or marketable emotion of the kind that swings elections. The Family Pack was as good as it got, a soup-to-nuts set of initiatives funded by freezing corporate taxes that would support Canadians of all ages. It only opened up another area of attack from the Tories that the Liberals were promoting an out-of-date tax-and-spend scheme.

Instead the patriotic card was turned into a defining negative by the Conservatives' massive attack advertising campaign aimed at demolishing Michael Ignatieff's stature as a Canadian. The devastating Conservative assault was based not on any discernable lack of regard for his home country, but on his physical absence from its shores. The Tories' subliminal suggestion that residence and patriotism were somehow interchangeable made no sense except as part of the Harper government's determination to ban any level of sophistication that departed from the down-home Tim Hortons mentality. You were either one of *us* or one of *them*. It was a triumph of division versus unity—and it was effective and deadly.

The Liberals failed to realize how fundamental to their story the questioning of Ignatieff's patriotism would turn out to be. Every time out of the gate when he was PM, Jean Chrétien screamed his patriotism from the rooftops and the mountain tops, sang the praises of the Rockies, of a bigger Canada, of a more international Canada that would make its citizens [and voters] proud. That ought to have been Ignatieff territory. His books preached it. There are few better records of Canadian patriotism than *Blood and Belonging*. But Ignatieff and his campaign chair and advisers did not develop that link to the party's past, or their leader's own past writings. Whether it was left on the cutting-room floor by inadvertence or on purpose by his handlers isn't clear. But what was clear is that the campaign was selling Ignatieff as a standard, slightly left-wing politician, and could not get that vague a message to stick under the blanket Conservative propaganda assault. They couldn't even seem to make an issue of how much money the Conservative party was willing to spend to basically propagate a lie: $10 million, in order to portray the Liberal leader as an opportunist come home for *his* advantage, instead of ours.

The attack ads defined Ignatieff in a way the Liberals did not—it turned out, could not—answer. Not because the accusations were true, but because they were repeated with brainwashing frequency.

HOW THAT LAPSE HAPPENED is the great untold story of the campaign. There was, during the 2011 election no public proof that anything positive was stirring inside the Liberal camp, but in fact nearly $5 million quietly trickled into Liberal headquarters. Those voluntary contributions were greater than the totals mailed in during the last three elections.

The Liberal party's fundraising was actually quite good, much better than that of the NDP or Bloc. The problem for the Liberals was that the power brokers divided the spoils. The Grits had the highest infrastructure costs of all the political parties—every federal-provincial association demanded their own office budgets and staff, plus there was a commission for every special interest within the party, each with its own budget. The Liberals' rotten internal culture meant that the power brokers would rather the party die than lose their little fiefdoms. The party thus left its leader helpless to defend himself. Too busy dividing what remained of fundraising dollars and the public subsidy between its fiefdoms and power brokers, the party was unable to save any for the response to the negative advertising that Ignatieff so desperately needed.

Gordon Gibson, who was a former senior aide to Pierre Trudeau as well a former leader of the BC Liberals, put the essential problem most succinctly: "The Liberal party is in great danger of becoming an irrelevance. Alas, that assumes there is still something called the Liberal party. What used to be a genuine, large and cooperative organization of like-minded people has been turned into an empty shell by centralizing leaders, and is now populated largely by celebrity followers and power seekers."

"It's not that the money wasn't there to fight the negative ads," one of the senior Liberal strategists told me. "We had $23 million in the kitty but nobody could figure out how to get at it. The NDP can run a national party organization and win three times as many seats as we did, on a quarter of our budget. How many regional offices does the Conservative party have? Certainly not the twelve we do.

"Because every Liberal fiefdom demanded their dollars, we didn't have access to the funds required to answer the Tory propaganda. Not because the party didn't have money but because we were spending it on stupid things, like provincial and territorial associations and the Women's Commission, and all these little party subdivisions that demanded their own budgets. Neither the Tories nor the NDP operate like that. Unlike the Conservative party, we're not a single entity but a coalition of many different subdivisions, commissions, individual fiefdoms, and provincial associations within a federal structure. Everybody covets their budgets and it's extraordinarily expensive. For example, we've had to hire fifty people to staff a simple nomination meeting. Why? Because we're still yesterday's party."

Ignatieff, with his easier manners and his rolled-up shirtsleeves, simply could not meet enough people face to face to counter the relentless impression of the advertising. And for some reason the campaign didn't use the popularity of Liberals of impeccable integrity and high profile, such as Senator Roméo Dallaire, to support the leader. Dallaire had actually been a fellow for a year at Harvard's Carr Center when Ignatieff was running it. He was an Ignatieff admirer, and though, with his focus on humanitarian, aboriginal and veterans' issues, he rode above the usual partisan hustle, he might have been amenable to campaigning on his friend's behalf, as he had done during Ignatieff's 2006 leadership run, when he'd introduced him to a rowdy crowd of young Liberals at the Jello nightclub in Montreal. "I'm not just here as a friend and a buddy," Dallaire said, "but because Michael Ignatieff is the only person who can articulate a vision of Canada, who can move the yardstick of humanity, who can move the country well beyond the borders in which we find ourselves." But in 2011 Dallaire wasn't asked for such help.

Liberal candidates reported from their doorstep tours that an inordinate number of people volunteered that they didn't approve of Michael Ignatieff. When they were asked why, they would parrot the Harper attack ads, word for word. ("He's not there for you . . ."). When confronted about that parroting, they would be offended, and insist, "I wasn't influenced by those ads."

Guy Giorno, who had been Harper's chief of staff and ran the Tory 2011 campaign, certainly had no doubts about their supreme significance in the election's results. "Mr. Ignatieff has no one to blame but himself for not taking the time to respond to the ads," he declared. "The issue was not the fact that he spent so much time living and teaching abroad. Rather, it was his failure to explain his reasons for returning to Canada. Ordinary Canadians said it looked like he came back just to run for prime minister. You can agree or disagree with the sentiment but that was a real-person reaction. His failure to define himself was his choice."

EVERYONE COMPLAINED that Ignatieff never took their advice and that was why he got into so much trouble. Not true. He did listen to advice, hours of it, but he took it from everyone at the same time. This resulted in his treating all sources of counsel as if they had equal credibility. Spending so much time abroad, he only had a brief base of experience from which to judge his advisers. For example, there were dozens of stories, some even published, that he refused to rehearse for the English debate in the 2011 campaign because he had been an ace debater at university and didn't need a refresher course.

In fact, he did rehearse, and quite diligently, with Glenn O'Farrell, a Canadian broadcast executive and former head of the Canadian Broadcasting Association. Not exactly a force of nature as a pretend interrogator. Dumping the ever-wise Rex Murphy, who was responsible for Dion's unexpectedly good performance two years earlier, was a serious mistake, and might have contributed to Ignatieff's lacklustre performance in the national televised debate. The Liberals' own pollster, Michael Marzolini—the chairman and founder of Pollara, one of the best in Canada—was quoted in the *Globe and Mail* after the election was over, saying that Ignatieff's dull showing in the leaders' debates was the beginning of the end. The rise of Jack Layton and the NDP began with Layton so clearly speaking for and to ordinary Canadians during the debates, while Ignatieff just could not make the connection on TV. (Marzolini also complained in mid-campaign to a senior Liberal that the party was paying his fees but paying no attention to his results: "They've managed to do the opposite of everything I've advised.")

The ebbs and flows of the campaign were meticulously tracked by other polling companies, of course, none more imaginatively than Angus Reid's outfit, whose vice president Mario Conseco, provided me with a private briefing that included a minute-by-minute review of that pivotally significant English leaders' debate. The most dramatic trend during the last two weeks of the campaign was a tectonic shift away from the Liberals. Their retention rate from the previous election was down to fifty-seven percent, compared to the Tories' eighty-two percent and the NDP's eighty-five percent. This meant that close to a half of the people who had voted Liberal in 2008, when Stéphane Dion was leader, abandoned their choice.

"It became clear as the campaign went on that the Liberals would finish below the dreaded Mendoza line," Conseco concluded (baseball player Mario Mendoza was known for his defensive skills as a shortstop but was a terrible hitter, often batting less than one hit for every five at-bats, excluding walks).

After the first week of the campaign, Ignatieff's approval rating jump from nineteen percent to twenty-five percent but NDP support moved up from thirty-seven percent to forty-three. Then came the English debate, and that was where Ignatieff's stumble, Harper's unbeatable lead and Layton's rise had powerful effects. Harper dominated the debate by the simple tactic of never moving his eyes away from the TV cameraman, which had him looking straight into the camera—directly into the audience's eyes—while all the other participants looked sidewise at one another when asking or answering questions.

Given that Ignatieff was a former professor in the area of international human rights, the expectation was that in the section featuring him debating Layton on Afghanistan, he would shine. Layton, who was not supposed to be a leader in foreign affairs, scored the highest of all when he expressed the simple wish: "Bring the troops home from Afghanistan." Ignatieff's comeback—"Help the Afghans defend themselves for three more years"—got the lowest level of approval of the entire segment.

In the final part of the debate, Ignatieff's summarizing view that the choice on May 2 was "between a Harper government and a Liberal government" went off the bottom of the charts—south of the Mendoza Line. (There must be a country and western song about that by now.)

David Peterson, Alfred Apps, David Smith, Gordon Ashworth and other Liberal gurus complained that no one was doing anything as the party's popularity kept slip-sliding away, with approval ratings ticking down steadily from the roughly 30 percent range where they'd started. "How is this possible after nine months of campaigning by Michael Ignatieff?" they would ask. "It must be somebody's fault." By election day, Liberal support had dropped to 18 percent. But the most disturbing statistic was the Liberal leader's *national* approval rating, on the cusp of the election, was exactly the same as that of Green Party Leader Elizabeth May, though she hadn't stirred out of her riding.

IGNATIEFF KNEW he wasn't going to win two weeks before voting day, including his own riding. The so-called National Liberal Team had assigned only a skeleton crew to Ignatieff's constituency and did no polling. They paid virtually no attention to the key riding that could easily have been won.

He ended up hoping for fifty seats. And if he had won his own constituency, he would have stuck around until his succession was arranged, rather than exiting to see Bob Rae take over as interim leader. The party's worst drubbing was in the Toronto area, once the Grits' private preserve, which went largely Tory. Yet on election night, a few brave souls—or dreamers who refused to credit the nightmare unfolding on their TV sets—were already reorganizing area ridings, not ready to abandon what had been their fortress.

ANOTHER GLARING GAP in the Liberals' aspirations of returning to their accustomed roost as the country's natural leaders? The party attracted no new star candidates who would create a buzz and deliver regional votes. The closest they got was Dan Veniez, who qualified as such a star in every respect but one: he was correctly perceived by the party's Old Guard as a threat to their existing structures. He wasn't one of them. Fearing reform more than Stephen Harper, they kept Veniez at bay.

Over his many years in politics, Jack Austin has seen political stars come and go. About Veniez, he said: "Dan was the best new candidate fielded by any party in British Columbia in the last election. His insight into issues of public policy, his presentation to his constituents in countless face-to-face meetings, and in thoughtful articles in local papers and media, and his clear advocacy, delivered with honesty and courage, against the prevailing popular 'wisdoms' have created a following who wants to see him in public life." Veniez is the prototype of the kind of candidates we need in all parties, the style of practical idealist the Liberals must attract if they have any hope of survival—a pedigreed political animal who believes that Canada's future should be built on dreams as well as appetites, and wants to prove his outspoken worth. "It's time for us to stop complaining from the cheap seats and give of ourselves back to Canada," he says. "Doing so is risky in every way I can think of. . . . Yet it feels very, very right to me. We must make public service a respected and desirable vocation again. The more of us there are, the more will want to join us."

RAISED IN THE SEPARATIST working class suburb Pointe-Aux-Trembles on the east side of Montreal where his father was an Anglophone truck driver and his mother a *pure lain* Québécois who worked in the local Canadian International Paper Company plant, Veniez attended the party's national convention in 1982 and was elected a vice-president for the Young Liberals. The following year he worked on John Turner's leadership campaign with Denis Coderre, later Ignatieff's Quebec lieutenant, but Veniez became disillusioned and switched to the Tories, falling under the spell of the youthful Brian Mulroney, then about to form his first government. He moved to Ottawa where he worked in the offices of three ministers.

He left politics to become a senior vice-president of Repap Enterprises, a lively pulp and paper company, and spent most of his career in the private sector as a senior executive, strategy consultant and entrepreneur. He turned into a Stephen Harper supporter in 2006. "I wanted him to succeed," says Veniez. "He was from the West, obviously smart, while the Liberals had become like the PC party that I left in 1992—tired and intellectually bankrupt. Like many Canadians I didn't trust the Reform crowd, their social conservative bent, or their dogmatic theology on economics, social and foreign policy. But I also thought that the party was maturing and that they had renounced their populist and evangelical impulses. I was wrong.

"Whether Harper stays or goes, the base of the Conservative party will remain the small-tent western and rural populist base, and its Christian fundamentalist core. And that's anathema to my essential DNA. The Conservative party and its leader are viscerally angry. That is an ingrained part of who they are and what they represent. They remain a protest party, even in power, and have turned themselves into a protest government. They manage by negatives and are genetically incapable of inspiring hope or thinking big. They attack, assassinate character, tell lies, lower the bar on public discourse, and engage in tactical and divisive wedge politics and governance. They tap into people's anxieties, fears, and prejudices, then seek to exploit them to the hilt for electoral advantage. The tone, strategy, and culture for this government are established by Stephen Harper, a cheap-shot artist and cynic of the highest order."

When I heard that Dan Veniez was intending to run for election as a Liberal in the West Vancouver-Sunshine Coast-Sea to Sky County constituency, I thought, at last, a positive sign for the Liberals. The riding he chose has the longest name (forty-eight characters) in the House of Commons; it's also one of Canada's largest by population (130,000) and area—stretching from West Vancouver, which has more billionaires than anywhere else in the country, to the Sunshine Coast, which has more hippies than trees—most of whom hang out at the Gumboot Café in Roberts Creek.Veniez was made for B.C. politics, except for two problems. He is one of the most articulate men I know, but is not expert in studied silences, the kind that Mike Harcourt, the NDP premier at the time I lived in the province, used to great effect. (It was only when Harcourt spoke that he got into trouble.) Veniez's more serious problem was—and is—that he may well be the last remaining idealist in Canadian politics. He believes that we are a smoothly functioning democracy, that honesty wins elections, and that elephants fly. How to do you deal with a guy like that?

Very carefully is one answer, but actually it's not that difficult—as long as you understand that you'll get the truth, the whole truth —and more truth than you really want to know.

This was the e-mail I received from Veniez on the morning after the 2011 election, just as Michael Grant Ignatieff, his party leader, was waking up to the worst humiliation in the annals of Liberal slaughters. "While smart, experienced, sophisticated, decent, and honest, I almost felt that I had to protect Michael, somehow," Veniez wrote. "I knew and felt that, underneath this exceptionally accomplished person, lay a flawed (as we all are) human being with scars and insecurities that would surface every now and then. Although that humanized him in my eyes, it also raised questions. Who is this guy really and deep down? What's he made of? Where are his kids and members of his family that we never saw? Why does he want to be prime minister?

"My single greatest and most profound disappointment in Ignatieff was that this extraordinary man of letters who I had gotten to know through his body of work bore no semblance whatsoever to Michael Ignatieff, MP and political leader. His writings reflected an intellectual range, courage, boldness, and insight that were remarkable. That was the man I had bought into. As Liberal leader much of his discourse had absolutely no relation to the author of *The Rights Revolution* and his magisterial biography of Berlin. It was almost as if he made a deliberate choice to ignore that guy, to become someone he wasn't, and recast himself as someone else that he could never be—a man of the people. . . . He was humbled by his countrymen like no leader of the Liberal party before him. He has to wear that and he knows it. Despite that burden, he was and remains a man of grace."

Now, that's about as barebones and painfully truthful an assessment any politician can make about any other. When I asked Veniez, who lost his own race to the Conservative candidate, to comment on the campaign's general outcome, his reply was just as straightforward: "Listen, the country made a perfectly rational decision. Think about it: did we really give them a compelling reason to vote for us? They sensibly chose the devil they knew rather than take a chance on Ignatieff, who they didn't. And as for the Liberal 'brand,' why the hell would they vote for us? Sponsorship was fresh in their minds; the party had, just a short time before, presented the Green Shift as the platform under a hapless leader. A massive 'carbon tax' in an incomprehensible election platform, just as the global financial system was crumbling! And this time, Canadians only saw the same front bench faces from a time they would rather forget. And they only saw that old sense of entitlement of a party that they felt had not learned the lessons of their recent defeats.

"All along Michael had to prove his Grit bona fides with a party establishment that didn't trust or like him. When he kept

saying, 'I knocked on doors for Pierre Trudeau, blah, blah, blah—
all that did was remind Canadians that Ignatieff was a blast from
the past—certainly not someone who would forge a new path.
Virtually everything he did reminded them of the Old Grits:
protecting his MPs on the Auditor General expense issue; the
'Mr. Harper, your time is up' line; and his leading of a rabidly
partisan and coarse parliamentary party in the House of Commons,
which had contributed to the country being so turned-off by the
daily circus of Question Period.

"In 2009 Liberals picked him for one reason and one reason
only—they were certain he could win. What most people forget is
how forgettable the Liberal Family Pack really was. How wholly
lacking in ambition. How devoid of a sense of purpose, and any
responsibility to deal boldly and substantively with the real and
fundamental questions we face as a country. 'Was this all a world-
class "thinker" could come up with?' was a reasonable question.
Jobs and competitiveness were given cursory mentions, at best,
and were far from top-of-mind considerations for Liberal policy-
makers. I had a tough time getting my arms around a gimmick like
the Family Pack. What is fundamental is the need for much more
efficient and competent use of our tax dollars, a welcoming invest-
ment climate, and the policies that foster a strong and dynamic
economy to pay for a strong and sustainable social safety net.

"In this election, our platform stood out for being better
than the rest only because the others were even worse. So, at
the end of the day, the country made a perfectly sensible and
rational judgment.

"At the same time," Veniez wrote, "there's no question that
Michael's true potential was not on display during the cam-
paign, because I don't believe he followed his own instincts.
From my vantage point, it looked to me like he felt he had to be

managed by polls and focus group-tested themes that he was told were absolute winners. Because of his inexperience, perhaps he didn't have confidence in his own judgment in the political realm. There was a huge chasm I'd say between Ignatieff the candidate in the general election and the man I watched so closely during his first leadership run. What I saw in the campaign was a guy trying to be someone he was not. The anti-politician intellectual shaping himself into someone he was told he had to be. Ideas matter.

"And on that front, the Liberals leadership did not give Canadians a substantive and over-arching rationale for supporting it. It was a campaign predicated in large part on getting rid of Harper, not defining what the Liberal party stands for. I believe this was one of Michael's greatest weaknesses. How ironic is that? This man of letters, of ideas, known globally as an outstanding public intellectual, could not and did not design a platform or articulate a compelling vision for Canada while he was leader of the party. My guess is that he got suckered into what he knew he must resist: the vortex of the Liberal party's sick culture."

But one thing Veniez refuses to even mention, which is just as illustrative of the decline of the Liberal party and the failings of its most recent leader, is the story told to me by a couple of members of the national press corps on Ignatieff's 2010 Liberal Express bus tour. Veniez arranged an extra stop in West Vancouver so the leader could meet more of his constituents and, he must have assumed, anoint him as the party's new local standard-bearer. Ignatieff arrived on time and gave a splendid speech, but totally forgot to mention his candidate.

ON ELECTION NIGHT, the dreary hotel room at Toronto's Sheraton Centre was occupied by the stunned members of both of Ignatieff's retinues: Peter Donolo's wizards and the Old Gang, together for the first and last time: Sachin Aggarwal, Leslie Church, Mark Sakamoto, Alexis Levine, Adam Goldenberg, Jeff Kehoe and Marc Chalifoux.

As the evening wore on, and the dire results began to filter in, the loyalists began to realize that this was not just the loss of an election. They had actually received fewer than half of the dismal returns that had turned "Stéphane Dion" into Liberal swear words.

Ignatieff could not seem to absorb them. He'd done the equivalent of flying to the moon, and must have been wondering how this shocking result could have come from all those goddamn burgers he flipped and all those lies he heard from strangers who promised to vote for him. His disappointment bit into his face, hardened its topography and caused his eyes to water, though he maintained a frozen smile.

Patricia Sorbara, chief operating officer under Donolo, refused to tell Ignatieff (or maybe to believe) that they had not only lost the election, but his own riding. Jeff Kehoe, the Ontario campaign chairman, finally pulled the leader aside and gave him the hard numbers. It was the final blow.

Over the span of the evening, watching the results, Ignatieff was stricken with what? Regret? Anger? Relief? Humiliation? He demanded phone numbers on the spot for several vanquished caucus members, but soon there were too many to be consoled by a leader who had let them down. And yet he seemed strangely resigned to the dismal results. There were no hysterics, just disappointment so profound it could be called mourning: for what might have been, but wasn't. The loss of hope.

He and Zsuzsanna held out to the end of the night, maybe imagining there must be something they could hang on to. In the last days of the campaign, she had suggested that if he won his seat, they would fight on, despite a Harper majority. But the destruction of the Liberal party was too raw, too complete, too public, too humiliating. Redemption would have to be postponed for another time and a different place. The Ignatieff Caper was history.

Conclusion: The Death of Liberal Canada

The self-immolation of the Liberal party does not
signal the end of Canada, just the cremation
of some compassionate ideals that for a time
were a worthy Canadian initiative.

THROUGHOUT MOST OF CANADIAN HISTORY the struggle for political dominance has pitted the Conservatives against the Liberals. What separated the political camps was that one was in power and the other wanted to be. For much of our history, only the most theoretical of academics could define the differences between Liberals and Conservatives.

If Liberal and Conservative programmes and promises sounded vaguely similar, it was because party leaders were following what had become the cardinal mantra of Canadian politics: only minor variations were permitted to disturb the nation's delicately balanced regional, racial, religious and economic differences. It was attitude rather than substance that differentiated the parties. They talked and walked and looked the same, but they felt, thought and reacted differently—or to be more precise, they reflected the dissimilar sets of prejudices and assumptions rooted in their very different histories.

253

The rebellions of 1837 were important dividing lines. Tories then and now were emotional loyalists. They grew out of the union of the fanatically crown-worshipping United Empire Loyalists of Ontario, combined with the ultrafaithful, ultramontane Castors of Quebec—a coalition between those who were more loyal than the king and those who were more Catholic than the Pope.

Sir John A. Macdonald was able to unite these factions behind the movement that brought about Confederation in 1867. It was an important hallmark of the precarious condition of his ship of state that he chose to call the political party he founded the Liberal-Conservatives.

Pure Liberals evolved from a much different union: between *Les Rouges* of Quebec, and the Clear Grits of rural Ontario. Just as *Les Rouges* were anti-clerical and violently opposed to Canada's British connection, the Clear Grits were, if not anti-Crown, certainly anti-Family Compact. Both groups were on the rebel side of the 1837 Revolution, which in Upper Canada consisted of a languid mid-afternoon exchange of musket fire, followed by lengthy debriefings in a round robin of loud toasts at local taverns. In Ontario at least, it was a very Canadian Revolution with few casualties. To emphasize their uncompromising nature, the Liberals adopted "Grits"—from the hard, gritty sand sought by masons in making mortar—as their nickname.

Moderated by time and the expediencies of political office, a Liberal was the one who had to *deny* that he was anti-clerical in Quebec and anti-British in Ontario. Sir Wilfrid Laurier's campaign for a Canadian fleet independent of the Royal Navy and Mackenzie King's lifelong suspicion of the British demonstrated the Grits' traditional distrust of what was still described as Canada's "Mother Country." On the Conservative side, Sir John A. Macdonald exhibited deference to the British crown, running under the campaign slogan, "A British subject I was born—a British subject I will die." His fellow Tories duplicated that sentiment: Sir Robert Borden took a tough pro-conscription stand; Arthur Meighen uttered the war cry, "Ready, aye, ready" when England appealed to the Dominions for soldiers during the Chanak affair of 1922 (Mackenzie King took a determined independent stand, and refused Canadian troops being used to counter the intended Turkish attack on the British and the French in the Mediterranean). At one point in the 1920s when the Conservative opposition members in the Commons couldn't think of a way to counter Liberal taunts, they spontaneously stood up in a body and sang *God Save the King*.

Such almost hereditary emotional reactions were more valid distinctions between Grit and Tory than specific policies, promises or even patronage. The history of Canada's Conservative party, for example, was dominated by the unremitting search for a reincarnation of Sir John A. Macdonald. Because none of the party chieftains who followed him came anywhere near to possessing his flair for leadership, Conservatives exalted the memory of their founder, as if he had been a saint, instead of a self-confessed tippler.

They just as badly needed another Sir George Etienne Cartier—the Montreal lawyer whose political skill enlisted Quebec behind the Tories in the move toward Confederation. Of the many unsuccessful strategies the Tories used to woo the French-Canadian vote, none was more disastrous than the selection, in 1938, of Dr. Robert James Manion as Conservative leader. A Fort William physician, Manion's sole claim for support in Quebec was that his wife had been born there. In his first campaign in 1940, he bravely declared that his party was "prepared to share the burden of office," and that since this was wartime, he promised that if elected he would form a coalition government. The vote gave his

Conservatives thirty-nine seats—their lowest Commons representation to that point, and until the Kim Campbell debacle—without a single MP from French Canada. Mackenzie King rewarded Manion's zeal for sharing the burdens of office by appointing him Director of Civil Air Raid Precautions.

The Tories' eagerness to find a winning formula was reflected in the fact that they changed their party name a dozen times post-Confederation and came under the leadership of nineteen individuals, many of whom gave anonymity of big boost. The Liberals never altered their label and had an even dozen chieftains—three of those in the last eight years.

The most successful politicians in that time have been Macdonald, Laurier, King and Trudeau, between them having held office for seventy-one years. The four men had vastly different personalities, but each exploited the democratic system to its limits. They were reformers, and proud of it, but never crossed the line to becoming revolutionaries or, heaven forbid, REBELS!

THROUGHOUT CANADIAN HISTORY, the Tories and the Liberals have exhibited an important difference in relations with the business community. From 1879 to 1942, the Conservatives really were the party, if not of big business at least of the secondary manufacturing industries of Ontario, which depended on Ottawa's tariff policies for its markets.

The specific concern of the Liberal party tended to be primary industries, especially those exporting the produce of farmers and lumbermen. It was no coincidence that the Liberals became a strong national movement only after the opening up of the Prairies, when wheat exports quickly became the major industry. The Liberals insisted that, unlike the Tories, they had always thought of people primarily as consumers with parallel interests, rather than as producers with clashing, *special* interests.

Tory attitudes toward big business began to change at the party's 1927 convention, which passed resolutions that supported "special legislation, designed to conserve human life, health and temperance, to relieve distress during periods of unemployment, sickness and old age." But when R. B. Bennett tried, in his 1935 New Deal–style legislation, to put these reforms into law, he was repudiated both by the electorate and his party.

The modernization of Conservative policy really began in September 1942, when 150 young Conservatives, fed up with the outdated ideas of their leaders, met at an unofficial round-table conference in Port Hope, Ontario. They drafted a programme that became the skeleton of the platform adopted at the Winnipeg leadership convention three months later. The party's new policy advocated many of the welfare measures that, until then, had been considered rank Socialist heresy. The dividing issue was how well—or badly—the party leaders could resolve differences between the public and private sectors.*

The 1942 choice of prairie Progressive John Bracken as Conservative standard-bearer shifted the effective leadership of the Tory party from the far right to the extreme centre. He couldn't convince much of the electorate that his party really had become progressive, even when he bravely added that adjective to the Conservative brand name. In the 1945 election that followed, the Progressive Conservative vote plummeted. Bracken refused to resign until the party bought him a new Buick.

---

* *The only effective formula to resolve that dilemma was concocted by an anonymous political theorist, who compared the process to visiting a dentist. "Just as he bends over you and is about put that painful drill in your mouth, you grab him by the balls and sweetly declare, 'Now, we're not going to hurt each other, are we?'"*

Mackenzie King carried through his own modernization of the Liberal party during the mid-twentieth century by bridging the apparent contradiction between its traditional pursuit of unhampered liberty for the individual and its compulsory enrolment of the public in its new welfare measures. Under King, the party invented the Canadian version of the welfare state as "a liberating force" and prepared an extensive network of social services for the return of Second World War veterans. This move stole much of the support that might otherwise have gone to the CCF, the newly nascent national party of the left. So that unlike in Britain—where Winston Churchill's coalition government failed to implement similar measures—Canada's wartime administration survived its first postwar election.

Louis St. Laurent, who succeeded King in 1948, was equally skilled at preventing the rise of the political left by extending the welfare state while at the same time keeping the business community reasonably happy and preventing the rise of the political right. Lester Pearson carried on in this tradition when he took over as PM in 1963 and introduced many new welfare measures, such as Medicare and a universal pension scheme. Pierre Trudeau, who was a progressive activist before he came to power, continued the Liberal modernization but concentrated on patriation of the constitution, multiculturalism, bilingualism and protection of human rights.

The division between the political Left and Right—the most common labels used to tell parties apart in democratic societies— was rendered less and less meaningful. Instead of Right against Left, the contest between Canada's Liberals and Conservatives became a determined struggle for the centre. Until now.

DURING HIS TIME AS LEADER, Michael Ignatieff resolutely spread the invitation across the breadth and width of the country for Canadians to join him "Under the Big Red Tent." It made good sense if you were caught up in the notion that there was a political polarization in the country, so that the safest and most productive place to be was in the unassailable Centre.

In fact, Canada could validly claim that it was still adhering to the centre of the road, a tradition I would argue that has been responsible for Canada's consistent ranking as one of the world's most desirable places to live and work. For instance, consider the bitter debate between the Grits, Tories and NDP over the rate of corporate income taxes in the country. Each of the contenders billed this argument as one of those riot issues that defined not just their policy, but their ethics. It turned out that the Tories were determined to proceed with their intended reduction of the corporate tax rate from 16.5 percent to 15 percent; the Liberals had pledged to restore the previous rate of 18 percent; and the NDP promised to raise the rate to 19.5 percent. That amounted to a spread of 4.5 percent, certainly significant but not enough to get your knickers in a knot. That was fairly typical of the debate over most existing policies while the Liberal party was still a power in the land.

But now it has become a third wheel without a regional power base and, under Prime Minister Harper's new legislation, bereft of its ability to finance itself. The British example is instructive. Its Liberal party, once a governing force in the island nation, by the mid-1920s had faded into exactly the same state of ill grace as the third party—after the Conservatives and Labour. That move away from the political centre might well become our template as the Tories and NDP, who now hold all the cards that matter, continue to energize their base support.

The Christian Democrats in Germany, the Greens in Holland, the Socialists in France, Ireland's Fianna Fáil party, the British Labour party's Scottish wing, and several other European centrist coalitions are all searching for new mandates—and not having much luck. Doug Saunders, the *Globe and Mail*'s European bureau chief, summed it up most dramatically, referring to the possible disappearance of Canada's Liberal party: "This was merely one event in a season of big-party cataclysms across the Western world. Like a row of wave-battered skyscrapers collapsing into the ocean, the world's mighty centrists are being humbled by formerly fringe challengers from the Left and Right. The big political parties seem to be headed for extinction." Can they make a comeback?

SINCE I STARTED TO WRITE ABOUT Canadian politics, when I arrived in Ottawa as a *Maclean's* columnist in the spring of 1958, I have strenuously maintained my journalistic objectivity, telling anybody who asked that, "I'm neutral—I attack everybody." At the same time, I was fortunate enough to become a confidant of leaders in both the major parties, and turned our conversations plus my observations into books. They include Louis St. Laurent, John Diefenbaker, Lester Pearson, Pierre Trudeau, Brian Mulroney and Michael Ignatieff, all of whom hosted my tape recorder, and shared intimate confidences with me. Once.

That's as it should be. We journalists should be itinerant chroniclers, not ideologues or partisan hacks. My belief system starts and ends with an abiding love affair with Canada that dates from the moment my parents, my aunt and I landed at Pier 21 in Halifax in 1940 as pretend barley farmers fleeing the Holocaust of central Europe.

For the first seventeen years of our life in Canada the Liberals were in office, and for half that time, the prime minister was

Mackenzie King. He was a revered figure in our household, as he was in the lives of the displaced, introspective refugees who were our friends. Quite simply, his government had saved us. Attaining Canadian citizenship was—and remains—our family's most significant accomplishment.

A family friend who had been sending the prime minister Christmas greetings was so proud one year when he received a machine-printed card from Mackenzie King in reply. At his citizenship hearing, when asked to name the king of Canada (the correct answer would have been George VI), he bowed to the presiding judge, produced his much-fingered prime ministerial Christmas card, and proudly proclaimed: "My friend, Mackenzie!"

HALF A CENTURY LATER predicting a comeback for the Liberals is tempting. They demand so little from their adherents. To be a Conservative these days, you must slavishly follow the daily edicts of Stephen Harper, and hum his songbook. Until Jack Layton fell ill again after the election and then lost his battle with cancer, it had to have been fun to be an NDPer, though you'd have to move fast to keep up with all the ways the newly popular party was watering down Scandinavian-style social democracy.

To be a Liberal, you just have to relax. The train has left the station, a few old position papers are blowing around the platforms, but nothing much is happening. Oh-oh, here is an announcement coming over the PA system: "The party's next leader will be chosen by a raffle to be held at Sable Island on the next windless Saturday."

This book has been my best attempt to describe what has happened to bring us to these unhappy options, which in my judgment, do not include the likelihood of a Liberal revival. To win a Canadian national election, any political movement requires two essential elements:

1. **A regional power base.** Even one or two such sanctums aren't enough. Social Credit and the Reform party on several occasions have enjoyed hefty support in British Columbia and Alberta, but their federal crusades went nowhere. A Liberal power base does not exists anywhere except perhaps virtually on Bob Rae's laptop.

2. **A method of financing its electoral ambitions.** From a strictly partisan point of view it wasn't surprising that Stephen Harper's prime priority last election night was to announce that he would end the distribution of per-capita funds to federal parties. That's no problem for the Tories, since they are majority incumbents, enjoy a solid core vote and run an efficient donations system based on the tithing approach of the old Reform party. It's less of a problem for the NDP, given its core supporters and the fact that it's now the official opposition. But for the first time having become a third party, the Grits have no realistic prospects of staying solvent. Whatever idealists may believe, most political donations are made subject to the expectation that there will be some payback, ranging from ambassadorial postings to an invite to the PM's annual garden party. The Grits have lost their means of providing incentives for the donations on which their revival depends.

Though the NDP suffered a huge blow with the loss of its charismatic leader on August 22—when Layton took over the party had thirteen elected members, and when the polls closed in the May 2011 election, it had 103—the NDP may still succeed in establishing the welcome precedent that Canadian politics is no longer the domicile of the Old Boys' Network that has run this country since forever. And then it is not only possible but likely that the new wave of youngsters ambitious for political careers who may have enlisted in the NDP on a whim will establish commendable track records. That will provide an Open Sesame for themselves and their successors, who will bypass the Liberals' opportunistic appeals.

The Liberal party has been steaming in the losing direction in the four elections since Jean Chrétien won his three majorities: from winning only 135 seats under the newly chosen Paul Martin; to retaining 103 of those seats in his last campaign; to Stéphane Dion, who won just 77 ridings; and finally to Michael Ignatieff, stuck with a residue of 34 members. Next stop in that trend of losing about thirty seats each time out, would leave the once glorious Government Party with precisely four ridings.

And it just may happen: under Michael Ignatieff, the Liberals didn't exactly launch a riptide of innovation. But who could do better? Past strength of the Liberals was to hijack middle-of-the-road ideas from any available source. But most voters, now, are searching for something more solid than the mushy middle ground.

IAN DAVEY WAS there at the creation of the idea of bringing Michael Ignatieff back to Canada and invested five years of his life in his leader's abortive run. He lost faith in him, heard he was fired through an unexpected CBC radio news flash, but never surrendered his hopes for the Liberal party.

Though those hopes now hinge, he says, on the party's ability to consider and then act on its complete failure. "I believe the federal Liberal party has been broken for some time and while it is easy to identify and begin to address structural, political and, now, economic challenges, it is far more difficult to correct a systemic cultural problem. You start by recognizing there is one. In my view, the federal party has been largely consumed by professionals. It ceased being a cause and, instead, became a career. It was about being a 'player' and wielding power; not surprisingly, the by-product was making money. I told Michael as much repeatedly from our first days. That I was able to accomplish so little in changing things is my real disappointment.

"The Liberal party of Keith Davey, Jim Coutts, Tom Kent, Dick O'Hagan and so many others, owed its success to being dedicated to enabling liberal thought, to taking ideas and ideals and making them real. To do so, you must constantly seek new people, embrace and encourage new concepts and never fear change. Canadians aren't interested in political or communications strategies. They care only about who you are, what you stand for and most of all, what you do intend to do. The Liberals have forgotten that renewal is more than just a word."

Michael Ignatieff's run brings to mind Lord Russell's dictum that democracy provides the choice of who to blame. To shift the burden of justified criticism on to his shoulders is too simplistic to ring true. He may have been the agent of destruction but he was not its originator. The blame lies with a Liberal party that had lost touch with its roots, rejected the enlightened ethic that brought it to power and, for the longest time, kept it there. It evolved into a bunch of independent political entrepreneurs who mainly looked after themselves, and ultimately didn't deserve—or earn—power or office.

Ignatieff's seminal error was not being aware of the very different—almost contradictory—skill sets of being an academic and a politician. John Meisel, the Queen's University professor of political science, put it best: "The real problem is that all occupations and professions have to be learnt. That takes time and experience. Ignatieff had no time for this and perhaps was not aware of the need. When I make this point to friends, they mention Trudeau, but Pierre had extensive knowledge of politics of a different kind: labour and unions. His friendship with Jean Marchand and his involvement in the asbestos strike taught him a lot. Academics face a steep learning curve when they enter politics. They need to retool and to reorient themselves. Listening becomes more important than lecturing. Scholarship seeks certainty, politics thrives on compromise."

THE SELF-IMMOLATION OF THE Liberal party does not signal the end of Canada, just the cremation of some compassionate ideals that for a time were a worthy Canadian initiative.

It is a tough time to be in party politics. Everybody demands leadership, yet the same voters also want to be consulted, not just on the great issues, but on such mundane matters as the direction of sewer lines and the politically correct way to peel a carrot. "I've never been able to figure out," David Peterson, the former Ontario premier, told me shortly after his defeat in 1990, "the difference between making a very tough decision in politics, which you have to do, and arrogance. I guess the dividing line is that if people agree with you, you're a great leader, and if they don't, you're an arrogant son of a bitch, because you didn't listen to them."

During one of the many crises that have shaken Canadian confidence over the years, I went to see one of the country's leading psychiatrists, Dr. Vivian Rakoff. "It's quite bewildering," I recall him telling me. "Here we are, one of the world's happy countries— not perfect, but essentially benign, welcoming and decent—and we seem to be tearing ourselves apart, as though we were oppressed by some offensive, outside regime. It's madness. One reason may be that our politicians are not talking about anything that really affects us. Instead, they're talking about the few defects of this funny, mixed-up, blessed, pluralist circus of a society that most of the world envies and is desperate to join."

ON A SUNNY AFTERNOON, not long after the 2011 election, a visitor driving a fire-engine red convertible pulled up at our house in suburban Belleville. It was Peter Donolo, who had spent the previous eighteen months as Michael Ignatieff's chief of staff. As cups of coffee grew cold between us, he summed up his first-hand experience, making some telling points about the current state of Canadian politics. Yes there are excuses here, but there is also insight into the ways in which the Canada of now has slipped beyond the grasp of the Liberals of old. Here is a partial transcript:

> "We put together a campaign that, in a normal circumstance, would have been a model. It was well-run, well-financed. . . . We had strong, enthusiastic crowds everywhere.
>
> "But we had three or four major factors working against us. One was the money that the Conservatives spent on ads—I think it was $10 million over two years before the election—aimed at demoralizing Michael Ignatieff. In Quebec, it was the yoke of the sponsorship scandal and the unpopularity of the provincial government. We had a public with a general fatigue with minority Parliaments. The voters' sense was that the economy was not bad, and that they weren't quite fed-up with the government yet. All these factors combined, so that even a campaign that was good, just wasn't enough to beat them back.
>
> "In the English debate, the leader was [hurt] by Layton's quip about not being in the house often enough and that should have been addressed. But otherwise, you look at the campaign, and his performance, and you could niggle here or there, but I'd say, we had the best losing campaign in Canadian political history.
>
> "There's a troubling elements in all this, particularly as it pertains to the way politics is done in Canada and more importantly,

about the state of our democracy. We seem to be in a post-political world, in which people make very superficial judgments about politics. Generally, I believe there was a pox on all political houses, and that the traditional measures, like building a grassroots organization, putting together a strong platform, bringing together a strong team of candidates really are less and less relevant.

"What's relevant is advertising, especially the advertising that the Conservatives used. Even if we had had the money to go dollar for dollar against them in the last two years before the election, we would have been disadvantaged. It wouldn't have been enough to tell people what a jerk Harper is, because everybody knows that. Instead, we would have had to straighten out the claims about Michael Ignatieff. All we would have been doing was buying ads saying, 'I don't beat my wife.' You'd be arguing on their grounds. They poisoned the well.

"Spend enough money for long enough before the election, destroying the reputation of someone, and it will pay off.

"And then, as Layton started taking off outside of Quebec, too, Harper came down hard, with a 'Stop NDP' push, and we got sided-swiped. We initially bled support to the NDP, in terms of people yearning for change who went to the NDP instead of to us. And then we bled support at the end, too, when Harper made the appeal to stop the NDP. You could see it. MPs I spoke to— Rob Oliphant, Alexandra Mendes from Montreal, Anthony Rota in North Bay, and Mark Holland in Ajax—all said that they had won the advance polls in their ridings. But what happened in the last five days of the campaign erased the support they needed. So we got caught up in this sort of tsunami . . .

"And so you end up with a Parliament in which a prime minister who has shown unprecedented contempt for democracy, and a complete disdain for Canadians, gets a majority. And the

NDP gets bartenders and university students elected. Three of my daughter's classmates in second year at McGill University are now Members of Parliament.

"There was a post-political mood out there. Such political components as active grassroots party organizations, policy platforms, teams of qualified candidates, a senior team of qualified advisers— those key elements that are the traditional constants in Canadian political success were almost irrelevant. What we've seen in this election was that you can't run a campaign without a political party, without an organization, without a credible platform and without an impressive team of candidates . . . I'm talking about the NDP, and to a certain extent about the Conservative party, too—and be very successful.

"You can do it when your government is in perpetual campaign mode. You use every element of incumbency to your advantage— everything from funding multicultural groups, to using government advertising in an unprecedented partisan way, to utilizing government offices to promote candidates, and so on. . . .

"The key elements that have been relevant in every successful reinvention of the Liberal party, at least since 1958, where members rolled up their sleeves and put into place the basic building blocks, became less relevant. There's much less attachment to any political party than ever before. And the communications revolution has ironically made it easier for people not to follow the news, and therefore, not to follow politics. There are too many communications choices now. You used to have to sit through the newscast to get to what you wanted to see or hear, but now you can pick and choose. And if people feel that essentially all politicians are corrupt then it doesn't really matter how much attention you pay. You'll end up with people like Rob Ford getting elected mayor of Toronto and bartenders getting elected to Parliament. And you'll end up with a prime minister who gets mired in the kinds of scandals that would have been the political death of previous PMs, and it doesn't affect him at all."

Peter Donolo is a highly capable professional, as were the mature advisers he brought aboard the Ignatieff submarine after the original members of the "Childrens' Crusade" were let go or quit in solidarity. And, as is clear from his post-election interview with me, he had much to say about what went wrong that was insightful. Having watched both Donolo's crew and the original Ignatieff team in action, it seemed to me that the Liberal party was in such a state of disrepair that neither of these dedicated platoons could save it. Still my preference, by quite a wide margin, were the originals. They learned on the job by teaching one another. They created a circular power structure—they reported to one another and taught one another. They were smart, funny and, above all, worshipped their leader. They knew a lot and learned a lot more—but not enough to realize what their replacements took for granted: that the jig was up, that all you could do on that final election night was laugh or cry. The members of the original praetorian guard, after they shed their tears, gave each other high-fives and walked away, heads held high.

WE MAKE OUR WAY ACROSS THE PONDS of history in a sequence of leaps, from one anxious moment to the next. They are the stepping stones—large and small, bitter and sweet—that define life's journey. As the universe continues to roll on into the current millennium, thoughtful Canadians feel trapped by the past and agitated over the future while harbouring grave doubts about the present. But this country wasn't born in a hurry, and it will not disappear overnight. Its traditional government party, on the other hand . . . well, it may just vanish.

Of course, it's not just me who is marking the signs. Jane Taber, the *Globe and Mail*'s astute Ottawa columnist, recently wrote: "Stephen Harper is working to recast the Canadian identity, undoing forty years of a Liberal narrative and instead creating a new patriotism viewed through a conservative lens." That insight is confirmed by the Tories' most thoughtful supporter, the University of Calgary political scientist and former Harper chief of staff, Tom Flanagan. He predicted that Canada could turn into "a Conservative utopia."

To my mind the finesse required to preserve the remnants of the Liberal party, a once omnipotent political force, is along the delicate lines once outlined by the late Jackie Gleason, who was instructing a group of French musicians in Paris on how to play the score of his film *Gigot*. He couldn't read music or speak French but he knew precisely the sound he wanted from the orchestra. He said to his interpreter, "Tell them I want the first note to sound like someone pissing off a cliff into a Chinese tea cup."

A tough assignment on a windy day. But it will take a delicate manoeuvre of that kind to assure some semblance of a future for the Liberals. In other words, don't count on it.

Key Legislation Passed by Liberal Prime Ministers during the Liberal Century

SIR WILFRID LAURIER

November 1896: **Manitoba Schools Act Amendment** (Laurier-Greenway compromise)—It allowed for limited Catholic and French language education in schools based on student numbers from these backgrounds.

June 1897: **Alien Labour Act**—It was prohibited for Canadian companies to hire foreigners who were under contract elsewhere.

September 1897: **Crow's Nest Pass Agreement**—An agreement between the CPR and the Canadian government, with CPR receiving government subsidy and access into British Columbia. In return, most importantly, the CPR reduced rates indefinitely for eastern-bound grain and flour.

June 1898: **Yukon Territory Act**—Yukon was established as a separate territory within Canada, largely due to the Klondike Gold Rush. '

September 1903: **Railway Act**—Allowed for the building of a third Canadian transcontinental railway.

July 1905: **Alberta and Saskatchewan Acts** establish these two provinces.

July 1908: **The Juvenile Delinquents Act**—The first federal legislation dealing with this issue, it primarily proposed reform for minors as opposed to punishment.

May 1910: **Naval Service Act**—It created the Royal Canadian Navy, which the Canadian government would control, but in case of emergency could be transferred to the control of the British. This act caused much tension within Laurier's own Liberal party and was one of the main reasons for his defeat in 1911.

WILLIAM LYON MACKENZIE KING

July 1923: **Chinese Immigration Act** (also known as Chinese Exclusion Act)—This was an extension of the earlier Chinese Head Tax, established by legislation in 1885, that further limited the immigration of Chinese to Canada with few exceptions.

March 1927: **Old Age Pensions Act**—It is one of the first pieces of significant welfare legislation in the country.

Second World War: Parliament accepted Mackenzie King's request that Canada enter the military conflict, and implements the **War Measures Act** (passed by a Tory government during the First World War), which eventually extended to the internment of Japanese Canadians and the appropriation or freezing of their assets.

June 1940: **National Resources Mobilization Act**—It allowed the government to requisition property for the war effort and allowed for the conscription of Canadians for domestic defence.

August 1940: **Unemployment Insurance Act** was passed.

July 1942: **National Resources Measures Mobilization Act** was amended, allowing for the conscription of Canadians for military service overseas.

1944: **National Housing Act**—This created the Canada Mortgage and Housing Corporation for the building of new homes and modernizing existing ones. This measure was to assist in the postwar economy.

August 1944: **Family Allowance Act**—It allowed for government payments to parents and guardians of minors under the age of 16.

June 1946: **Canadian Citizenship Act**—The law defined Canadian citizenship (separate from British) as those born in Canada and immigrants (immigrants would need to meet certain qualifications first).

May 1947: **Chinese Immigration Act** of 1923 was repealed.

LOUIS ST. LAURENT

March 1949: **Newfoundland Act**—Newfoundland joins Canada.

December 1949: **Trans-Canada Highway Act**—It was an ambitious project to connect the country from the Atlantic to the Pacific coast. The project would take just over twenty years to complete.

May 1952: **Old Age Security Act** (revision of the Old Age Pensions Act from 1927)—Old Age Assistance Act.

1954: **St. Lawrence Seaway Authority**—It was established to oversee the development of the seaway on the Canadian side between Montreal and Lake Ontario and Lake Erie. The seaway was a joint project agreed upon by the Canadian and United States governments, and was completed in 1959.

June 1956: **TransCanada Pipeline Bill** is passed. It allowed the natural gas pipeline to be built from Saskatchewan to Quebec. This bill was one of the contributing factors for the Liberals' defeat in 1957.

August 1956: **Female Employees Equal Pay Act**—This provided pay equity for women employed by the federal government.

April 1957: **Hospital Insurance and Diagnostic Services Act**—It was the beginning of universal health care in Canada. It allowed the federal and provincial governments to formulate agreements regarding universal plans covering certain hospital admissions and medical testing.

LESTER B. PEARSON

December 1964: **Canadian Flag** (the maple leaf flag, as we know it today) was adopted by Parliament.

March 1965: **Canada Pension Plan**—It came into effect in 1966 and complemented Old Age Security benefits.

December 1966: **Medical Care Act**—It extended the Hospital Insurance and Diagnostic Services Act. The federal government would share health insurance costs with the provinces. It encompassed free universal health care coverage including visits to general physicians.

February 1968: **Divorce Act**—The law no longer limited divorce proceedings to adultery; the Act was revised again in 1986.

April 1968: **Broadcasting Act** set up a regulatory body, the Canadian Radio-Television Commission (CRTC), to oversee broadcasting regulations.

PIERRE E. TRUDEAU

May 1969: **Criminal Law Amendment Act**—Some of the items included in this omnibus bill decriminalized homosexuality and allowed for contraception and abortion.

September 1969: **Official Languages Act**—The bill gave equality to both English and French within federal institutions.

October 1970: **The War Measures Act** was enacted during the FLQ crisis in Quebec.

June 1971: **Unemployment Insurance Act**—It was a major revision of the UI Act, originally passed in 1940 and overhauled in 1955.

April 1975: **Petroleum Administration Act**—Under this act the federal government could determine Canadian oil and natural gas prices without the approval of energy-producing provinces. This caused much animosity towards the federal government, especially from oil-rich provinces like Alberta.

December 1975: **Anti-Inflation Act**—The federal government implemented wage and price controls to curb high inflation.

July 1976: The federal government abolishes the death penalty for civilian murders.

July 1977: **Canadian Human Rights Act** is passed by the federal government. It prohibits discrimination on the basis of race, religion, sex and disability.

August 1977: **Immigration Act**—Now centred on compassionate grounds specifically dealing with family reunification and non-discriminatory policies towards refugees, the act formulated Canada's policy towards immigration and also fulfilled Canada's international obligations regarding refugees.

June 1980: **National Anthem Act**—*O Canada* was officially proclaimed the national anthem of Canada.

November 1980: **Bank Act** (revised)—The federal government allowed foreign banks into Canada and further revised Canadian bank regulations.

April 1982: **Constitution Act**—This repatriated the Canadian constitution from Great Britain. No longer would Great Britain need to approve bills passed by the Canadian Parliament or have say in the matters of the Canadian constitution. The Constitution Act also included the Canadian Charter of Human Rights and Freedoms.

May 1982: **Young Offenders Act**—The minimum age for a minor convicted of a crime was twelve years old, and the maximum sentence was three years. The bill was controversial and was revised later. It replaced the legislation from 1909. This bill came into effect in 1984–85.

June 1982: **The Access to Information Act**—It allowed Canadians to gain access to federal records and also information that the federal government maintained on them.

April 1984: **Canada Health Act**—The federal government wanted to ensure that the provinces were maintaining the universality of Canadian health care. Provinces that allowed extra billing or user fees in the Medicare field would have their federal health-care funding curtailed.

July 1984: **CSIS Act**—The Canadian Security Intelligence Service was created as a civilian intelligence agency. Its primary focus was to deal with espionage, terrorism and other threats against the security of Canada.

JOHN TURNER
No significant legislation

JEAN CHRÉTIEN
May 1994: **Coastal Fisheries Protection Act**—It was amended in response to overfishing off Canadian waters by foreign vessels. The Fisheries Ministry was given substantial powers to board, seize and arrest those foreign vessels that didn't adhere to fishing quotas and conservation methods.

February 1995: **Young Offenders Act**—This amended the earlier bill, increasing the length for first- and second-degree murders for those sixteen and seventeen years old as well as sentences for violent crimes.

December 1995: **Firearms Act**—Implemented to reduce crime by requiring all firearms to be registered by 2003, the regulations drew outrage from farmers, rural residents and hunters who owned shotguns and rifles.

May 1996: **Bill C-33**—The bill disallowed discrimination based on sexual orientation in federal institutions.

April 1997: **Bill C-95**—This amendment to the criminal code made it illegal to belong to a criminal organization.

June 1999: **Extradition Act**—To prevent criminals from other countries finding "safe haven" in Canada, the act replaced legislation from the previous century.

June 2000: **Clarity Act**—This came about from the Quebec referendum issue. In it the federal government affirmed the need for any provincial/territorial referendum regarding secession to be clear. The Canadian government thereby made the conditions for any possible secession very difficult.

November 2001: **Immigration and Refugee Protection Act**—The act protects refugees from harm and provides them safe haven in Canada.

December 2001: **Anti-Terrorism Act**—It was in response to the 9/11 attacks in the United States. It provided specific sentences for those involved in terrorist activities and gave police broad powers in pursuing terrorists.

February 2002: **Youth Criminal Justice Act**—It amended the Young Offenders Act, and emphasized rehabilitation.

PAUL MARTIN

March 2004: **Assisted Human Reproduction Act**—It banned human cloning, renting wombs, the sale of sperm and eggs and cloning stem cells. A government agency was created to oversee assisted human reproduction activities.

July 2005: **Civil Marriage Act**—Federal legislation recognized same-sex marriages as having all the same rights as heterosexual unions.

November 2005: **Public Servants Disclosure Protection Act—** Was an act to protect federal government workers who came forward to disclose wrongdoing in the workplace.

Acknowledgements

LIKE ALL BOOKS, this one has a role model. It is Michael Herr's *Dispatches*, a defining chronicle of the Vietnam War that was an impressionistic collection about a cataclysmic conflict that followed no rules. The episodic style of the book evolved out of the events it described—Herr needed to find a way to show that nothing was too absurd not to happen. Form followed function, just as it does in this volume.

I originally intended to document the making of Canada's next prime minister, Michael Grant Ignatieff, who was briefly thought to be a shoo-in for the position. His curious fate is only the most visible aspect of the Liberal party's vanishing act. From providing the glue of common aspirations of our nationhood, the Grits turned themselves into political entrepreneurs, in it for themselves instead of their country. "We are in the trough of the party's life and those who would be memory carriers are resigned to old and hazily recalled war stories," lamented former Liberal senator Jerry Grafstein. "For the first time in Liberal history we seem fated to live on the margins of political culture — neither adding nor subtracting, just whimpering."

The voices of those who participated in *When the Gods Changed* echo with tales of intrigue, loyalty, betrayal and patriotism that made up the history told in these pages. I am profoundly grateful to all those voluntarily cornered sources who welcomed me into their offices, their homes and their confidence. These include Michael Ignatieff, his enchanting wife, Zsuzsanna, and most of their entourage; outriders, critics and the many un-indicted co-conspirators involved.

As I documented the terminal pratfalls of this once invincible political movement, I realized that what was in play here was not merely the arguably justified disappearance of a political party but of a dream: the notion of Canada as a compassionate and enlightened country, cherished as unique among the available options; the detonation of one historical cycle and the birth of another.

In a way this book sits shiva for a Canada that has ceased to exist, or at least has moved out of the mainstream — the end of the notion that if we built it, the Canada of our hopes would abide. So it seemed to those of us who came here as immigrants, and stayed on as patriots. The new country being born is still too much putty in too many hands to have taken on any definite shape or purpose, except that we have seen clear signals that the continuity of an age has been cut. What comes next will test our resolve, our patience and our tempers.

ANY BOOK CONCENTRATES the mind beyond the randomness that spawns us. But this one stretched the potential of everyone involved. The dedication, talent and discipline that Anne Collins, the publisher of the Knopf Random Canada Publishing Group, brought to her assignment as an editor was both inspiring and humbling. I cannot express my gratitude adequately, except to bluntly proclaim that there would be no book without her. I am particularly grateful to Brian Bethune, who has diligently and good-humouredly fact-checked all of my works, including this one. I also owe an incalculable debt to David Olive, business columnist for the *Toronto Star*, whose input was an astounding avalanche of essential information and compatible opinion; Ray Heard, who has been a companion in arms since we both worked for the *Montreal Star*, was an invaluable source and resource. I also thank John Meisel, the Queen's University political scientist, who has been an inestimably astute adviser.

As well I must express my profound gratitude to my loving family and treasured friends who continue to put up with me. Any errors are entirely my fault.

No book leaves our house, now in Belleville, Ontario, or our sailboat—moored on the Bay of Quinte—without the inspiring imprint of my wife, Alvy Newman, who is the love of my life.

Index

PETER C. NEWMAN has been writing about Canadian politics for nearly half a century, including books on prime ministers John Diefenbaker, Lester B. Pearson, Pierre Elliott Trudeau and Brian Mulroney. His *Renegade in Power* (1963) revolutionized Canadian political reporting with its controversial "insiders-tell-all" approach. He did it again four decades later with *The Secret Mulroney Tapes: Unguarded Confessions of a Prime Minister* (2005), a number one bestseller that became one of the most controversial books ever published in Canada. The author of twenty-five books that have sold over 2.5 million copies, Newman has won a half dozen of the country's most illustrious literary awards, including the Drainie-Taylor Biography prize for his 2004 memoir, *Here Be Dragons: Telling Tales of People, Passion and Power*. A former editor-in-chief of the *Toronto Star* and *Maclean's*, Newman has been honoured with a National Newspaper Award, has been elected to the News Hall of Fame, and has earned the informal title of Canada's "most cussed and discussed" political commentator.

A NOTE ABOUT THE TYPE

When the Gods Changed is set in Electra, designed in 1935 by William Addison Dwiggins. A popular face for book-length work since its release, Electra is noted for its evenness and high legibility in both text sizes and display settings.